KENTUCKY
Government and Politics

Joel Goldstein, editor
Kentucky Political Science Association

College Town Press
P.O. Box 1998, Bloomington, Indiana 47402

To my father and mother

CONTENTS

INTRODUCTION

James H. Mulligan's poem "in Kentucky" ends by asserting that "politics—the damnedest in Kentucky." This book, written by political scientists from across the Commonwealth, is meant to shed some light on the peculiarities of Kentucky government and its politics.

Every state contains its share of unique personalities. No state has the simple textbook structure for its government, Kentucky is no different. Consequently, there is a need for a book which describes and analyzes its government and political structure.

This book was conceived as a supplement for use in the Introductory American Government course. For many of our students that is the only class in government they take. An understanding of the similarities and differences of governments at the national and state levels is essential if they are to function as well-informed citizens.

I took the idea to the Kentucky Political Science Association. That group was aware of the need for a basic college level text on Kentucky government which can be used in state government classes. Consequently, the book was written to serve two audiences. Hopefully it meets the needs of both groups, only time will tell.

Chapter 1

KENTUCKY: An Introduction

Joseph L. Rose, Murray State University

BRIEF HISTORICAL PICTURE

Kentucky, geographically, is located in the southeastern United States, or, more properly, the east south central section of the country.[1] Its northern boundary is the Ohio River and the states of Ohio, Indiana, and Illinois. The eastern boundary is the Big Sandy River and the Cumberland Mountain Range and the states of West Virginia and Virginia. Kentucky's entire southern border is the state of Tennessee. The western boundary is the Mississippi River and the state of Missouri. Kentucky has seven states on its borders. Only two other states have more states on their borders than does Kentucky.

The area of Kentucky is 40,395 square miles, ranking thirty-seventh among the fifty states. Its 1980 population was 3,660,257, ranking twenty-third. The state's largest city is Louisville (298,451), located in the north central section on the Ohio River. The state capital is Frankfort (25,973), located in the inner bluegrass, or central, section of Kentucky. Kentucky has 120 counties, a number exceeded only in two other states, Texas and Georgia. Popularly, Kentucky is called the Bluegrass State because of a blue grass (*Poa pratensis*) grown in the central part of the state. Officially, its title is the Commonwealth of Kentucky.

Kentucky, renowned in literature, song, and myth for the quality of its tobacco, whisky, and racehorses was the first state west of the Allegheny and Appalachian Mountains to be settled by the westward moving pioneers. The state is one of anomalies. There are many fine farms and estates, some of which are among the most valuable per acre in the United States. Other parts of the state, in both the east and the west, have been devastated by reckless lumbering and strip mining practices. Chronic unemployment has historically prevailed in some of the richest coal areas in the world.

1

Kentucky is poor, dependent, and underdeveloped, yet it is one of the few surplus energy producing states.

Though settlement in Kentucky is usually discussed with the names of Daniel Boone and James Harrod receiving first mention, Indians are thought to have lived in permanent settlements in the woodlands and river areas in the western part of the state up to fifteen thousand years ago. Europeans moved into and through this territory many years before white man's permanent settlements began. The first serious settlement took place in 1750 when Dr. Thomas Walker passed through a gap in the mountains (now called Cumberland Gap and the Cumberland Mountains) and settled around what is now Middlesboro. Cherokee Indians from the south and Shawnee and Iroquois Indians from the north contested and resisted the white man's coming.

Daniel Boone explored eastern Kentucky in 1767 and later spent two years in the exploration of what is now the bluegrass area of central Kentucky. In 1773, Boone led a group of settlers into the territory, only to be forced out by the Indians.

James Harrod established the first permanent settlement in 1774 at Fort Harrod, near present-day Harrodsburg. Fort Harrod's most famous resident was George Rogers Clark. One year later, in 1775, Daniel Boone established Fort Boonesborough on the Kentucky River, in central Kentucky. Boone was acting as an agent for the Transylvania Company. The road that led from the mountain gap to the settlement in central Kentucky became known as the Wilderness Road.

Kentucky at this time was known politically as Fincastle County, Virginia. Kentucky County was created by Virginia in 1776. Separation and statehood was gained on June 1, 1792, and the Commonwealth of Kentucky became the fifteenth state to join the Union.

Indian raids were a continuing menace to Kentucky settlers until General (Mad) Anthony Wayne routed the Indians in Ohio at the Battle of Fallen Timbers. In 1795, the fledgling United States entered into a treaty (Pickney's Treaty) with Spain, and in 1803 the Jefferson administration purchased the Louisiana Territory from France. Thus, stability came to Kentucky's borders, and the Ohio and Mississippi Rivers became prominent avenues of commerce, transportation, and settlement. Kentucky prospered with the westward movement, and the state's population burgeoned.

Kentucky's economic, political, and social growth has been marked by continuing conflict and violence, which has given the state and its citizens a stereotype of Kentucky to the rest of the United States that has continued to the present day.[2] Kentucky

2

fought with the Jeffersonians against the Federalist supported and adopted Alien and Sedition Acts (1798) by passing the Kentucky Resolution (1799). The states citizens supported vigorously the War of 1812 and the Mexican War (1846-48). Despite an official stance of neutrality during the Civil War, the state was caught in the middle of the conflict, and it supported each side with thousands of troops. The Hatfield-McCoy feud, which is symbolic of Kentucky's "hillbilly" stereotype, lasted for fourteen years (1882-1896). A Democratic governor, William Goebel, was assassinated in 1900. The long-running and frequently deadly strife between the mine owners and operators on the one side and the mine workers and their union, the United Mine Workers, on the other has solidified the stereotype and has given use to the descriptive phrase "Bloody Harlan."

PHYSIOGRAPHIC FEATURES

Much of Kentucky's historical, political, and economic tapestry has been determined by its physiographic features.[3] Kentucky is an oddly shaped state, measuring in a straight line over 400 miles from Pike County in the east to Madrid Bend in the west. The north-south line from Covington in northern Kentucky to the Tennessee border in the south measures 175 miles. In western Kentucky, a line from Paducah, in the north on the Ohio River, to the Tennessee line in the south measures only 45 miles.

Kentucky's diverse sectional variations are described in five, or often seven, geographical divisions. The basic five divisions are the Jackson Purchase, the Pennyroyal, the Western Coal Field, the Bluegrass, and the Mountains. The five become seven when the Knobs are added and the Mountains are divided into the Cumberland Plateau and the Eastern Coal Field (Figure 1.1).

The Jackson Purchase is the eight counties lying between the Mississippi River in the west, the Tennessee River in the east, the Ohio River in the north, and the state of Tennessee in the south. Called by geologists the Southwestern Mississippian Embayment, the area joined Kentucky in 1818, having been purchased by treaty from the Chickasaw Indians by a group led by Andrew Jackson and Governor Isaac Shelby. Rising slightly from the alluvial lowlands along the Mississippi River, through the low grass-covered hills of the Barrens to the Tennessee River (now mostly Kentucky Lake), the area reaches an elevation of about 500 feet. Covered by numerous small streams, until recently the area was isolated politically and economically from the rest of the state, and even today it maintains a

3

FIGURE 1.1

PHYSIOGRAPHIC MAP OF KENTUCKY

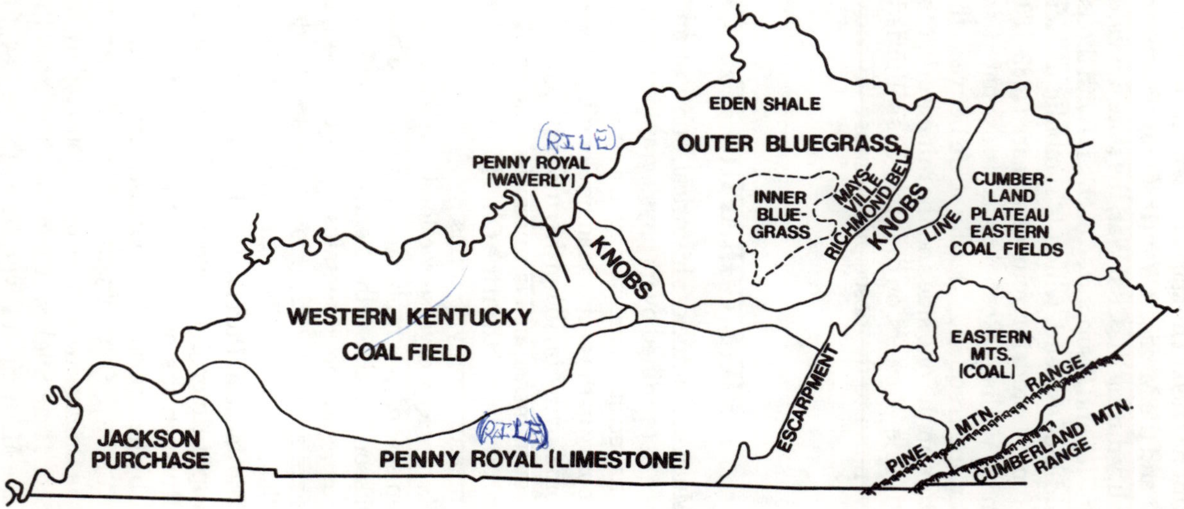

political and economic stepchild relationship to the rest of Kentucky. Economically, Tennessee and Illinois are more important. Agriculturally, soybeans, corn, tobacco, and livestock are important. Swamplands with cypress give way to poplar, oak, pecan, hickory, and sweet gum. Tourism is of tremendous importance, as shown by three major state parks, two lakes, and a major outdoor recreation area called The Land Between the Lakes.

The Pennyroyal (pronounced Pennyrile) is directly east of the Jackson Purchase and covers most of southern Kentucky. Called by geologists the Southern and Southeastern Lower Mississippi Plateau, this 8,100 square mile area rises to about 1,300 feet and is noted for one of its main features, the cavernous limestone caves. In fact, one of the two distinct subdivisions of this area is called the Cavernous Limestone Area; the second smaller subdivision is called the Waverly Area. The Waverly Area, at the northern end of the Pennyroyal, appears to be a separate and distinct area. It is small, covered by hills and ridges, small streams, and forested slopes. The larger Cavernous Limestone Area, on the other hand, is one of the better known parts of Kentucky because it is covered by many spectacular caves (Mammoth, Onyx, Horse, Crystal) that are today major tourist attractions. The western end of the Pennyroyal has some of the state's best agricultural land, and a diversified agriculture dominates this area. Per capita farm income, derived from soybeans, corn, wheat, tobacco, hogs, and cattle, is the highest in the state.

Directly north of the Pennyroyal and stretching to the Ohio River is the Western Kentucky Coal Field. Covering about twenty counties and parts of others, this area is one of the two great coal-producing areas of Kentucky and the United States. Strip mining dominates, but deep (underground) and auger mining operate here, also. The land is rolling, covered by valleys and numerous small streams. The dominant river is the Green River, which flows through the eastern end of the coal field. Much of the land has been stripped-mined many years ago and is now orphan land, a designation identifying worn out, eroded land. As a result, much soil erosion and stream pollution has taken place. Efforts in recent years to reclaim the newer stripped lands have been more successful. Agriculturally, hogs, corn, and soybeans are grown in the alluvial soils bordering the Ohio River. One of the state's major manufacturing areas, Owensboro and Daviess County, is located on the northern edge of the coal fields on the Ohio River.

Beginning east of the Waverly Area at the Ohio River in southern Jefferson County (Louisville) and running south, then east, then north, in a semicircular fashion around the Bluegrass area to the

Ohio River in northern Kentucky at Vanceburg is an unusual area, a narrow belt called the Knobs. This area gets its name from the numerous, highly visible cone-shaped hills that jut upward out of the landscape. There are many streams and valleys in the Knobs, and flooding is a perennial problem. The soil is poor to fair, with corn and tobacco being the major crops. Hardwoods (oak, chestnut, hickory) and pine are plentiful on the forested slopes.

Inside the boundary of the Knobs, northward to the Ohio River is the Bluegrass area, from which Kentucky gets its popular name, the Bluegrass State. A large area, over 8,000 square miles, the terrain is gently rolling, covered by many streams, and is drained by the Dix and Kentucky Rivers. Both of these rivers have cut deep gorges in the southern Bluegrass, with the Dix River being a major source of electric power. The Bluegrass has three distinct subdivisions, the Inner Bluegrass (the Lexington-Cynthiana limestone belt), the Eden Shale belt, and the Maysville-Richmond Limestone belt. The Eden Shale is on the northern and western side of the Bluegrass, and the Maysville-Richmond Limestone belt is on the eastern side of the Bluegrass; these two areas are collectively known as the Outer Bluegrass. The Inner Bluegrass (Fayette, Mercer, Woodford, Scott, Harrison, Bourbon, Clark, and Madison Counties) is what represents Kentucky in most people's minds. The Inner Bluegrass is a land of spas and springs, of above- and below-ground running water, of limestone soils and bluegrass, of landscaped farms bordered by white (though there are miles of black) fences or limestone rock fences. This is also home to an internationally prominent thorough-bred industry. Beef production, tobacco (white burley), and bourbon distilleries are economically prominent. Lexington is the heart of this area. The Eden Shale is an area of rolling to rugged terrain. The soil here is poor to good, with tobacco and corn the cash crops. The Maysville-Richmond Limestone belt is gently rolling terrain with many small streams and the Kentucky River. The topsoil is good, and corn, tobacco, and cattle production dominate this area.

Moving east from the Bluegrass and from the Pennyroyal areas, the topography changes rapidly as an escarpment rises sharply, ending in the eastern mountains. This area is called the Cumberland Plateau. Geologists call it the Eastern Coal Field because of its rich mineral deposits of coal. The plateau is a rugged mountainous area with forested slopes of laurel, pine, hemlock, huckleberry, and chestnut and swiftly running streams that are the headwaters of the Kentucky and Cumberland Rivers. Cumberland Falls, the second largest falls in the eastern United States, is located in the southern part of this area. Sandstones undergird a large part of the plateau, and the wind and the rain have carved numerous, some quite large, natural bridges in the landscape. Agriculture is of little importance, operating at a subsistence level. Coal mining dominates the economy.

At the eastern end of the state is the area termed the Eastern Mountain. This area is divided into the Pine Mountain range and the Cumberland Mountain range. This is also an area of thick coal seams, and deep (underground) mines are prominent. Auger and strip mining occur, and the hillsides are eroding and the streams are silt filled and polluted. Floods are prevalent. The Eastern Mountains are isolated from the rest of the state, and regional ideas, traditions, and customs have been maintained in the valleys and "hollers." These traditions play a major role in mountain life. Subsistence agriculture is practiced here. Coal mining dominates the economy here, also. The mountains rise to 6,000 feet.

WATER RESOURCES

Kentucky is blessed with abundant water resources; the state certainly is one of the richest of all fifty states. Running waters attracted explorers and settlers into and through the state; some streams acted as river highways of transport and commerce. A few of the rivers became as important to early Kentucky settlements as did the famed Wilderness Road. Not only is the above-ground water important, but the underground springs, which are numerous, served as settlement points in the state, giving birth to such central Kentucky communities as Lexington, Georgetown, Danville, Richmond, and Harrodsburg. None of these towns is on a navigable stream, but they grew and prospered, each becoming a county seat. Mineral spring spas were once numerous and popular in Kentucky, but such towns as Crab Orchard, Dawson Springs, Cerulean, and Drennon Springs are now reminders of an age gone by.

The major rivers of Kentucky are the Ohio River, the Kentucky River, the Tennessee River, the Cumberland River, and the Green River. Other rivers of varying importance are the Licking River, the Barren River, and the Bid Sandy River. Smaller streams that carve up the Kentucky landscape are the Salt River, the Little River, the Tradewater, the Red River, Elkhorn Creek, Clarks River, and Tug Fork River.

The Ohio River, which is the entire northern boundary of Kentucky is the most important river historically and economically. Running from Ashland in the east, the Ohio empties into the

Mississippi River west of Paducah. Historically, for exploration and commerce by flatboatmen and keelboatmen, the Ohio River was the prominent river from the eastern United States to the Mississippi River and the gulf port of New Orleans. The Ohio River today is one of the major commercial rivers in the United States. Major Kentucky ports on the Ohio River are Ashland, Maysville, Covington, Carrollton, Louisville, Owensboro, and Paducah.

Perhaps the most important river wholly within the state is the Kentucky River. Its main channel begins at Beattyville in the eastern Cumberland plateau, flows westward and northward to within a few miles of Lexington, splits the state capitol of Frankfort in half, and turns north emptying into the Ohio River at Carrollton. The Kentucky River was the major commercial and transportation river for early settlements in central Kentucky. Today the river's 9-foot and 6-foot channels are used primarily for pleasure boating.

In size and importance today, no other rivers in Kentucky can compare economically with the Cumberland River and the Tennessee River, with the possible exception of the Ohio River. The Cumberland River rises in the eastern mountains of Kentucky in Harlan County, flows westward through the south central part of the state, creating Cumberland Falls and filling up Lake Cumberland behind Wolf Creek Dam. It then swings southward out of Kentucky and flows through the state of Tennessee (Nashville and Clarksville) before reappearing in the western part of the state as the boundary of the Jackson Purchase, forming Lake Barkley behind Barkley Dam before discharging into the Ohio River. The Cumberland River served early Kentucky as a water avenue of commerce and transportation and today is of major commercial importance. The river is also one of the prominent water recreational playgrounds in the state and the nation.

The Tennessee River flows through Kentucky for only a short distance of its total length. It parallels roughly the Cumberland River in western Kentucky. Only a few miles west of the Cumberland River, about 4 to 10 miles, the Tennessee River forms a 184-mile-long lake, called Kentucky Lake behind Kentucky Dam, before emptying into the Ohio River. Barge traffic is heavy on the Tennessee River, but its main importance today is as a great water recreational area. The land lying between these two rivers forms a 170,000-acre outdoor recreational area called The Land Between the Lakes and complements the two river-lakes as the state's and the nation's great recreational resource.

The Green River is still important economically to the state. Its 6-foot channel runs from the Ohio River, into which the Green empties, to the Mammoth Cave area, draining the eastern side of the

Western Coal Field. A 9-foot channel exists for a short distance on the lower Green, and numerous coal-carrying barges navigate this part of the river. The Green River flows through Mammoth Cave and is partly responsible for the spectacular cave formations.

The Barren River, in south central Kentucky, has agricultural and recreational significance. It drains some of the richest farmlands in the state, while flowing northwest before emptying into the Green River near Morgantown. Barren River Reservoir has been created by the damming of this river.

The Licking River, in early Kentucky history, was nearly as important to the development and settlement in central Kentucky as the Wilderness Road. Flowing in a westward direction from its headwaters near Salyersville, and then north, it discharges into the Ohio River at Covington. This river, however, over the decades lost out to rail transport and later to highway transport, and today is of mostly recreational value.

The Big Sandy river forms the northeastern border of Kentucky, discharging into the Ohio River. Its short 9-foot channel carries chiefly petroleum products from the refineries in this area.

The Mississippi River forms the short western boundary of Kentucky. The only port here is the small town of Hickman. The Mississippi River has become more important politically and historically. As an example, a major Civil War defensive fortification was built at Columbus. The Mississippi River today is commercially important to Kentucky, primarily because of the Ohio River.

Kentucky's waterways today do not have their earlier transportation and commercial importance. The rivers today are mainly drainage systems, recreational playgrounds, and developed sources of hydroelectric power.

MINERAL RESOURCES

Kentucky's mineral resources have been and are important contributors to the economy of the state, although the ownership of these resources in many cases is external to the state, making Kentucky a dependent state.[4] The most prominent resource is coal, and Kentucky has two major coal-producing fields. Every year Kentucky ranks at the top or near the top in United States coal production. Coal contributes heavily to the coffers of the state and is responsible for employing thousands of people in Kentucky.

Oil and natural gas resources are small but well developed; however, they are declining in economic importance as the reserves are being depleted. The state has excellent deposits of clays and clay shales that are used for refractory, pottery, structural, and thermometallurgical purposes. Limestone, sandstone, and dolomite are also major resources in Kentucky. Used for almost any building purpose (limestone fences along the "pikes" and around horse farms in central Kentucky to cement production), this wealth in rock will be of great value to the state for many years. The rock asphalt industry is a growing industry, and the western and eastern coalfields are major producers of this commodity.

Perhaps the least known but certainly one of the more important mineral resources in the state is fluorspar. One of the world's great areas of fluorspar is in western Kentucky. Used in the production of aluminum, this resource may prove to be of increasing value to Kentucky.

ECONOMY

The economy of Kentucky is based on agriculture, manufacturing, mining, and tertiary activities, such as government work, services, and tourism.[5] Manufacturing includes steel and sheet metal, stoves, electrical machinery, domestic wares, farm machinery, and industrial machinery. Major manufacturing centers are Louisville, Lexington, Ashland, Bowling Green, Owensboro, and such rural areas as Hancock County.

Chemicals and allied products, such as petroleum, coal, rubber, and plastics, are the second most important part of the state's manufacturing processes. Major chemical centers are Louisville, Lexington, Paducah, Mayfield, Bowling Green, small towns such as Calvert City, and rural areas such as Taylor County.

The state's agricultural products have created a food-processing industry based on dairy products and grain products. Louisville, Danville, and Harrodsburg are centers for this activity. Tobacco and tobacco products are the major cash crop for the Kentucky farmer, amounting to over a billion dollars a year. Cigarettes, cigars, and chewing tobacco are manufactured in Louisville, Owensboro produces cigars and chewing tobacco, and Greenville, Bowling Green, and Paducah manufacture chewing tobacco. Major tobacco warehouses are in Lexington (the largest burley market in the world), followed by Maysville and Owensboro. Corn, soybeans, hay, and wheat are major agriculture products.

Alcohol production, known in Kentucky as bourbon whiskey, is located almost exclusively in the central Bluegrass area. The three major production areas are Louisville, Frankfort, and Bardstown. The major noncentral Kentucky production area is Owensboro. The state derives millions of tax dollars from bourbon production.

Coal is the major mineral resource of Kentucky and a most important cog in the economic life of the state. Kentucky ranks at the top (sometimes in first place) in the production of coal. Underground and auger mining in eastern Kentucky and strip mining in western Kentucky are the methods by which coal is extracted in the state. Kentucky is sitting on top of one of the world's greatest reserves of coal.

There are large manufacturers and manufacturing plants in the state. General Electric, Ford Motor Company, Ashland Oil Company, Armco Steel Corporation, International Business Machines, Brown and Williamson Tobacco Company, Firestone Textiles Company, Airco Alloy, Peabody Coal Company, and Island Creek Coal Company are representative of the corporations operating in the state. Near Paducah is located one of only three gaseous diffusion plants in the United States. However, a measure of Kentucky's economic dependency is that nearly all of the state's larger manufacturing industries have home offices located in other states. One major exception is the Ashland Oil Company. The pace of manufacturing development is uneven in Kentucky, with the eastern and southeastern sections of the state having little to no manufacturing capabilities.

The state's major retail trading centers are Louisville, Lexington, Paducah, Owensboro, Covington, and Bowling Green. Occupationally, Kentuckians are employed in trades and services, government work, agriculture, manufacturing, and mining. Of special importance in the service area is Humana, Inc., a Louisville-based private-for-profit health and hospital corporation that is one of the largest in the United States.

A distinct feature of the Kentucky economy is the horse industry. Concentrated in central Kentucky, the breeding, raising, racing, and sales of thoroughbreds amounts to over a billion dollars a year in business. Pari-mutuel and other taxes bring millions of dollars to Kentucky government. Lexington is the center of the horse industry.

A review of Kentucky's economy would not be complete without a mention of the state's recreational park system and its state shrines. The parks maintained by the national government and the Land Between the Lakes outdoor recreational area maintained by the Tennessee Valley Authority has made Kentucky today one of the major recreational areas in the United States. Tourism generates over a billion dollars a year. The tourist industry (lodging, restaurants, and recreational services) is a joint public-private effort. Tourism is important economically to Kentucky because millions of dollars are paid into the state's tax coffers by out-of-state tourists.

POPULATION AND THE PEOPLE

The population of Kentucky in 1980, as tabulated by the Bureau of Census, was 3,660,257.[6] This was a 13.7 percent increase over the previous decade, and the largest increase since the 15.5 percent increase of 1900 over 1890. For only the second time since 1820 (the other time was 1930), Kentucky's population increased at a greater percentage rate than the national percentage rate of increase. Kentucky's population by decades is given in Table 1.1.

TABLE 1.1

Year	Population	Percent Growth Rate from Previous Census
1790	73,677	
1800	220,955	199.9
1810	406,511	84.0
1820	564,317	38.8
1830	687,917	21.9
1840	779,828	13.4
1850	982,405	26.0
1860	1,155,684	17.6
1870	1,321,011	14.3
1880	1,648,690	24.8
1890	1,858,635	12.7
1900	2,147,174	15.5
1910	2,289,905	6.6
1920	2,416,630	5.5
1930	2,614,589	8.2
1940	2,845,627	8.8
1950	2,944,806	3.5
1960	3,038,156	3.2
1970	3,218,706	6.0
1980	3,660,257	13.7

The Urban Studies Center at the University of Louisville in 1979 projected a 1980 Kentucky population of 3,567,144, missing the actual population by about 93,000. The Urban Studies Center projections for the next four decades are a 1990 population of 3,966,653, a year 2000 population of 4,355,851, a year 2010 population of 4,747,005, and a year 2020 population of 5,138,795. Two University of Kentucky geographers, Dr. P. P. Karan and Dr. Wilford Bladen projected Kentucky's year 2010 population at 5.07 million persons.[7]

Kentucky is essentially a rural, small town state, even though the census lists the state as being 50.9 percent urban and 49.1 percent rural. The urban-rural, small town dichotomy is accentuated when one looks at where the people live in the state. Only 13.5 percent (down from 14.6 percent in 1970) of Kentuckians live in cities with a population greater than 100,000 (Louisville and Lexington). A smaller 8.5 percent (down from 9.1 percent in 1970) live in cities with a population between 25,000 and 100,000. Places with less than 25,000 population account for 25.2 percent (up nearly 3 percentage points from 1970) of the state's citizens. Other urban is listed at 3.7 percent (down nearly 3 percentage points from 1970).

There are six standard metropolitan statistical areas (SMSAs), and one standard consolidated statistical area (SCSA) involving just 17 of Kentucky's 120 counties. The six SMSAs are Owensboro and Daviess County; Lexington–Fayette County (including the counties of Woodford, Jessamine, Scott, Clark, Bourbon); Evansville, Indiana (Henderson County, Kentucky); Huntington, West Virginia–Ashland, Kentucky (Boyd and Greenup Counties); Louisville (Jefferson, Bullitt, and Oldham Counties, Kentucky and Clark and Floyd Counties, Indiana). Only two of these SMSAs are wholly within Kentucky (Owensboro and Lexington), and only one other SMSA has a dominant Kentucky influence (Louisville). The one SCSA is Cincinnati–Hamilton County, Ohio, which includes the Kentucky counties of Boone, Kenton, and Campbell.

The ten largest cities and the ten largest counties in population in Kentucky are listed in Table 1.2.

TABLE 1.2

City	Population	County	Population
Louisville	298,451	Jefferson	685,004
Lexington-Fayette (Urban)	204,165	Fayette	204,165
Owensboro	54,450	Kenton	137,058

continued on the next page

Table 1.2 *continued*

City	Population	County	Population
Covington	49,563	Hardin	88,917
Bowling Green	40,450	Daviess	85,949
Paducah	29,315	Campbell	83,317
Pleasure Ridge Park	27,332	Pike	81,123
Hopkinsville	27,318	Warren	71,828
Ashland	27,064	Christian	66,878
Frankfort	25,973	McCracken	61,310

If Pleasure Ridge Park is not listed, and sometimes it is not since it is a census designated plate (CDP), then each city moves up one, and the tenth largest city is Henderson (24,834). Robertson County (2,265) and Gallatin County (4,842) are the two smallest counties in population.

Kentucky's population is basically white, at 92.3 percent, with the black percentage at 7.1 percent. Persons under 18 years of age make up 29.6 percent of the state's population. Those 65 years and over are 11.2 percent of the population. Those persons in the prime years, 18 to 64 years, constitute 59.2 percent of the population. The median age is 29.1 years, and there are 2.82 persons per household. There are 95.6 males for every 100 females in Kentucky. The fertility ratio is 303. Kentucky is an insular state with a limited mixture of other races. The 1980 census lists such minorities as American Indian (3,518), Eskimo (59), Aleut (33), Japanese (1,056), Chinese (1,318), Filipino (1,443), Korean (2,102), Asian Indian (2,225), Vietnamese (1,090), Hawaiian (342), Guamanian (265), Samoan (129), and other (8,714).

What, then, is a Kentuckian? He or she is an amalgam of many ethnic groups, with some dominant groups forming the cultural concept Kentuckian. The first white settlers were eastern seaboard colonials, Pennsylvanians by way of the Ohio River and Virginians and North Carolinians by way of Cumberland Gap. The people who lived in Eastern Kentucky spoke a Shakespearean dialect that became isolated in the "hollers" and could be heard in its original state until after World War II. These first settlers were of English, Irish, and Scottish ancestry.

During the latter quarter of the nineteenth century, another influx of Irish immigrants settled in the state, in Louisville primarily. At this time another influx of English settlers moved into eastern

Kentucky and became the coal, iron, and timber entrepreneurs. They settled in and around the Middlesboro area.

Germans constitute a large percentage of the cultural body of Kentucky. Most Germans came to the state in the 1840s to 1860s and settled primarily in the Louisville and Covington areas. Both cities and their environs developed major brewing industries. German architecture, reflected in the church spires, brick buildings, and narrow cobbled streets, is modeled after the Old World. The German influence is more visible (but sadly greatly diminishing) today in the Covington area rather than the Louisville area.

Early Kentucky history reflects the French culture, even though the French did not come in great numbers. As a mark of admiration for French support in the War for Independence, the French influence is more greatly felt in Kentucky place names, such as Versailles, Paris, Louisville (King Louis XVI), Fayette, and Bourbon.

Kentucky's earlier history shows that smaller numbers of Swiss, Poles, Syrians, Lebanese, and Greeks came to the state. Most settled in the cities, but the Swiss settled in the mountains of eastern Kentucky in the town of Bernstadt.

Blacks came to Kentucky with the first settlers. Later settlers brought blacks as slaves and opened the plantation system of central Kentucky. Slave market operations were prominent in the pre–Civil War Kentucky economy, particularly at Louisville, Lexington, and Washington. The large slave market operation at Washington is the inspiration for Harriet Beecher Stowe's *Uncle Tom's Cabin.* Blacks arrived in large numbers after the Civil War to build rail lines across the state. Today blacks are concentrated in the urban centers and large towns in Kentucky.

POLITICAL CULTURE

Religion has played a major part in Kentucky's cultural development and continues to have a major influence on the state today.[8] Protestantism was the major religious preference of the early settlers and today constitutes the main body of religious belief among Kentuckians. The largest Protestant denomination is the Baptists, primarily Southern Baptists, with smaller collections of Methodists, Christians (Disciples of Christ), Presbyterians, Episcopalians, Lutherans, and United Church of Christ. The Christian Church, Disciples of Christ, is a religious movement indigenous to Kentucky. There are many independent pentecostal and fundamentalist groups dotting the religious landscape of eastern, south central, and western Kentucky.

Catholicism has been and is a prominent influence in Kentucky. Except for the Baptists, Catholics constitute the largest religious group in the state. Catholic centers are Louisville, Bardstown, Covington, and Owensboro. Two Trappist Monasteries, the Abbey at Gethsemane, south of Bardstown, and one at South Union, west of Bowling Green, are located in the state.

A small but influential religious sect lived in central Kentucky at Shakertown near Harrodsburg until early in the twentieth century. The United Society of Believers in Christ's Second Appearing, commonly called the Shakers because of an undulating shaking dance they used in prayer making, were influential in agricultural development and handicrafts. A smaller colony existed earlier at South Union in the Pennyroyal.

While physical, demographic, and economic information is helpful in understanding Kentucky's political and cultural tradition, a fusion of these features into the concept of "political culture" might offer a more helpful and meaningful explanation of Kentucky and Kentuckians. Political culture is defined as "the particular pattern of orientation to political action in which each political system is embedded."[9] There are three political cultures: individualistic, moralistic, and traditionalistic. These terms identify dominant political cultures, only two of which exist in Kentucky, and may help to explain what policies may be expected to be supported in differing sections of the state, the kinds of people who became active in political affairs and the way the political game is played in each section of Kentucky.

Kentucky's political culture is identified as individualistic in northern Kentucky. It is a mixture of an individualistic political culture and a traditionalistic political culture in a narrow belt running down the Ohio River from Louisville to Owensboro. The remainder of Kentucky, most of the state, is of the traditionalistic political culture.

In the individualistic section of the state the people view government in a utilitarian sense, that is, they see government as one of a number of means through which the people can improve their economic and social position. Some political corruption is expected and accepted as a natural part of the governing system. Being a politician is accepted as a profession. These people tend to be conservative and to talk in marketplace terms. They do not see government as the initiator of new programs, do not support programmatic (policy) ends, and see the winning of political office as a reward in itself. These people talk in terms of efficiency and argue that private initiative is the economic mode of operation. Government is used to encourage economic development. Government tends to be viewed more as a caretaker, and politicians have clerkship roles rather than leadership roles. Government is not viewed as the initiator of new programs unless these programs are demanded by public opinion. The government worker is viewed ambivalently. Politics should have its own rewards (patronage politics are favored), but at the same time there is a recognition that career bureaucrats provide the prized criterion of efficiency. Some merit system in needed, but not too broadly applied. Politics is viewed as a dirty business, and the people who engage in it despoil themselves. As a result, a professional political class comes to the fore in this area and political parties are holding companies that dole out favors and recruit people for public office. Strong party cohesiveness is demanded and usually secured. In this individualistic political culture, issues are seldom argued. Politics is party competition. The party wins office, and all political rewards flow from this. Politics tends to be more competitive in this section of the state.

In the traditionalistic political culture section of the state, government is viewed as a means of maintaining the existing status quo. Traditional economic, social, and political patterns are to be supported and maintained. Politics is a privilege, and only those born to rule should govern. Political competition takes place between elitist dominated factions within the dominant political party; thus, the political values of the dominant elite are maintained. Government is highly personalized within the elite-subordinate patterns of existence. Government policies serve the elite. Government is used in the programmatic sense to promote programs that serve the interests of the governing elite. The government worker is viewed in a pejorative manner as someone who has depersonalized government and made the citizen a number. There is little to no support for the adoption of or the maintenance of a merit system. Politics is the playground of the privileged few, and only the acceptable elite are to participate. The party organization is not very strong, since politics is based on family, social, and economic ties. In a sense, politics becomes vigorous among elected individuals of similar political values. Political participation tends to be very low, and one-party politics prevail. Thus, traditional political values prevail. Too little has changed to say that Kentucky in the 1980s still does not carry on this traditionalistic political culture.

FOOTNOTES

1. Material for this section was gathered from numerous sources of general historical interest. The reader should review the following works: Steven Channing, *Kentucky: A Bicentennial History* (New York: W. W. Norton, 1977); Thomas D. Clark, *A History of Kentucky*, rev. ed. (Lexington: The John Bradford Press, 1960); Lewis Collins, *History of Kentucky*, reprint ed. (Lexington: Henry Clay Press, 1968); Louise Carson Drake, *Kentucky in Retrospect: Noteworthy Personages and Events in Kentucky History, 1792-1967* (Frankfort: Kentucky Historical Society, 1967); Federal Writer's Project, *Kentucky: A Guide to the Bluegrass State* (New York: Harcourt, Brace and Co., 1939).

2. A recent publication subtitles Kentucky as "diverse, genteel and violent." See Neal R. Pierce and Jerry Hagstrom, *The Book of America* (New York: W. W. Norton and Co., 1983).

3. The best atlas of Kentucky is P. P. Karan and Cotton Mather, eds., *Atlas of Kentucky* (Lexington: The University Press of Kentucky, 1977).

4. Material for this section was gathered from sources furnished by the Department of Geography (now Geosciences) at Murray State University.

5. Material for this section was gathered from sources furnished by many offices in Kentucky State Government. See also P. P. Karan and Cotton Mather, eds., *op. cit.*

6. U. S. Bureau of Census, *1980 Census of Population: Number of Inhabitants. Vol. 1, Chapter A, Part 19, Kentucky* (Washington: U. S. Government Printing Office, 1982); U. S. Bureau of Census, *1980 Census of Population: General Population Characteristics. Vol. 1, Chapter B, Part 19, Kentucky* (Washington: U. S. Government Printing Office, 1982).

7. Urban Studies Center, University of Louisville, Louisville, Ky., 1979; Louisville *Courier-Journal*, "Five Million Kentuckians by 2010," May 9, 1978.

8. A series of articles appeared in the Louisville *Courier-Journal* that should be read. See Louisville *Courier-Journal*, "Kentucky: Cradle of Frontier Religion," June, 1976, and "Closer to God," May 7, 1979.

9. The following discussion is based on Daniel J. Elazar, *American Federalism: A View from the States*, 2nd ed. (New York: Thomas Y. Crowell Co., 1972), pp. 93-114.

Chapter 2

THE KENTUCKY CONSTITUTION

Carl Chelf, Western Kentucky University

In 1947 Allen M. Trout, a well-known writer for the Louisville *Courier-Journal*, observed:

> Many Kentuckians are never aware they live under a Constitution. They never see it. They never feel it directly. The Constitution may exist as a vague conception of state government in the abstract, but it seems remote to every day life on rural mail routes and pleasant streets in little towns .... Yet without this set of fundamental principles to guide our local and State governments, the whole structure would fall down in confusion.[1]

In America written constitutions have become a basic part of our political culture, and even though the average citizen may be only remotely aware of such documents and their provisions, they are viewed as an important element in our democratic government. Some of our most fundamental political rights, such as individual freedom and personal liberty, are addressed in state constitutional provisions. More and more, even the federal courts are looking at our state constitutions in their continuing efforts to resolve such difficult issues as religious freedom, freedom of expression, abortion, public school financing, and other knotty social issues. Thus, state constitutions, including Kentucky's basic document, have taken on new significance in the efforts to resolve these difficult questions of the relationship between citizens and the state. Some of these specific issues will be treated in more detail in later chapters.

Most American constitutions are a product of both governmental theories and pragmatic political considerations growing out of the setting in which they are framed. As Charles Borgeaud notes in his book *Adoption and Amendment of Constitutions*, most constitutions are "in more respects than one, the work of time and

19

circumstance."[2] This has certainly been reflected in Kentucky's constitutional development. Each of Kentucky's constitutions has built on its predecessors, but each has included provisions reflecting the influences prevalent in the state at the time it was adopted. A look at the state's historical and political development is essential for an understanding of the current constitution.

CONSTITUTIONAL ORIGINS

In his poem "On the Emigration to America and Peopling the Western Country," Philip Freneau wrote of the new frontier: "Here reason shall new laws devise,/And order from confusion rise."[3] To a degree, Kentucky reflected Freneau's concept of development on the frontier, becoming a testing ground for some of the post-Revolution ideas on constitutions, governments, freedom and individualism.

With the image of a land so rich and fertile that it would produce everything needed, Kentucky attracted an unusually mixed lot of early settlers. Most were not social planners with ideas for developing a new society but were practical people seeking to improve their own lot. Kentucky society was a blending of eastern gentry and rugged frontiersmen, coming from several states and varied backgrounds. While several of the early settlers had claims to large tracts of land, many of those who came later were tenants and sharecroppers. Although by the 1790s a majority of Kentucky householders were landless, the frontier conditions that encouraged respect for skills having nothing to do with one's birth or breeding, led to a growing spirit of equality and independence. With no landed gentry class well established in the frontier society, the old-style politics of deference was not widely embraced.

While this did contribute to the growth of a more democratic spirit of individual freedom and equality, it also kept a leadership class from emerging to direct the state's early development. The lack of established order provided early Kentuckians very little preparation for their eventual statehood and self-government. In December 1776 the Virginia Assembly organized the Kentucky territory as a county of Virginia. Kentucky was allowed to send two representatives to the Virginia Assembly; however, the Virginia capital was 700 miles away, and travel difficult. Only a few Kentuckians gained governing experience during this period.

Many Kentuckians were not happy under Virginia rule. In 1784 Colonel Benjamin Logan called for a constitutional convention to meet in Danville, whose delegates would petition for statehood. The movement for statehood touched off a political debate that lasted almost a decade and influenced the course of Kentucky politics for years to come. Heated disputes arose over the timing, method, and terms of separation from Virginia. In 1790 with Kentucky's population at 73,677, Kentucky and Virginia, after repeated efforts, finally agreed on the terms for their separation. The matter of a constitution still remained unsolved, however. Interest in statehood and constitutions became so rampant that in 1791 one observer noted, "The people of Kentucky are mere fanatics in politics. Constitutions are forming in every neighborhood."[4] This popular movement attracted many not previously active in politics.

Since Kentucky had had no period of colonial rule and the time it spent as a county of Virginia had done little to prepare them for self-government, many who favored statehood had qualms about the availability of leadership for sound government. They also feared the talent needed to draft a sound constitution was lacking in the state. Several Kentuckians turned to such outsiders as Thomas Jefferson, James Madison, and Edmund Pendleton for help. Although they sympathized, these well-known Virginians declined to write draft constitutions because they were not familiar with Kentucky and its citizens. In the end Kentuckians were on their own. Nine constitutional conventions had been held prior to statehood, but they had raised as many differences regarding the terms for statehood as they had agreements. With separation from Virginia approved, the tenth convention met in Danville in April 1792 to draft the state's first constitution. On June 1, 1792, Kentucky was admitted to the Union as the first state west of the Appalachians.

KENTUCKY'S EARLY CONSTITUTIONS

The First Constitution

The convention that produced Kentucky's first constitution was a hurried affair. It met only seventeen days and produced a brief document of only eighteen pages. The convention was an amalgamation of rather disparate elements. Of its forty-five members, over half were from Virginia originally, and only a dozen had any legislative experience. Only a half dozen had attended college, and surprisingly, there were only two lawyers among the forty-five. By contrast, the convention that drew up the United States Constitution was 60 percent lawyers and almost half held college degrees.

Approximately two-thirds of the delegates to the 1792 convention were slave owners. The major force in this first convention was George Nicholas of Mercer County, who had moved to Kentucky from Virginia only a short time before the convention.

Despite their lack of experience and haste, the 1792 delegates produced a document with some positive features. It was brief and contained a minimum of legislative detail, a feature lacking in the current constitution. For the first time in any state constitution, the right to vote was granted to all free males over the age of twenty-one with no property qualification. Voting was to be by secret ballot, and the lower house was directly elected by the voters. Representation was based on population rather than on counties, as in the Virginia assembly. While a clause protecting slavery was written into the document, emancipation of slaves was provided for and legislative limits were set on slave trading.

There were other paradoxes in the document as well. While the house of representatives was to be popularly elected, the governor and the senate were both to be chosen by an electoral college. Although there were ministers serving as delegates to the convention, they were prohibited from serving in the general assembly. In one of the first provisions on corrupt practices in elections, candidates for senator, representative, or sheriff could be disqualified if convicted of "canvassing" (campaigning) for their offices.

This first document also included some unique features. There was no provision for a lieutenant governor. The senate elected a "speaker," who was to act as chief executive in the governor's absence or in the event the office became vacant. With less than one in ten land titles in Kentucky secure, the court of appeals (state supreme court) was given original jurisdiction over land dispute cases.

Much of the first Kentucky constitution was patterned after the federal Constitution. The document also reflected the sentiments prevalent in the state at the time. There was no desire by the delegates to dismantle the basic system of representative government, but many of the delegates were quite wary of popularly elected legislatures. By the 1780s popularly elected state legislatures were beginning to appear unruly and were viewed by more conservative elements as a threat to republican government and private property. George Nicholas and fellow members of the Kentucky elite took steps to ensure that legislative power was kept within limits. By making the governor and senate indirectly elected, by giving the governor extensive appointive power, and by giving the court of appeals original jurisdiction in land title cases, they were able to limit the power and influence of the masses. Although the state's first constitution included some very progressive concepts, it also reflected the conservative elitism of many of the delegates. Evidently the framers foresaw early dissatisfaction with their efforts because they included a provision for automatic review by the voters at the end of five years.

Kentucky's Second Constitution

The concern for public dissatisfaction was not unwarranted, as flaws in the first constitution appeared quite early. A disputed governor's election in 1796 showed that the constitution was vague and unclear. There was considerable dissatisfaction with the indirect election of senators and the governor, and the senate and court of appeals had become suspect because of their land decisions. In elections in 1797 and 1798, the voters approved the call of a convention to review the 1792 constitution. The convention met in July 1799 and took less than a month to complete its work.

Both similarities and differences existed between the 1792 and 1799 conventions. Most of the delegates were property owners and were respected figures in their home counties. Only one of the fifty-eight delegates was a nonslaveholder. On the whole, the delegates were more experienced in government than their 1792 predecessors; twenty-seven were acting justices of the peace, many were local officials, and several were veteran legislators. Nine were lawyers/judges, and three were ministers.

The delegates to the second convention were more pragmatic than ideological; they weighed their experience under the current document in framing provisions they hoped would serve the state's future needs. The result was an amalgamation of ideas, with several provisions being carried over from the 1792 document and others being dropped or revised. The 1799 document continued to reflect an aversion to deferential politics by the elite, but at the same time, there were only a few outspoken democrats among the 1799 convention delegates. In some respects the 1799 document represented a step backward from democratic government. The clause protecting slaveholding was strengthened. Whether it had been intended or occurred through oversight, the right to vote that had been allowed to free blacks, mulattoes, and Indians under the first constitution was taken away in 1799. Secret ballot voting was replaced by *viva voce* voting. The provision that prohibited candidates for elective offices from canvassing for votes was also dropped. One area of struggle was between those who favored centering more power in the state government and those who favored more local autonomy. Those favoring decentralization were able to get substantial power restored to the county courts, but sheriffs and coroners, who had been elective, along with other local officials, were made appointive by the governor—a victory for those pushing centralization.

The office of lieutenant governor was added, and the office of governor, lieutenant governor, and members of the senate were made popularly elected. Changes in the powers of the governor and the legislature showed that in any head-to-head clash, the framers intended that the legislature should be the prevailing body. This was a marked change from the attitude of the 1792 delegates but reflected the trend in other states at this period. The 1799 document was not submitted to the voters for ratification, nor did it include any provisions for amendment. It could only be changed by calling another convention.

Kentucky's Third Constitution

Over the years, the county courts that had been strengthened by the 1799 constitution became powerful local oligarchies in some areas and began to generate considerable criticism. Also, the host of appointive offices provided for under the second constitution had led to widespread nepotism. An oligarchy of officeholders had developed that rotated from office to office regardless of election results. (A somewhat similar situation has developed under the current constitution among elective officials who cannot succeed themselves. They play a game of "musical chairs" rotating from office to office, election after election. This will be discussed in following sections.) A rush for internal improvements in the 1830s led to heavy indebtedness of many local governments as well as the state. The abuses under the existing system caused many to feel it was time to change some rules. In 1847 and 1848 the voters approved the call for another constitutional convention. Delegates were elected and met from 1849 to 1850.

Journalist George Willis says the delegates to the 1849 convention were well qualified, describing them as possessing "great intellectual vigor, high attainment and unquestionable patriotism."[5] Among their ranks were forty-two lawyers, thirty-six farmers, nine doctors, four merchants, three clerks, two ministers, one hotel keeper, and one mechanic. Their average age was forty-five, and approximately one-half were native Kentuckians.

The burning issue facing the delegates in the 1849 convention was whether slaveowning should be protected in the constitution. While the frontier experience had created a strong sense of social equality among the state's citizens, the delegates to the 1849 convention were ultimately swayed by their prejudices and self-interests. Most of the delegates were slaveowners themselves. Almost a quarter of the debate of this convention revolved around the slavery issue. A clause protecting property in slaves was included as it had been in the two earlier constitutions.

The 1849 convention was also considerably influenced by the concepts of Jacksonian democracy. Under the previous constitution, the governor had appointed judges and local officials. The 1849 document adopted the long ballot making most officials, including judges, elective. The rash of governmental indebtedness incurred by the rush to finance internal improvements led to provisions prohibiting state support of internal improvements and a limit on the size of debt that could be incurred. The third constitution also placed a sixty-day limit on legislative sessions.

Like its predecessors, the 1849 constitution was somewhat of a paradox, including some rather conservative limits on governmental authority, as well as some provisions quite progressive for the time. For example, the document included a provision that prohibited child labor, a requirement that wage earners be paid in lawful money, and a requirement that public printing be done by the lowest bidder. These provisions were somewhat ahead of their time. Like the two earlier constitutions, the 1849 document made no provision for amendment.

Many of the provisions of the state's third constitution were made obsolete by the Civil War and the adoption of the Thirteenth Amendment to the federal Constitution. As early as 1867 the governor recommended that a convention be called to revise the constitution. This question was submitted almost regularly to the voters for the next twenty years but failed to get the required number of votes. The constitution provided that a convention must be approved by a majority of "those entitled to vote for representatives." The number of eligible voters was determined from the tax rolls, and the tax collectors were inclined to inflate their lists. As a consequence, the convention call could not attain the required majority. Finally in 1886 the legislature adopted a voter registration law, and with the more accurate count of eligible voters, a convention call was approved in 1888 and again in 1889. On May 3, 1890, the general assembly passed an act calling for a constitutional convention; delegates were elected and met in September 1890.

KENTUCKY'S CURRENT CONSTITUTION

Kentucky's fourth and current constitution is the product of the 1890 constitutional convention. Many of the provisions of the third constitution were carried over in this document, but like its predecessors, it includes many provisions that are a product of its time.

In 1890 Kentucky's population was still 80 percent rural, but industrial development was becoming a major force in people's thinking. The growing power of the railroad, mining, and timber interest was of increasing concern to many. Furthermore, the convention met at a time of considerable agrarian unrest in the state. Among the delegates were five Populists, seventy-seven Democrats, and eighteen Republicans. There were no real radicals among the group, which was largely rural and on the whole rather conservative. Most of the delegates were middle aged or older, and several had been or were active in state politics. Former Governor Proctor Knott and incumbent Governor Simon B. Buckner were among the delegates. The delegation included sixty lawyers, twenty farmers, thirteen doctors, and seven bankers or merchants.

The state was facing some trying economic, political, and social issues in the 1890s, and these are reflected in the constitutional debates. While earlier conventions, even though wrestling with the issue of slavery, had disposed of their tasks in relatively short time, the 1890 convention lasted for eight months, and debate filled over 6,000 pages. Some of the delegates wanted only to update the current constitution and get on with their task. Others, with the industrial revolution swirling around their heads, were convinced limits on corporate power must be provided. Some felt the main purpose for calling a convention was to place some restraints on legislative power. Taken as a whole, the delegates were agrarian and conservative with a strong distrust of unlimited legislative power. As a result, the constitution contains many specifics that traditionally had been left to the discretion of the legislature. This characteristic is one of the major handicaps of the current constitution, as will be pointed out later.

The result of the delegates' deliberations was a document twice as long as the previous document and four times as long as the state's first constitution. Many of the provisions addressed issues that were of special concern at that time, such as free railroad passes to public officials, regulation of corporations, lotteries, and duels. By the time it finished its sessions, some people had grown tired of the convention's lengthy deliberations and were less than enthusiastic about the results. Henry Watterson, publisher of the *Courier-*

Journal said the state constitution should be written on "two pages of paper" and he called the proposed new constitution "confusion worse confounded." Voters, however, approved the new document overwhelmingly by a vote of 213,432 to 74,017. Following ratification, the convention reconvened and changed several provisions that were never resubmitted to the voters. It took eighteen months of legislative sessions to bring the state's laws into conformity with the new constitution.

Problems with the Current Constitution

Some delegates were opposed to the excessive specificity of the 1890 document. A. J. Auxier warned his colleagues that they should not attempt to frame a government for generations yet to come. He told them:

> I predict that, before another Constitutional Convention shall be assembled in this hall, men will be navigating the air instead of traveling in railroad coaches; that instead of doing thirty or forty miles an hour, they will go two hundred miles an hour, and hundreds and thousands of unthought of things will be brought into existence; and new fields of operation and new systems of governments, or modifications, at least, will be required in those days yet to come . . . .[6]

Another member, James Blackburn told the delegates they should not put into the constitution anything that properly belonged to legislation. He urged, "Let us lay down general rules to control the Legislative, Executive and Judicial Departments, and when we have done that, we have done our duty in making this organic law."[7] In the end, however, their fears and apprehensions of unlimited power led the delegates to frame a lengthy and detailed document, which placed severe limits on governmental authority. Clifton Lowry wrote,

> The "fathers" devoted themselves to the task of developing a governmental machine which, if powerless to do much good, was equally powerless to do much harm. . . . An attempt was made to create a political system which would yield to them the advantages of civil society, but which could be held within the sphere of action proper to it. In all of these, one purpose is evident and paramount: to place limitations upon political authorities.[8]

The state legislature in particular was the object of considerable concern. The last general assembly meeting under the 1850 constitution had passed 1,926 acts, most of which were private measures. Only 117 of these affected more than one county. "The people of Kentucky today are expecting more radical changes and relief in that department [the legislative]," said one delegate, "than in any other department of the government.["9] Echoing this concern, another delegate noted, "The principal, if not the sole, purpose of the constitution which we are here to frame, is to restrain its will and restrict its authority." One later observer commented that the 1890 convention delegates evidently expected all future legislatures to consist only of fools or knaves.[10] Many of the limits that appeared appropriate then became burdens with the passage of time.

Defects appeared in the new document quite early. Provisions wise for that day and time became archaic and obsolete as the state grew and changed, but once written into the constitution, these provisions became difficult to change. In 1890 Kentucky had 1,858,000 residents, 80 percent living in rural areas. Only Louisville and Covington had populations of 25,000 or more. State government was a $3½ million enterprise then, compared with over $4 billion today. The state had no compulsory system of education and spent only 2 dollars per pupil. Tobacco sold for seven cents a pound. Autos and airplanes were still in the future. Today one can fly to Europe in less time than it took some delegates to reach Frankfort in 1890. Few businesses of that day had telephones, and electric lights were rare. Television, radio, computers, and video games were not even dreamed of at the time. It is not difficult to see how the vast changes brought by the passage of time rendered many of the more specific provisions of the 1890 document obsolete.

One of the areas in which this obsolescence occurred was in provisions dealing with revenue and financial matters. In 1890 about 70 percent of state revenue came from property taxes. Where the first three constitutions had simply provided that "all laws for raising revenue shall originate in the House of Representatives," the fourth constitution was more specific. It required that taxes "shall be uniform on all property." In a rural, agrarian society this was not a problem, but as the state became more urban and industrial, it was. This provision was changed by amendment in 1915. The constitution also sets a state debt limit of $500,000. In 1890 this was about 20 percent of state tax receipts and more realistic. By 1982 this limit was less than 1/30th of 1 percent of state revenue and had become quite unrealistic. Rather than being frozen, the debt limit might better be tied to a percentage of the previous year's general fund revenue receipts. The current limit does not allow the needed financial flexibility for running the state government on its present scale. Likewise the $7,200 ceiling placed on salaries paid to state employees was quite liberal in 1890, but by the mid-twentieth century this limit had become a burden, making it difficult for the state to attract and retain qualified and competent employees.

In 1960 and 1963 the court of appeals, in what became known as the "rubber dollar" decisions, held that such limits could be based on the relative purchasing power of the dollar.[12] Thus, on this basis, a $7,200 salary in 1890 might have as its equivalent a $60,000 salary in 1980.

As times and circumstances have changed dramatically, the courts have been compelled to apply provisions of the constitution to conditions never imagined by the framers. In addition to the salary limit decisions, they have upheld such things as city occupational and payroll taxes and the issuance of revenue bonds—the former to get around the constitution's prohibition of city income taxes and the latter to avoid the debt limit. While such decisions enable the state to skirt the unrealistic limits, they do not add to respect for the constitution.

Another area of growing problems in recent years has been the distribution of powers between the executive and legislative branches. All four state constitutions are quite similar in their provisions on the separation of powers. The 1890 delegates felt, however, that the general assembly had betrayed the people's trust and should be carefully controlled. They limited its sessions to sixty days every other year. Only the governor can call special sessions. They also directed special attention to the legislature's powers and spelled them out in precise detail. Special legislation was specifically prohibited on twenty-eight subjects. Executive functions, on the other hand, were not defined nearly as precisely. Other than denying the governor the right to succession in office, the constitution imposes few restrictions on the powers of the governor. Consequently, the twentieth century has seen substantial growth in the powers of the governor and the executive branch of the state government.

The governor's administrative leadership of the executive branch was complicated by the provision for the election of six constitutional administrative officials: the secretary of state, the auditor of public accounts, the attorney general, the superintendent of public instruction, the treasurer, and the commissioner of agriculture and labor statistics. Not only does this create a long ballot for the voters, it makes it difficult to hold the governor responsible for actions of such constitutional offices though they are a part of the executive branch of government. In some instances there may even be open conflict between the governor and some of these officials, as was the case with Governor John Young Brown and Commissioner of Agriculture Alben Barkley in 1982. Governor Brown transferred some of the functions of the commissioner's office to other state agencies, and the commissioner filed suit against the governor. The court voided the governor's actions in this instance. Such an arrangement does not promote harmony in the executive branch. Also, since these officials are not eligible to succeed themselves, a system of "musical chairs" has developed, in which the same individuals rotate among these offices from election to election. Thus, although there are changes in titles and duties, there are often few changes in personnel involved.

The current constitutional arrangement has resulted in some difficult questions involving the separation of powers. Section 27 states:

> The powers of the government of the Commonwealth of Kentucky shall be divided into three distinct departments, and each of them be confined to a separate body of magistracy, to wit: Those which are legislative, to one; those which are executive to another; and those which are judicial, to another.

Section 28 further specifies that

> No person or collection of persons, being of one of those departments, shall exercise any power properly belonging to either of the others, ...

When the 1982 session of the general assembly adopted legislation seeking to give the legislature and its interim committee a greater oversight role on executive actions, questions regarding the constitutional separation of powers were raised. A suit was filed in the state courts seeking a decision on the constitutionality of the 1981 acts. In the fall of 1983, the state supreme court ruled that the legislature's action violated the concept of separation of powers as expressed in Sections 27 and 28.[13]

As state government has grown, effective legislative oversight of the executive branch has become a major problem under the current constitution. With a full-time governor and a part-time legislature, it is inevitable that the powers and functions of the executive branch have far outstripped those of the legislative branch. Such things as budgetary and financial decisions, the handling of federal grants and funds, and many other matters require full-time, day-to-day management. Since the general assembly is limited to sessions of only sixty days every two years, it is impossible for it to provide day-to-day oversight. To handle state business, it has turned to a system of interim committees, which can conduct hearings and investigations. And in 1981 the general assembly tried to delegate oversight functions to its arm, the Legislative Research Commission, but even the LRC has grown up outside the constitution, and the state supreme court said neither the interim committees nor the LRC could act in place of the full legislature.[14] So, the problem of more effective oversight awaits further resolution.

Apparently the framers gave only passing thought to another aspect of the executive branch that has become extremely important for current governmental operations. In a rather off-hand manner, they approved a provision for the creation of other "inferior officers." Under this provision the general assembly has created some of the largest and most important departments of state government. Today these appointive statutory officers head the major departments of state government and have come to play a major role in policymaking and implementation. These administrative agencies, which former Chief Justice of the Kentucky Supreme Court John Palmore calls "swooses" (neither swan nor goose), pose a major problem in effective oversight by the general assembly.

Critics contend that the state constitution lacks the necessary flexibility and has become outmoded and obsolete. They say that even though the courts have managed to keep it workable through liberal interpretations, this encourages dishonesty and disrespect for the law. Despite the obvious shortcomings and heavy criticism for years, efforts to change the state constitution have not met with overwhelming success.

EFFORTS AT REVISION

Many of the constitution delegates realized their efforts would need modifications. A. J. Auxier observed:

> There is nothing so sacred about any of this Constitution but what the people can alter, modify or change, and adapt it to the wants of the people when the emergency arises . . . . We are simply the representatives of the people. They sent us here to form a Constitution; not for the government of all generations yet unborn, but to prepare a Constitution suitable for the government of the people at the present time.[15]

For the first time, the 1890 delegates provided that the constitution could be changed either by amendment or convention. The first three documents could be changed only by calling a convention.

Revision by Convention

Section 256 provides for the calling of a convention to revise the constitution. First, two sessions of the general assembly must approve an act providing for a referendum on the question of calling a convention. When a referendum is held, the convention call must be approved by a majority at least equal to one-fourth of the number of qualified voters who voted at the last preceding general election. In other words, a mere majority favorable vote of those voting on the call may not be sufficient to require a convention.

Calls for a convention to revise the current constitution have never been successful. The first attempt to use this method came in 1931 and was rejected by the voters—97,788 no votes to 28,204 yes votes. Even if a majority had favored the call, fewer than 20 percent of the eligible voters voted on the issue—not enough to require a convention. In 1947 another effort was made. This time 50 percent of those eligible voted, but the vote was against a convention 191,876 to 144,692. In 1961 a vigorous campaign was waged for a convention, but the call was rejected in a close vote 342,501 to 324,777. This time about 60 percent of the eligible voters voted on the issue. After this effort for a convention failed, proponents for change sought other channels for revision.

Revision by Assembly

Though not provided for specifically in the constitution, a couple of efforts have been made to propose revision through specifically appointed bodies. In 1949 Governor Earle Clements named a seven-member constitutional review commission to study and propose needed changes. The 1950 general assembly gave the commission permanent status; however, little came from its efforts, and it was abolished in 1956.

In 1964 the general assembly created the Constitution Revision Assembly as an arm of the Legislative Research Commission. The governor, lieutenant governor, speaker of the house, and chief justice were to name members of the assembly. All living ex-governors were members; one member was to be named from each of the thirty-eight senatorial districts, and five at-large members would make a total membership of fifty. After twenty-three months of work, the assembly produced a draft constitution that was largely an editing and updating of the 1891 document. It left about 70 percent of the existing document unchanged. The assembly's draft was submitted to the general assembly in 1966 and was approved overwhelmingly for submission to the voters at the next general election. This procedure was definitely not in keeping with the provisions for revision outlined in the constitution. However, the procedure was upheld by the court of appeals as falling under Section 4 of Kentucky's bill of rights, which gave the people the right to revise their form of government. In the November 1966 election the voters rejected the proposed revision 517,034 to 143,133. The proposed revision failed to carry a single county in the state. In 1977 another attempt at revision by special commission failed, leading many to conclude that about the only feasible process for changing the document was by amendment.

Revision by Amendment

In Section 256, the framers provided that amendments could be proposed by members in either house of the general assembly. If approved by a three-fifths majority in both houses, amendments are submitted to the voters for ratification in the next election for members of the house. If approved by a majority of those voting on them, amendments become a part of the constitution. The governor's approval is not required on amendments. As originally adopted, Section 256 allowed only two amendments to be submitted to the voters at one time and required that amendments deal with only one subject. If an amendment was rejected, it could not be resubmitted for five years. In 1979 Section 256 was amended so that up to four amendments could be proposed at one time; amendments could cover related subjects and as many articles or sections of the constitution as necessary and appropriate. No limit was placed on resubmission of rejected amendments. This made it possible to propose more comprehensive changes in the constitution at one time through the amending process. In 1975 a major reform of the state judiciary article was approved by the voters. While the amendment process has been used to correct several basic weaknesses over the years, it is far from a surefire method of change. Only twenty-five amendments have gained approval, twenty-eight have been rejected, and four thrown out on technical grounds. One of the most recent rejections was a 1981 proposal to allow county sheriffs and the governor to succeed themselves.

Since the 1930s, over four-fifths of the states have undertaken revisions in their constitutions. The 1960s and 1970s were periods of numerous attempts at revision. Between 1945 and 1981 new constitutions were approved by the voters in fourteen states. Still, as a general rule, citizens tend to take a rather conservative attitude toward changes in their state constitutions. This is reflected in the fact that at the start of the 1980s twenty-nine states still had their constitutions that were written in the nineteenth century, and three New England states had documents going back to the eighteenth century. Nineteen states were still using their original constitutions, and the average age for state constitutions was about eighty-two years. Since 1930, proposals for convention calls have been submitted to the voters in twenty-seven states. Out of sixty-two referenda, thirty-two calls have been approved, and twenty-seven were rejected. Even when conventions are approved, revision is not certain. Over the last two decades, revisions proposed by unlimited conventions have been rejected in six states. Because of the voter's conservatism on the issue, many states choose to undertake revision in stages rather than all at once. This is what most observers feel will be necessary in Kentucky considering past experiences. With the changes in the amending clause, the process has been made somewhat easier. Nonetheless, the task of updating the constitution, in light of the voters' conservative attitude, remains a formidable one. Many Kentuckians still reflect Jefferson's observations when he remarked: "Some men look at Constitutions with sanctimonious reverence, and deem them like the ark of the covenant, too sacred to be touched...."[16] Many voters apparently prefer to go with the old and familiar, even if somewhat flawed, rather than take a chance on something new and different. Their innate suspiciousness of politicians and apprehensions about anything uncertain make them wary of political change. Constitutions, even though somewhat defective, provide an element of stability and restraint.

FOOTNOTES

1. Allen Trout as quoted by James T. Fleming in "The Story of Kentucky's Constitution: An Explanatory Essay," from *Constitution of the Commonwealth of Kentucky*, Informational Bulletin #136, Legislative Research Commission (Frankfort, 1982) p. xxi.

2. Charles Borgeaud, *Adoption and Amendment of Constitutions* (New York: Macmillan, 1895), p. xvii.

3. From *American Life in Literature*, Ed. Jay B. Hubbell (New York: Harper and Brothers Publishers, 1936), p. 172.

4. Quoted by Joan Coward in *Kentucky in the New Republic* (Lexington, Ky: University Press of Kentucky, 1979), pp. 14-15.

5. George Willis, "History of Kentucky Constitutions and Constitutional Conventions," *Register of the Kentucky Historical Society* (October, 1930), p. 319.

6. A. J. Auxier, *Official Report of the Proceedings and Debate in the Convention to Adopt, Amend or Change the Constitution of the State of Kentucky* (Frankfort, 1891), Vol. II, p. 1753.

7. James Blackburn, *Ibid.* Vol. I, p. 796.
8. Clifton Lowry, *The Influence of John Locke upon the Early Political Thought of Kentucky,* unpublished dissertation, University of Kentucky Library (Lexington, 1940), pp. 17ff.
9. J. M. Wood, *1890 Convention Proceedings, op. cit.* Vol. III, p. 3683.
10. As quoted by James Fleming, *op. cit.* p. vii.
11. Committee for Kentucky, *A Report on the Constitution,* 1946, p. 14.
12. *Board of Education v. DeWeese,* 343 S.W. 2nd 598 (1960) and *Matthews v. Allen* 360 S.W. 2nd 135 (1963).
13. *Legislative Research Commission v. John Y. Brown,* 82 Supreme Court 896 (1983).
14. *Ibid.*
15. A. J. Auxier, *1890 Convention Proceedings, op. cit.* Vol. II, p. 1759.
16. Thomas Jefferson in letter to Samuel Kercheval, July 12, 1816, from *The Life and Selected Writings of Thomas Jefferson,* edited by Adrienne Koch and William Peden (New York: Random House, 1944), p. 674.

BIBLIOGRAPHY

Borgeaud, Charles. *Adoption and Amendment of Constitutions.* New York: Macmillan, 1895.

Clark, Thomas D. "Background of the Present Constitution" in *The Constitution of Kentucky: Suggestions for Revision.* Lexington, Ky: Bureau of Government Research, University of Kentucky, 1948.

Committee for Kentucky. *A Report on the Constitution.* 1946.

Constitution of the Commonwealth of Kentucky. Legislative Research Commission. Publication #136. Frankfort, Ky.

Council of State Governments. *Book of the States.* v24. Lexington, Ky. 1982.

Coward, Joan W. *Kentucky in the New Republic.* Lexington: University Press of Ky., 1979.

Dietzman, Richard P. *"The Four Constitutions of Kentucky." Kentucky Law Journal* v.15 (January, 1927), pp. 116ff.

Graves, Brooke. "What Should a Constitution Contain?" *New Jersey Constitutional Proceedings,* VII, 1947.

Legislative Research Commission. *Kentucky's Constitutional Development.* Informational Bulletin #29. Frankfort.

Legislative Research Commission. *A Comparison . . . The Present, The Proposed Kentucky Constitutions.* Informational Bulletin #52. Frankfort, 1967.

Lowry, Clifton. *The Influence of John Locke upon the Early Political Thought of Kentucky.* Dissertation, University of Kentucky Library. 1940.

Official Report of the Proceedings and Debates in the Convention to Adopt, Amend, or Change the Constitution of the State of Kentucky. Frankfort. 1890.

Phelps, Lilburn. *Kentucky's 1891 Constitution.* Jamestown, Ky. 1947.

Reeves, John E. *Kentucky Government.* Lexington, Ky. 1966.

Willis, George L. *History of Kentucky Constitutions and Constitutional Conventions.* Frankfort: State Journal Company, 1937. Also reprinted in the Kentucky Historical Society Register, (October, 1930 and January, 1931), pp. 305-29 and 52-81 respectively.

Young, Bennett. *History of the Texts of the Three Constitutions of Kentucky.* Louisville, Ky: *Courier-Journal* Printing Company, 1890.

Chapter 3

THE GOVERNOR

Robert J. Synder, Georgetown College

INTRODUCTION

The governor of Kentucky is probably the most visible figure in public life in the state. In this television age, he/she is subject to the close scrutiny of the press almost on a nightly basis, especially during elections or sessions of the general assembly. The office has considerable power in the administration of billions of dollars coming from the sales, income, and coal severance taxes. The influence of the office can be used to promote new industry, to schedule an annual basketball game between the state's major universities, or as a springboard to the United States Senate. The governor also has at his/her disposal a large bureaucracy including two significant law enforcement agencies: the state police and the national guard. In short, it is an office with great power similar to the chief executive officers in the forty-nine other American states and many of the smaller nation-states overseas.

There are several different ways to study the office of governor. One can examine the legal constitutional and statutory require-ments of the Commonwealth of Kentucky. Another research technique would be to look at how the thirteen most recent occupants of the office conducted their affairs within the culture and political system as they found it. No political institution or statewide leader operates in a vacuum: the governor must interact with the legislature, the bureaucracy, the courts, and various organized groups that seek influence. A study of the recruitment process is also important because it tells us what socioeconomic factors seem to be important in the selection of people who have been elected governor in this state. Finally, in order to get a broader perspective, we shall try to compare the Kentucky experience with that in the other forty-nine states in the American federal system.

Perhaps the high point of a governor's popularity and public exposure is inauguration day, which takes place in early December after the general election every four years. In 1983, the parade passed through downtown Frankfort and up Capitol Avenue past about twenty thousand people on a cold, crisp day. Friends and family of the new governor, former governors, congressmen and senators, legislators, university presidents, and campaign leaders sat on the reviewing platform. In a space of four hours, over two hundred marching bands, floats, and drill teams passed by, representing most of the state's universities and counties. Actually, Chief Justice Robert Stephens had already sworn in Martha Layne Collins at 12:01 A.M. in a private ceremony; later in the morning, she attended a service at the Bagdad Baptist Church in Shelby County, where she was born. After the formal swearing-in ceremonies at 2 P.M. before several thousand people and television cameras from the major networks, there was a reception in the Old Capitol Building downtown. That evening, a large crowd participated in the grand march opening the black-tie Inaugural Ball in both the Capitol Rotunda and a huge tent on a nearby parking lot. But much of crowd's attention centered on the new governor's gown, which had been specially designed for the occasion.

EARLY DEVELOPMENT

The office of governor is one of the oldest positions in the American political system. As an agent of the British Crown, the colonial governor served at the pleasure of the monarch and exercised vast powers, which included control of the militia, law enforcement, tax collection, the court system, and the granting of pardons and reprieves.[1] He had direct access to the central government in London. Early frontiersmen in Kentucky had to travel over miles of mountainous territory to reach colonial Williamsburg, Virginia, the colonial capital. After the end of the American Revolution in 1783, all the new states searched for new systems of government. They retained the office of governor but limited his term and made the office elective in some manner. In general, the Kentucky political culture inherited both the need for some central authority and a deep suspicion of too much authority centered in the hands of one person.

In the first Kentucky constitutional convention in 1790, a former Virginia legislator, George Nicholas, stressed the need for adopting a governmental model using a governor, a court of appeals, and an elected general assembly made up of representatives and senators. He justified his proposals with arguments from classical, European, and American national experiences. Nicholas wanted direct election of the governor, but the convention designed an electoral college, which was later scrapped in the 1799 constitution in favor of direct election by the people in the best early nineteenth century democratic tradition. Unlike most of the former colonies, which sought to restrict the power of the governor in their initial constitutions, Kentucky followed the example of the national constitution: the 1790 Kentucky constitutional convention gave the governor a four-year term with no restrictions on reelection. He could veto acts of the legislature and appoint the officers necessary to do the work of the government.[2]

Throughout the nineteenth century, Kentucky state government slowly enlarged its scope of activity, but most governmental services were handled at the county level. Nevertheless, the office of governor became the center of conflict between competing political parties and political interest groups. Differences over slavery led to a constitutional convention in 1849 that took away most powers of appointment in local government from the governor. The Civil War put further strains on the chief executive, as Governor Magoffin vainly sought neutrality before he resigned to be replaced by a pro-Union state senator.[3] After the war, the office became a new prize between the populists and the supporters of railroad development. This competition for power set the stage for the constitutional convention of 1891, which designed the current constitution of Kentucky.

The constitution approved in 1892 by the people limited the governor to one four-year term at a time. The occupant of the position had to be a least thirty years old and a resident of the state for six years. The powers of the chief executive were further diluted by the requirement that seven other statewide officers be elected by the voters. On the other hand, the constitution gave the governor the power to call special sessions of the legislature after they had completed their limited sixty-day term every two years. The framers of the 1892 constitution also included an innovative provision called an item veto, whereby the governor would be able to strike out changes in money bills that he thought were unwise. Not even the president of the United States has that power.[4] In summary, the office under the 1892 constitution was both restricted in its power and broad in some ways in order to attract an executive to manage the affairs of the state with some energy.

Under the new constitution, competition increased for the office of governor as the Republican party finally began to compete successfully with the Democrats and elected a candidate for the first time in 1895. They almost repeated the process again in 1899. It appeared that the Republican Taylor had been elected, but the legislature chose to investigate the matter. The Democratic nominee, William Goebel, was subsequently shot in front of the capitol building; then he was sworn in as governor on his deathbed. His successor, J.C.W. Beckham, served for seven years—the longest continuous service for any governor.

The most exciting race came in 1915 as Democrat A.O. Stanley and Republican Ed Morrow debated each other all over the state with spendid campaign oratory. After his election, Governor Stanley initiated reforms in election laws, labor relations, legislative redistricting, education, tax laws, and the welfare system in addition to starting the first budget system in Kentucky state government.[5] Thus, by the beginning of the twentieth century, the office of governor had begun to evolve into a position of authority and leadership.

RECENT GOVERNORS

The roots of Kentucky politics and attitudes toward the governor go deep into regional and national history, but after looking into the first 140 years of the state's history, it would seem to be helpful to look in more detail at recent governors. Most observers agree that the modern governorship began in 1935 with the reforms of Governor Chandler as a response to the economic Depression.[6] Ten of the twelve governors who have served since 1935 are still living, and the selected papers of five of them have been published. We will be looking at a variety of things: socioeconomic backgrounds, methods of operations, the workings of the political system, goals and accomplishments, and the way the system perhaps needs to be changed. Finally, a word of caution needs to be added. The press tends to concentrate on the activities of governors, but the workings of government are the product of the work of thousands of dedicated state employees and political leaders. We will try to summarize state government operations by the terms of particular governors, but credit for accomplishments and failures should be spread around the thousands of participants in the governing process.

Chandler, A.B.   **44th Governor**
(Term of Office—December 10, 1935 to October 9, 1939)

Albert B. "Happy" Chandler was born on a small farm near Corydon in Henderson County in western Kentucky. Because of family circumstances, he had to support himself through high school before leaving for Transylvania University in Lexington with a "five dollar bill, a red sweater, and a smile."[7] Again he made his own way while playing football, basketball, and baseball. After graduation in 1921, Chandler went on to Harvard Law School for one term before returning to Lexington to graduate from the University of Kentucky Law School. For a time he coached football for Centre College in Danville, then he began his law practice in Versailles where he was elected to the state senate in 1929. In 1931, Chandler was elected lieutenant governor. While Governor Laffoon was out of the state, Chandler called a special session of the legislature to change the election laws. On his return, the governor had his leaders strip the lieutenant governor of most of his powers in the senate, but the new primary election law passed anyway, and Chandler used it to good advantage, as he won the primary election runoff against the governor's candidate in 1935.

As governor, Happy Chandler quickly plunged into an effort to revitalize and reform state government in the late 1930s after the worst of the economic depression has passed. Thousands of patronage workers were removed from the state payrolls; young college graduates and specialists came to Frankfort to modernize state operations. The state debt of $28 million was reduced, and the budget was balanced with the help of federal funds from Washington and from centralized financial controls in a new Department of Finance. Chandler got the legislature to adjourn after thirty-nine days so he could call special sessions to tackle problems one at a time. In turn, the legislature approved a repeal of the sales tax; new taxes on income, alcohol, and cigarettes; a compulsory primary election law; free textbooks for school children; old-age pensions using federal matching funds; and a full-scale government reorganization.[8] The governor also showed great courage when he went to the state prison during a riot and promised the prisoners fair treatment; a new reformatory was subsequently built at LaGrange. It was a time of rapid change, which called for strong leadership.

But Chandler's attention soon moved on to the United States Senate in Washington. In 1938, he challenged the majority leader, Alben Barkley of Paducah, and lost. Then the other Senator from Kentucky died; Chandler resigned as governor and was appointed to the senate by the new governor, Keen Johnson.

Johnson, Keen   45th Governor
(Term of Office—October 9, 1939 to December 7, 1943)

Keen Johnson was born at Brandon's Chapel in Lyon County in the western part of Kentucky into the family of a circuit-riding Methodist minister. After military service in World War I, he graduated from the University of Kentucky with a degree in journalism in 1922. He had worked on several newspapers, but he soon made a reputation as the successful publisher of the Richmond *Daily Register.* His introduction to statewide politics came with his appointment as executive secretary of the State Democratic Central Committee in 1932. In 1935 he was elected lieutenant governor on the ticket with Happy Chandler. After Chandler resigned in 1939 to enter the United States Senate, Keen Johnson became governor for one month before winning a full four-year term in November.

In his inaugural speech, Johnson emphasized Kentucky's motto: "United We Stand, Divided We Fall" as World War II was breaking out in Europe.[9] In the legislature, he pushed for constitutional amendments to equalize educational expenditures among school districts; to remove the $5,000 salary limit in the constitution; and to permit the buying of voting machines. He lost the salary issue, but won the other two. Governor Johnson was proud that his administration had done major repairs at the state's hospitals and prisons while trying to match federal offers of money for food and old-age pension programs. He vigorously sought a reapportionment of the legislature in 1942 to balance rural and urban interests. Methodically, he tried to shift highway building programs from political necessity to requirements of need and usage. Toll bridges at Owensboro, Paducah, Ashland, Covington, and Newport were freed of tolls. The governor constantly emphasized good stewardship of state funds; he eliminated the state debt and actually left a surplus in the state treasury to his successor.

Eastern Kentucky State College in Richmond named its new Student Union Building in honor of Governor Johnson in 1940. After his term had ended, Keen Johnson served briefly as undersecretary of labor in the administration of President Harry Truman before returning to Richmond.

Willis, Simeon S.   46th Governor
(Term of Office—December 7, 1943 to December 9, 1947)

A native of Lawrence County, Ohio, Simeon Willis spent most of his early life in the Ashland, Kentucky, area in the northeastern corner of Kentucky. He was the son of a Union veteran of the Civil War. Willis completed a common school education in Greenup

County, Kentucky, taught school for a time, and then spent three years reading law. After passing the bar exam, he set up a law practice in Ashland in 1902. Willis served as city solicitor for Ashland, and his introduction to statewide politics came when Governor Flem Sampson appointed him to the state court of appeals. He subsequently won election for an eight-year term on the court. Just as World War II was beginning, friends prevailed upon Judge Willis to run for governor on the Republican ticket in early 1943. In the general election he defeated former Highway Commissioner J. Lyter Donaldson by a margin of 8,600 votes on a platform calling for repeal of the state income tax without substituting a new tax and a promise to pay an additional $3 million to public school teachers. Simeon Willis was the first Republican elected governor since 1927.[10]

Once in office, Governor Willis was unable to get the income tax repeal through the legislature controlled by the Democrats, but teacher's pay was doubled. He appointed the first black member of the state board of education and selected an engineer as head of the highway department after he had eliminated the highly politicized district commissioner system. The high bridge over the Kentucky River at Clay's Ferry was opened in 1946. The game and fish division of state government was returned to the sportsmen, who began to elect a supervisory commission for the program. Five new tuberculosis hospitals were opened under Governor Willis, and a bond issue helped finance several new state parks. Tax collections went up sharply to reach a new high of $80 million in 1947, but the governor failed to arouse much interest in constitutional reform or a new justice building in Frankfort.[11]

Clements, Earle   47th Governor
(Term of Office—December 9, 1947 to November 27, 1950)

Earle Clements was the consumate politician and organizer. He was born on a farm in Union County in western Kentucky. After he graduated from Morganfield High School, Clements attended the University of Kentucky where he played football before entering military service in World War I. For twenty years after returning home, he held a succession of local government offices: sheriff, county clerk, and finally county judge. In 1935, he became campaign chairman for the Rhea coalition that lost to Happy Chandler. Then in 1942, he entered the Kentucky senate, where he quickly assumed leadership as Democratic majority leader under Republican Governor Willis. After a brief term in the United States House of Representatives, Clements won the election for governor in 1947 by 100,000 votes. A crowd of over 20,000 people and numerous bands welcomed his return to Frankfort at the inauguration in December.

Governor Clements moved quickly to adjust the sources of income for the state. The 1948 general assembly passed a two cents per gallon increase in the gasoline tax to help pay for improving rural roads. A 3 percent tax was imposed on pari-mutuel betting at the state's racetracks, and the income tax was raised in 1950. In turn, the governor increased the state's contribution to public education by $10 million. In order to house the increasing number of state employees, an office annex was constructed behind the capitol building in Frankfort. The state highway patrol was absorbed into a new state police organization. Another major achievement was the organization of an Agriculture and Industrial Development Board in 1948 to study state resources and to solicit new industries to locate in Kentucky. This effort played a part in the doubling of plant payrolls between 1948 and 1954.[12]

During his term as governor, Earle Clements decided to run for the United States Senate in 1950. His well-organized political supporters gave him a large victory. In the Senate, he quickly became one of the inner club and was named Democratic whip under Majority Leader Lyndon Johnson in 1953. But, he was defeated in a reelection bid in 1956 during the Republican sweep that year.

Wetherby, Lawrence   48th Governor
(Term of Office—November 27, 1950 to December 13, 1955)

Governor Clements's successor as governor was Lawrence Wetherby, the lieutenant governor who served as governor for a little over five years. He was a native of Middletown near Louisville in Jefferson County; both his father and grandfather had been physicians. After graduation from Anchorage High School, Wetherby went on to the University of Louisville to earn a law degree in 1929. He was admitted to the bar and opened a practice in Louisville. From 1943 to 1947 he served as juvenile judge of Jefferson County. During that time he was active as a member of the Anchorage school board, the Jefferson County Democratic Central Committee, and finally secretary of the Democratic State Central Committee. Lawrence Wetherby won the 1947 election for lieutenant governor by a margin of 100,000 votes. Then in 1951 he defeated Republican Eugene Siler by 58,000 votes to win a full four-year term as governor.[13]

Governor Wetherby presided over major changes in Kentucky during the early 1950s. The general assembly improved the voting system by providing for permanent registration, a comparative signature test, and eighteen-year-old voting. In the field of education, the Minimum Foundation Program was started in 1954 via a constitutional amendment; state aid to local school districts was thereafter based on need and average daily attendance rather than on just numbers. College graduation became a requirement for teachers. In the area of economic development, the state played a major role in bringing the General Electric Co. and the Ford Motor Co. to Louisville and Jefferson County. A new innovation, the Kentucky Turnpike, was built as a toll road from Elizabethtown to Louisville, where it entered the city near the new fairgrounds and its 18,000 seat Freedom Hall. Kentucky took other progressive steps with a new withholding collection system for its income tax and a legislative research commission to give badly needed assistance to the general assembly. It was a time for Kentucky to move ahead.

Governor Wetherby left office in 1955 and ran for the United States Senate in 1956, but he was defeated. He went into private law practice in Frankfort but took the unusual step of serving in the state senate for a four-year term in the late 1960s.

Chandler, A.B. "Happy"   49th Governor
(Term of Office—December 13, 1955 to December 8, 1959)

Former Governor A.B. Chandler resigned as Commissioner of Baseball on July 10, 1951. He returned to Versailles to practice law and run his weekly newspaper, the *Woodford Sun*. Challenging the combined political power of Governor Wetherby and Senators Clements and Barkley, he defeated Judge Bert Combs in the Democratic primary election in 1955. Chandler had campaigned for ten months making over nine hundred speeches. He smiled, sang, shook hands, and called many old friends in his audiences by their first names. After each speech, he sang, "There's a Gold Mine in the Sky."[14] He won the closely contested primary by 18,000 votes out of 500,000 votes cast. After the other leaders of the Democratic party pledged their support, he won the November election by 129,000, the largest plurality a candidate for governor ever received up to that time in Kentucky. When Chandler heard the news of his victory he sand, "My Old Kentucky Home," while tears streamed down his face.

At his inauguration in December 1955, Happy Chandler rode in a blue and red wagon drawn by four white horses. Music was supplied by seventy-one bands, and seventy floats passed the reviewing stand bearing such slogans as "Happy for President in 1956 if Mama Says Yes." But, the new governor serving his second term was faced with problems fairly quickly, as the federal courts ordered integration of local schools. The process was handled peacefully in Columbia, Kentucky, in 1956, but the National Guard had to stand guard in Sturgis. At the 1956 Democratic presidential nominating convention, the Kentucky delegation was bound to Governor Chandler until it was obvious that Governor Stevenson of Illinois would be nominated.

Chandler's major achievements in his second term came in the fields of development and education. The International Business Machines Corporation chose to locate its new electric typewriter factory on part of the grounds of the Eastern State Hospital in Lexington, and soon it became a major employer in central Kentucky. The new medical center with its hospital and medical school at the University of Kentucky was named in honor of Governor Chandler because of his untiring efforts to get a medical school for the university.

Combs, Bert T. 50th Governor
(Term of Office—December 8, 1959 to December 10, 1963)

Bert Combs was the first Democrat elected governor from eastern Kentucky since 1927. He was also the first veteran of World War II to win the governor's chair. Combs was a native of Clay County, where he graduated from Manchester High School before attending Cumberland Junior College. He then spent several years working in Frankfort before attending the University of Kentucky, where he graduated from the law school in 1937. During World War II, Bert Combs served in the War Crimes Department on the staff of General MacArthur in the Philippine Islands. Returning to Prestonsburg, he was elected as commonwealth's attorney for Floyd County. In 1950, he was appointed to fill a vacancy on the court of appeals in Frankfort. There his opinions came to the attention of the Democratic leadership, and he was asked to run against former Governor Chandler in 1956. He lost, but he came back in 1959 to team with former Louisville Mayor Wilson Wyatt to win the governor's chair. Together they pledged to improve both education and roads in the state.

Once in office, Governor Combs cut the state's payroll by 15 percent, as many Chandler supporters were dismissed. He sent the legislature a sixteen-point program, which included a merit system for state employees, a law requiring voting machines in all precincts, a $1,500 increase in teacher's salaries, and a new institution to encourage research and development of business in the state. In February of 1960, Governor Combs signed into law a controversial veteran's bonus bill. To help finance the bonus and other programs, the governor had the legislature approve a 3 percent sales tax and an increase in the income tax by 40 percent. The Mountain Parkway was built into eastern Kentucky, while the Western Kentucky Parkway connected I-65 at Elizabethtown to the western part of the state. Substantial portions of the interstate highway system in the rest of the state were also finished. The governor showed some courage by cancelling a doubtful dump truck deal and removing some Campbell County officials from office for not enforcing state gambling laws in Newport. He left his mark on the Capitol Building area by building a floral clock that soon became a tourist attraction.[15]

After leaving office, Bert Combs was appointed to the federal court of appeals in Cincinnati in 1967, but he resigned to run for governor again in 1971. He was defeated by Wendell Ford in the Democratic primary race. He then turned to the practice of law in Louisville and Lexington.

Breathitt, Edward T. (Ned)   **51st Governor**
(Term of Office—December 10, 1963 to December 12, 1967)

Edward T. (Ned) Breathitt, Jr., came from a political family: three of his relatives held statewide office as attorney general, lieutenant governor, or governor. Ned Breathitt was reared in Hopkinsville, where he graduated from high school before going into the United States Air Force just before World War II ended. He then joined the army of returning veterans attending the University of Kentucky, where he graduated from the law school in 1950. After setting up a law practice in Hopkinsville, he won election in 1951 to the Kentucky house of representatives for the first of three terms. From 1952 to 1954 he served as president of the Young Democrats of Kentucky. In 1959, Governor Bert Combs appointed him as the first commissioner of personnel under the new merit system law. The next year he moved over to the Public Service Commission for two years before making the race for governor in 1963. In the Democratic primary election, he narrowly defeated former Governor Happy Chandler, but the Chandler candidate for lieutenant governor, Harry Lee Waterfield, won his race. In the fall, the Breathitt-Waterfield team narrowly defeated the Republican ticket led by Louie Nunn by 13,000 votes.[16]

In his inauguration address, Governor Breathitt urged Kentuckians to go forward in the spirit of the late President John F. Kennedy, who had been assassinated only the previous month. Not long after that, ten thousand demonstrators descended on Frankfort demanding action on civil rights legislation pending before the legislature, but the general assembly refused to pass a bill recommended by the governor. Then the scene shifted to Washington, where the Congress did pass the Civil Rights Act of 1964. In the other matters, the state legislature passed a law regulating campaign finance and new legislation concerning control of strip mining in the coal fields. The four regional colleges were upgraded to universities. In downtown Frankfort, a new high rise office building was built as part of a Capital Plaza authorized in 1966. Finally, Governor Breathitt led a major effort to reform the state's constitution by calling a special convention to study the document and present a revised version directly to the voter. Unfortunately, the issue was soundly defeated in the general election of 1966.

After leaving government service, Ned Breathitt became Vice-President for Public Relations of the Southern Railroad with his home base in Washington.

Nunn, Louie B.   **52nd Governor**
(Term of Office—December 12, 1967 to December 7, 1971)

Louie B. Nunn became the first Republican elected governor of Kentucky in twenty years when he won the general election in November 1967 by 29,000 votes over former Highway Commissioner Henry Ward. The new governor was born in the park community of Barren County where he graduated from Hiseville High School. After attending Bowling Green Business University and the University of Cincinnati, he entered military service in World War II. On returning home he attended the University of Louisville and graduated from the law school in 1950. Back in Barren County, Nunn became the first Republican ever elected county judge. He entered statewide Republican politics as campaign manager for the races of President Eisenhower, Senator John Sherman Cooper, and Senator Thruston Morton in the 1950s. Then in 1963, Louie Nunn ran for governor, but he was defeated by a narrow margin; in 1967 he was more successful.

On taking office, Governor Nunn was soon absorbed in budget politics as projections showed a substantial deficit in his first year in office. Despite a campaign pledge not to raise taxes, he showed some courage by asking the legislature to extend the sales tax from 3 to 5 percent. The new stability in the budget allowed the governor to double the money spent on vocational education, to complete a statewide educational television network, and to increase the salaries of teachers substantially. In addition, a new hospital for exceptional children was built in Somerset, and a new toll road was constructed from that south central Kentucky city westward to the governor's hometown of Glasgow. In higher education, the University of Louisville was brought into the state system, along with a new Northern Kentucky State University, which in turn named its administration building after Nunn. In his papers, the governor indicated that he was especially proud that his administration was free of major scandal and actually left a surplus in the treasury for his successor.[17]

After his term in office expired, Governor Nunn moved to Lexington to practice law, but he kept his hand in politics by running unsuccessfully for the United States Senate on one occasion and for governor again in 1979.

Ford, Wendell H.   53rd Governor
(Term of Office—December 7, 1971 to December 28, 1974)

Wendell Ford did not fit the normal mold of governors in recent years—men trained in the law. He was born in rural Daviess County in western Kentucky. His father had been a state senator. Wendell Ford received his schooling in Daviess County schools and attended the University of Kentucky before entering the army during World War II. After military service, he returned to work in the family insurance business in Owensboro. Long active in civic and religious affairs in his community, he became the first Kentuckian ever elected national president of the Jaycees. He took leave from the insurance business in 1959 to enter state government service as chief administrative assistant to Governor Combs. Then in 1965, Ford was elected to the state senate and began an active campaign for the office of lieutenant governor. In the 1967 general election, he was elected as a Democrat to serve with a Republican governor. As the top Democrat in the state, he successfully guided the Democratic legislature for four years before launching his campaign for governor. In 1971, he defeated his former boss, Bert Combs, in the primary election and went on to win the general election by 68,000 votes over both his Republican opponent and Happy Chandler, who was running as an independent.

Wendell Ford came to the office of governor with over ten years experience in the capital. He fulfilled 85 percent of his campaign pledges in his first budget. The sales tax was removed from food, and a new severance tax was placed on coal to obtain new money for education and welfare programs. The council on higher education was restructured to strengthen its functions. In addition, Governor Ford sponsored aid to both downtown Louisville and Lexington for urban redevelopment to be matched by both federal and local sources. He enjoyed taking state government to the people in trips around the state, and he responded quickly to the crisis created by the tornados of 1974. In his papers, he congratulated the legislature on the passage of such programs as the Kentucky Housing Corporation, a new penal code, and no-fault insurance for automobiles. He cut ribbons for the opening of the last link in I-64 in eastern Kentucky and the Green River Parkway near his hometown of Owensboro in western Kentucky. Special attention went to energy development after the international oil crisis of 1973 and to reorganization of state government into cabinets and departments. Because of the advent of federal revenue sharing, he was able to leave a surplus of $147 million in the treasury for his successor.[18]

During his term as governor, Wendell Ford sought to unify the Democratic party. As a result, in 1972 Kentuckians elected a Democrat to the United States Senate for the first time since 1956. Then in 1974, Governor Ford ran for the other senate seat and won; consequently, he resigned his office as governor a year short of finishing his term. He was subsequently reelected to the senate in 1980.

Carroll, Julian M. 54th Governor
(Term of Office—December 28, 1974 to December 10, 1979)

A native of McCracken County in western Kentucky, Julian Carroll graduated from Heath High School, attended Paducah Junior College, and graduated from the law school of the University of Kentucky in 1956. Following service in the United States Air Force, he returned to Paducah to practice law. His activity in church work led to his being elected moderator of the Kentucky Synod of the Presbyterian Church in 1966. In the meantime, he entered politics by his election to the Kentucky house of representatives, where he was elected as speaker in 1968 and 1970. Carroll chose to make the race for lieutenant governor in 1971 with former Governor Bert Combs, but in the Democratic primary election he was picked to run with Wendell Ford. Following Ford's resignation in 1974, Carroll took the oath of office as governor and turned his attention to developing a campaign organization for the 1975 election. In November, his organization gave him a 198,000 vote margin.[19] Thus, Julian Carroll came to the office with experience in both houses of the legislature and in the governor's chair.

On taking office, Governor Julian Carroll took careful stock of the financial condition of the state in light of the national economic recession. Much effort went into both promoting and regulating the coal industry through resource recovery roads and new regulations on surface mining. The state also participated significantly in downtown redevelopment projects in both Lexington and Louisville. In law enforcement, the governor pushed through laws abolishing the bail bond system and received several threats on his life as a result. After the tragic Beverly Hills night club fire, new safety codes were implemented and enforced. While the governor was out of the state in 1979, Lieutenant Governor Thelma Stovall called a special session of the legislature to limit increases in property taxes, and House Bill 44 passed. At the same time, the press began to criticize the use of a small fleet of airplanes by the governor and his staff, but Carroll insisted that they saved the state money in travel costs and time. In the end, Carroll wanted to be remembered as the education governor, and indeed spending on elementary and secondary education doubled. His task force on education in 1977 made a number of long range recommendations, many of which were put into force either by the legislature or the state board of education. At the same time, over $100 million was spent on new facilities for higher education.[20]

Brown, John Y., Jr.   **55th Governor**
(Term of Office—December 11, 1979 to December 9, 1983)

John Y. Brown, Jr., was born into a political family. His father had been both a speaker of the Kentucky house of representatives and a Congressman. John Y. Brown, Jr., graduated from Lafayette High School in Lexington and went on to graduate from the law school of the University of Kentucky in 1960. He then entered practice with his father, but his talents soon were applied toward business, as he built the Kentucky Fried Chicken Corporation into one of the nation's largest fast food chains.[21] In the early 1970s, he also became involved in professional basketball first with the Kentucky Colonels of the American Basketball Association and then with the Boston Celtics of the rival National Basketball Association. Throughout the 1970s, he participated in Kentucky politics in various ways, but in 1979, at almost the last minute, he entered the race for governor. Along with his wife, Phyllis George—a former Miss America—he waged a vigorous media campaign against old style politics. He promised to run state government like a business, emphasizing good management and economic development. His power base in the Lexington and Louisville areas helped him defeat eight other opponents in the Democratic primary elections. In the general election, Brown defeated Louie Nunn by 173,000 votes with a major boost from the Louisville area.

In his inaugural address, the new governor declared that Kentucky had what the world needed: food, energy, and recreational opportunities. He came to Frankfort with one of the ablest cabinets ever assembled, and he promised to reduce the size of government without infringing on the merit system or denying blacks and women equal opportunities. Unfortunately, the state ran into the buzz saw of the economic recession, especially in the coal industry. On six occasions over succeeding months, the governor had to announce major cutbacks in order to keep the budget balanced without new taxes; as a result, the number of state employees fell from 37,000 to 29,979. Economic development plans using industrial revenue bonds were also slowed, but state funds were used to help finish the new Fine Arts Center in Louisville and refurbish Freedom Hall.

The attempt to remove the restriction on the governor's succeeding himself failed in the election of 1981. Yet, better management was achieved in such things as reduction in patronage; better returns on state investments, linkage of pay to employee performance, reorganization of commissions dealing with education and utility rates, and computerization of the food stamp program. In education, two things stood out: the governor's scholar program for promising high school students and the Prichard Committee's Report laying down challenges in higher education.[22]

Collins, Martha Layne   56th Governor
(Term of Office—December 9, 1983 to December 14, 1987)

A native of Shelbyville in central Kentucky, Martha Layne Collins graduated from the University of Kentucky. After her marriage, she taught school in Louisville while her husband attended dental school. The family then moved to Versailles, where she taught junior high school and her husband opened a dental practice. In 1971, she entered statewide politics as sixth district chairperson for Wendell Ford in his race for governor. She then went to work for the Democratic party and served as national committeewoman and delegate to the presidential nominating convention in 1972.[23] In 1975 she was elected clerk of the court of appeals, and in 1979 she won a close race for lieutenant governor. She used the next four years to travel to all of the 120 counties in the state and to preside over sessions of the senate. Part of the time was taken up with duties as chairperson of the National Conference of Lieutenant Governors and acting governor for about 500 days. In the 1983 election, Martha Layne Collins won the primary election by 4,500 votes over Louisville Mayor Harvey Sloane and Dr. Grady Stumbo. She went on to defeat former Republican State Senator Jim Bunning in November.

On taking office, Martha Layne Collins faced the same problems encountered by recent governors in the areas of taxation, education, and economic development. The severe national economic recession eased in 1984, but coal severance tax income remained behind projections. It also became apparent that new growth money in the state's budget would be limited by declines in federal grants of all types. The deregulation of the telephone industry touched off another battle over finances in the Public Service Commission. Proponents of jail reform presented the governor with a large building program emphasizing regional jails.

The biggest problem, however, remained in education, as several study commissions both in and out of government completed their work. Attention centered on higher pay for teachers, lower class sizes in the early grades, dropout rates, tougher curricula, competency tests for new teachers, and keeping master teachers in the classrooms. Everyone was aware that economic development in the late 1980s was related to improvements in education to meet the changing trends in industry and business.

OTHER CONSTITUTIONAL EXECUTIVE OFFICERS

One characteristic of American state government is the splitting of executive responsibilities among several elected officers alongside the governor. In contrast, the federal government allows the election of only a president and a vice-president running as a team. The average number of elected statewide offices in the United States is ten; Kentucky is close to the average with eight.

The objective of nineteenth century constitution writers was to check and balance the top positions of state and local government and make them responsive to the moods of the voters in the best Jeffersonian/Jacksonian tradition. Today, one can criticize this tradition because it tends to create several centers of power not beholden to anybody. The only requirement for these officers is that they be thirty years old and have lived in the state two years prior to their election. They may not succeed themselves immediately, but several seem to move back and forth between different offices every four years in what the press calls a game of musical chairs.

Commissioner of Agriculture, Labor, and Statistics

Kentucky is one of only eight states that requires the election of an officer to administer regulatory and promotional programs related primarily to agriculture. They range from animal vaccination to the sale of farm exports in an effort to promote the state's most important agricultural products such as tobacco, horses, corn, and cattle. A nine-member board of agriculture appointed by the governor advises the commissioner, who is also a member of the state fair board, which administers the fairgrounds in Louisville. It would seem that there should be some requirement for training, but there is none. In 1981, Governor Brown stripped the department of major promotional and marketing functions and gave them to a new Energy and Agriculture Cabinet under his own appointee, but the Kentucky supreme court in 1982 said that only the general assembly can transfer functions from a constitutional officer.[24]

Attorney General

The attorney general is the chief legal officer of the state and the legal advisor to all its departments, boards, commissions, agencies, and political units. Forty-three states require the election of such an officer in their constitutions. An average of 750 legal opinions a year come out of the attorney general's office in response to requests from all levels of state, county, and city government. The office also is involved in such things as intervening in utility rate cases, stopping consumer fraud, and investigating wrongdoing in the coal industry.[25] But, governors tend to feel more comfortable with their own staffs and usually have a general counsel position in the governor's office.

Auditor of Public Accounts

Kentucky's third constitution in 1850 required that an auditor of public accounts be elected to represent the people, not the governor. In the 1936 reorganization, the office was made responsible for auditing all accounts of both state and county governments, but no training was required. Half of the states elect an auditor. Under the leadership of Mary Louise Foust, at least the assistants to the auditor were required by law to be trained accountants. In the late 1970s, the office took on an image of hard-nosed investigation under George Atkins, and the governor tried to cut his budget severely before the legislature restored the cuts.[26] Audits of county government each year do seem to turn up irregularities; there does seem to be a need for an audit function in state government.

Secretary of State

Kentucky's first constitution called for a secretary to be appointed to keep a register of all the official acts and proceedings and to continue in office "if he shall behave himself well."[27] Currently, the elected holder of that office keeps the official seal of the commonwealth, serves as chairman of the state board of elections, and is third in line of succession for governor in an emergency. The office also keeps track of 100,000 corporations either based in or doing work in the state.[28] Thirty-six states continue to elect such an officer.

Superintendent of Public Instruction

The domain of the chief educational officer in the state is by far the largest of the state's constitutional officers other than the governor. The superintendent supervises a staff of 4,000 people and a budget of over $1 billion a year. Actually the statewide superintendent is not in complete control, since the 180 local school boards appoint their own superintendents. Even at the state level, a fourteen member board is appointed by the governor to oversee policy. On the other hand, it is true that over 70 percent of all funds for education now come from the state level, thus, most of the significant policies are determined in Frankfort. Nevertheless it is strange that a statewide superintendent without any educational requirement is elected and the state board is appointed, while just the opposite is the case at the local level of government.[29] Only seventeen states still follow this practice.

Treasurer

Basically, the office of treasurer handles the billions of dollars that flow through state agencies each year from a variety of sources. Every check must come through the treasurer, although most are now signed by a signature machine.[30] Thirty-seven states still elect a treasurer. One subject of concern in recent years has been the return of interest on state funds temporarily placed in over 300 banks across the state. Under Governor Brown's leadership, the 1982 legislature established a state investment commission to oversee this area, but there are still differences of opinion about what is more important: a high rate of return or the need for each bank to have a portion of the money.

Lieutenant Governor

The office of lieutenant governor is the most popular among the lesser constitutional officers in state government. Forty-two states require an elected second-in-command.[31] All of the Kentucky's constitutions have required the officer to be thirty years of age and a resident of the state for six years. The major activity of the office is to preside over the senate every two years and cast a vote in case of a tie. The main legal function is to act as governor if the governor dies, resigns, is absent from the state, or from any cause is unable to discharge his duties.

In practice, on several occasions since 1935 lieutenant governors have either threatened to do something rash while the governor was out of the state or called special sessions of the legislature in the absence of the governor. In 1967, the electorate elected a Republican governor and a Democratic lieutenant governor. It seems to be common practice not to involve the lieutenant governor in running the state, although the primary informal activity of the office appears to be the development of a power base from which to run for the highest office.[32]

The constitutional revision assembly of 1966 dealt with the lesser elected constitutional officers other than the lieutenant governor and came to the conclusion that only two should be elected.[33] They felt that the attorney general was a separate ministerial officer who should be independent of the executive. The auditor also performs duties that should be independent, but the incumbent should at least be required to be a certified public accountant. The assembly also felt that the other officers were properly part of the executive function of government, and in fact, they perform some jobs that are similar to existing departments such as finance. The superintendent of public instruction should be appointed by the state board of education from among the ranks of the best professional educators in the nation. As to the lieutenant governor, eight states have done away with the office since it had so few duties. It would be worth considering a requirement that candidates for governor and lieutenant governor run as teams to cut down the chances for obstruction and emphasize teamwork as the lieutenant governor trains to run for the top job in state government.

THE RECRUITMENT PROCESS

After having read the brief summaries of the work of governors and a short analysis of the lesser constitutional executive officers, the next step is to examine the data in a search for predictive factors. It is hoped this short review will give some insight into how and why certain people are selected for the office of governor in Kentucky (Table 3.1).

TABLE 3.1

A Profile of Recent Kentucky Governors
1935 to 1983

Governor	Term	Home	Home Region	Election Age
Chandler, A.B.	1935–39	Versailles	Central	37
Johnson, Keen	1939–43	Richmond	Central	41
Willis, Simeon	1943–47	Ashland	Eastern	64
Clements, Earle	1947–50	Morganfield	Western	51
Wetherby, Lawrence	1950–55	Middletown	Louisville	42
Chandler, A.B.	1955–59	Versailles	Central	57
Combs, Bert	1959–63	Prestonsburg	Eastern	48
Breathitt, Edward T.	1963–67	Hopkinsville	Western	39
Nunn, Louie	1967–71	Glasgow	Western	43
Ford, Wendell	1971–74	Owensboro	Western	47
Carroll, Julian	1974–79	Paducah	Western	43
Brown, John Y., Jr.	1979–83	Louisville/ Lexington	Central/ Louisville	46
Collins, Martha Layne	1983–87	Versailles	Central	46

Governor	Sex	Race	Religion	Higher Education
Chandler, A.B.	Male	White	Episcopalian	Transylvania U., U.K. Law School
Johnson, Keen	Male	White	Methodist	U. of Kentucky
Willis, Simeon	Male	White	Methodist	None
Clements, Earle	Male	White	Christian	Attended U.K.
Wetherby, Lawrence	Male	White	Methodist	U. of Louisville Law School
Chandler, A.B.	Male	White	Episcopalian	Transylvania U., U.K. Law School
Combs, Bert	Male	White	Baptist	Cumberland College, U.K. Law School
Breathitt, Edward T.	Male	White	Methodist	U.K. Law School
Nunn, Louie	Male	White	Christian	U. of Louisville Law School
Ford, Wendell	Male	White	Baptist	Attended U.K.
Carroll, Julian	Male	White	Presbyterian	U.K. Law School
Brown, John Y., Jr.	Male	White	Baptist	U.K. Law School
Collins, Martha Layne	Female	White	Baptist	U. of Kentucky

A Profile of Recent Kentucky Governors
1935 to 1983

Governor	Profession	Prior Government Experience
Chandler, A.B.	Lawyer/Politics	State Senate, Lieutenant Governor
Johnson, Keen	Journalist	Lieutenant Governor
Willis, Simeon	Lawyer	Judge of the Court of Appeals
Clements, Earle	Farmer/Politics	County Judge, State Senate, Congressman
Wetherby, Lawrence	Lawyer	Party Leader, Lieutenant Governor
Chandler, A.B.	Lawyer/Politics	Governor
Combs, Bert	Lawyer	Judge of the Court of Appeals
Breathitt, Edward T.	Lawyer	State House of Representatives, Public Service Commissioner
Nunn, Louie	Lawyer	County Judge, Party Leader
Ford, Wendell	Business/Politics	Governor's Staff, State Senate, Lieutenant Governor
Carroll, Julian	Lawyer	Speaker of the House of Representatives, Lieutenant Governor
Brown, John Y., Jr.	Lawyer/Business	None
Collins, Martha Layne	Teacher/Politics	Clerk of the Court of Appeals, Lieutenant Governor

Governor	Political Party	Post Term Government Service
Chandler, A.B.	Democrat	Governor, U.S. Senate
Johnson, Keen	Democrat	U.S. Undersecretary of Labor
Willis, Simeon	Republican	Public Service Commission
Clements, Earle	Democrat	U.S. Senate, Highway Commissioner
Wetherby, Lawrence	Democrat	Kentucky Senate
Chandler, A.B.	Democrat	U.K. Trustee
Combs, Bert	Democrat	State Board of Education
Breathitt, Edward T.	Democrat	Council on Higher Education
Nunn, Louie	Republican	
Ford, Wendell	Democrat	U.S. Senate
Carroll, Julian	Democrat	
Brown, John Y., Jr.	Democrat	
Collins, Martha Layne	Democrat	

A chart does not tell the whole recruitment story. To become governor, a candidate must survive a long and tedious process, which may last up to ten years. In the case of Martha Layne Collins, she began working in the party machinery before winning election to two of the lesser constitutional executive offices. In the process, she built up name recognition and contacts in every county while expanding an organization in her natural base areas in the central and northern parts of the state.

The grind of hundreds of trips to attend receptions, fundraisers, festivals, parades, service clubs, and television interviews requires a strong physical and mental constitution, but the real tension comes in the closing days of the campaign as each candidate competes for press coverage and the attention of the voters. The high hour at election headquarters comes as the vote returns pour in and are tabulated from the 3,000 precincts across the state. The financial cost of the process continues to grow: it cost the winner in 1983 about $5 million.

The campaign is also an intense education in issues for the gubernatorial candidates. Each one puts out position papers and tries to offer some innovative programs to catch the eye of the undecided voter. Some of these programs are rational and well planned; some are not. At every stop, different issues pop up, and the press may interpret them differently depending on the mood of the reporter and the editor. Spontaneous or extemporaneous remarks can be killers in such a circumstance, but the most difficult spot is the televised debates on Kentucky Educational Television, where a panel of reporters ask the candidates questions. In the 1983 debates, the topics ranged from abortion to acid rain to right-to-work laws. It would take a genius or a fool to allow himself or herself to be put in such a position before television cameras; candidates are expected to be expert on all the ills of society, and the public expects them to be able to handle the pressure.

As a result of the campaign, each new governor rides into office atop a pyramid of voter and pressure group support. Financial contribution lists and endorsements give some clues of their importance. A sampling of groups in 1983 would include the following:

Attorneys
Black organizations
Business leaders of Louisville
The Chamber of Commerce
Coal Operators
Contractors
The Farm Bureau

Kentucky Education Association
Labor unions
Local government officials
Political Action Committees of all types, both within and
    without the state
Right-to-Life supporters
State government workers
Political families
University staff, students, and alumni

The new governor must somehow decipher which demands are worthy of consideration and how they relate to his/her program. He/she must then plan whether to use his/her limited political influence with the legislature and the bureaucracy to get something done or to let the issue disappear into the swamp of competing groups. This is a staggering drain on the energy and time of the governor.

A quick look at the recent governors who have survived the long selection process shows that they have come from a fairly narrow portion of the population of Kentucky. Only two have been Republicans, although the dominant Democratic party may be loosely divided into two factions. Only two governors have come from Louisville, the state's urban center. Most of them have been college graduates with some relationship to the University of Kentucky. Nine have been trained as lawyers, although several did not practice much. All but one of them have been men, and all have family names that indicate descent from the early white English settlers of the state. All have been Protestant Christians, with the majority being Baptist/Methodist in the southern tradition.

As for career advancement, most were in their forties and at midcareer when they were elected. Six were former lieutenant governors, and three went on to the United States Senate when the opportunity arose. John Y. Brown, Jr., however, bucked the trends on experience or prior political party leadership. So, the picture is mixed, although the election of male, white, protestant, small city lawyers in their forties seems to be the norm.

ROLES OF THE GOVERNOR

Once elected, the governor performs a variety of roles during his/her four-year term. On paper, he/she is required to do the things the constitution directs: participate in some ceremonies, intervene on occasion in the judicial system, lead the legislature, and generally manage state government. But, the constitution says nothing about the stream of ceremonies that require the governor's attendance all over the United States. Industrial development may even require international travel.

The election process does not stop with the primary or the general election. If the governor's program is to be successful, he/she must lead the political party for four years and try to influence public opinion on a daily basis. The governor has many roles, far more than ever imagined in a public office.

The Ceremonial Role

The ceremonial role of the governor has several parts, some of which are unique to Kentucky. His/her presence is required at the inauguration, and he/she must present a state of the commonwealth address to the legislature every two years. There is also a never-ending list of requests to cut ribbons on new highways, to attend events such as the Fancy Farm Picnic in western Kentucky, or to crown the queen of the Mountain Laurel Festival each year at Pine Mountain State Park. People also ask for Kentucky Colonel Commissions to be presented to notables and friends, although recent governors have been less generous than in former years. Governor Brown got caught between the University of Louisville and the University of Kentucky during the 1983 NCAA Basketball Tournament in his ceremonial role, so he sat on a different side each half of the game with a red and blue cap.

The biggest ceremony is the Derby weekend in early May of every year. The morning begins with a breakfast on the capitol grounds, where 5- to 10,000 people eat ham and eggs before many of them go on to the Kentucky Derby in Louisville at Churchill Downs. That afternoon, worldwide television audiences hear the playing of the state song, "My Old Kentucky Home," and see the governor award the trophy to the owner of the winning horse.

The Developer Role

Most ceremonies are also important as part of an image-building process that is an essential ingredient of economic development. The governor must lead the effort to create a favorable business climate that will attract new industries and businesses to the state. Such an effort is usually the product of years of coordination, hard work, and planning, spreading across the terms of several governors. In the 1960s, Kentucky sped up the building of its new interstate highway system in order to encourage economic development, and it worked. In the 1970s, attention was given to both

61

promoting and regulating the coal industry in the midst of an energy crisis.

Large corporations also consider things such as tax rates, utility availability, and the quality of life in areas such as education, entertainment, and the fine arts before they make a decision to commit hundreds of millions of dollars to a new plant. Governor Brown went so far as to set up offices in Brussels and New York in his search for prospects. It takes a governor with a broad background and a strong drive to succeed in the role of developer against the competition of forty-nine other governors all working in an uncertain economy.

Federal Coordinator

A role similar to that performed by the governor in development work is the role of federal coordinator, which involves trying to get funds and programs for the state from the Congress and bureaucracy in Washington. In this work, the governor frequently deals with the state's congressional delegation, consisting of seven Congressmen and two Senators. Finding the main power center is sometimes difficult: it may be in the Atlanta regional office of a large department rather than in Washington.

In order to exchange ideas with other governors, Kentucky governors usually participate in the activities of the National Governors Conference and the Council of State Governments. In fact, Governor Breathitt enticed the council to relocate its offices from Chicago to the Spindletop Research Center near Lexington.

Since Kentucky is a state of modest means, its governors must also be able to negotiate with some sophistication to get new water projects, energy research facilities, and military bases such as Fort Knox and Fort Campbell. In time of natural disaster, the governor is the top political officer on the scene who can ease the way toward federal disaster relief and low-interest loans for victims.

Judicial Role

The Kentucky constitution gives the governor power to commute sentences and grant pardons. In years gone by, families of prisoners roamed the corridors of the capitol building, trying to get husbands and sons out of the penitentiary in Frankfort, but those powers were moved to a state parole board, although on occasion a pardon has been given directly by the governor or the acting governor. Recent governors have had a staff attorney hear all such cases, including requests for extradition of criminals to the states where they committed crimes. Occasional judicial hearings have been held for the removal of local law enforcement officials who did not carry out their duties. In death penalty cases, there are sometimes last-ditch appeals to the governor for clemency. There have been no executions in the electric chair at Eddyville for twenty years, although a handfull of prisoners still languish on death row.

Within the judicial system itself, all the judges are elected, but the governor appoints a judicial nominating commission to help him appoint people to vacancies.

Leader of the Political Party

The governor's role as leader of a political party in the state is extraconstitutional. Traditionally, the governor selects the chairman for his/her political party organization and carefully nurtures the county and city organizations. The role of personalities is a major factor in this process; some local officials may want the help of the governor and the state staff, but most use their own resources. Special fundraisers are held each year to raise money for whatever race is up that year: the United States Senate, the president, or the governor.

It is the nature of the two-party system that factions within each party must pull together in order to win. Governor Brown chose to cut down party patronage even further than the merit system had done in the 1960s and 1970s, and he took very little part in congressional races, but he did seem to be interested in helping the national party with telethons to raise money. On the other hand, Governors Chandler, Clements, Ford, Carroll, and Collins were involved constantly in local, state, and national politics, using their state political base to best advantage.

Leader of Public Opinion

Closely connected with his/her role as leader of a political party is the governor's relationship to public opinion. During an election campaign a successful candidate builds up a momentum of public interest and support. One can sense this at rallies, at the inauguration, and in speeches to the legislature. In the beginning, public approval ratings are high, but the crunch sets in as political realities take over, and the long bargaining process with the legislature begins. Promises are slow to be fulfilled, and public interest begins to wane. Attention may shift quickly to things that in hindsight do not seem important: the rug in the governor's reception room, the days since the governor promised to sell the private helicopter, and the private life of the governor. Governors often hold press conferences and give interviews to the Frankfort press corps to build public confidence and support for programs, but nearly every governor complains about the coverage he/she receives in the press. It is a monumental effort to maintain high levels of public interest and approval throughout a four-year term.

Legislator

When the legislature is in session, the governor must spend a great deal of time working with the details of legislation and trying to hold a majority together in both the senate and the house of representatives. The inner politics of this process include identifying the opinion leaders and groupings by regions and political party. The governor must also contend with the legion of lobbyists that circulate through the capitol building during the sessions.

For the governor, the most important item of business is the budget bill, since its effect on state business is so extensive. After its passage, he/she can turn attention to other bills and make decisions whether to exercise the power of veto. Kentucky governors have used this power sparingly, although Governor Nunn did veto about 20 percent of the bills presented to him in 1968.[35] Governors also have the power to call special sessions, and Governor Chandler was the master at that tactic. But, normally governors are reluctant to bring the legislators to Frankfort between regular sessions because of the heavy expense involved. The boundary lines between legislative and executive power are somewhat blurred, but the Franklin Circuit Court in November 1983 clearly curtailed legislative attempts to become too involved in executive decisions in the interim between regular sessions of the general assembly.[36]

Manager

A final gubernatorial role is his/her function as manager of the state's bureaucracy and programs. This is probably the toughest role since it is present twenty-four hours a day as personnel come and go; tax collections go up and down according to the health of the economy; and budgets come unglued or hang together until the end of the fiscal year. Through all of this, the public expects the governor to manage effectively.

THE GOVERNOR AS CHIEF ADMINISTRATOR

Every governor must decide how to manage the vast programs and bureaucracies that he/she inherits and whether he/she wants to create new ones. Management includes setting an issues agenda and formulating policies for the entire state government structure during a four-year time frame. The recruiting process for governors in Kentucky seems to concentrate on lawyers and political leaders without regard to management experience. In fact, the political process virtually excludes experienced managers from rising through the company ranks into top management. Even the lieutenant governor is usually left out of the day-to-day administrative operations. In addition, the constitution decrees that most of top management must change every four years, leading to instability in state policies. Within this model a governor sets the direction for his/her administration daily.

Appointments

One of the first major tasks facing a new governor is the job of selecting a staff of assistants and managers to move in and take over the reins of government. Staff usually includes people to handle appointments, press relations, legal work, and liaison with agencies and the legislature. The variety of appointments to various boards, commissions, and departments is staggering—over 1,800 in all, and each of these organizations has its own clientele and constituencies. The governor must be careful to appoint people who can represent the public interest along with some specialized interests.

An even tougher job is the selection of middle management non–merit system policy-makers who may come from the campaign staff, close supporters, personal friends, and casual acquaintances. To prevent conflicts of interest, it may be necessary for the governor to call the whole group together and let legal counsel advise them on what is legal and what is borderline activity. The turnover of these people in Frankfort is another problem; two years seems to be the norm for department heads. This may lead to inconsistency and confusion in management policies. Finally, every governor tends to rely on some small group of advisers outside of government or one dollar a year men inside who can give objective advice—perspective keepers.

The Merit System

Most of the state's 30,000 employees are covered by the state's merit system law enacted under Governor Combs in 1960. They are not to be discharged for political reasons, but patronage has been a part of the state's political system for years. One still hears of a few people being required to sell tickets voluntarily for some political fundraiser. The system was put to its sternest test in 1968 when over 700 employees sued in court to get back their jobs after political firings and won damages in addition to their former jobs. Cases still come up in every administration, such as ones in which an inexperienced campaign worker walks into the office of a veteran middle manager doing highly technical work and informs him that he has thirty minutes to clean out his desk on orders of the new governor. It is vitally important that the governor attempt to gain the confidence of state employees by treating them with respect, by hiring competent managers, by encouraging the development of a career executive service, and by paying them competitive wages.

Managing Education

One of the most complex management tasks for the governor to tackle is bringing some sense of direction to the educational apparatus in Kentucky. About 70 percent of the state's budget goes for education, and the major part of it goes to elementary and secondary programs.

Education leadership comes from several power centers: an elected superintendent of public instruction, an appointed state board of education, elected local boards, school administrators, and the Kentucky Education Association. Governor Brown made a special effort to appoint members of the state board from various parts of the state and to include blacks and women. Some of the recommendations of the Carroll Commission, such as competency testing, have been adopted.

In higher education, various governors have tried to tighten up coordination between the eight universities, with different degrees of success, through the appointed council on higher education. Appointments by the governor to the university boards are highly prized positions. Unfortunately, the recommendations of the 1982 Prichard Commission on Higher Education have not been fully implemented. The governor still sets the direction for education through his/her appointments, the budget, and leadership of public opinion.

Managing the Environment

Another tough management task for a modern Kentucky governor has been the environment. This has become more apparent since the 1970s, when environmentalists supported the creation of the United States Environmental Protection Agency. Kentucky followed suit by updating its programs to a new Cabinet for Natural Resources and Environmental Protection, which monitors the use of water, land, forests, and air. Kentucky has been one of the major battlegrounds in this area as state government sought to control surface mining of coal and require reclamation. In addition, coal trucks began to damage the state's highway system. As a consequence, the governor frequently found himself between the coal operators, the miners, the truckers, the railroads, the federal government, and the environmentalists. The debate over the new coal severance tax initiated by Governor Ford further accentuated coal as a resource for future energy needs and new state income. Since that time, candidates for governor soon learn that the public expects leadership in these matters to come from the governor.

Managing Human Resources

After education, human resources programs take an enormous amount of tax dollars each year. Sometimes it is difficult for even the governor to know what is happening because of the complexity of financing arrangements and detailed administrative regulations. Each of the programs, such as Medicaid, food stamps, and aid to families with dependent children, has its own federal matching component. On the other hand, unemployment insurance is related to its own special tax on employers. The funding of manpower programs goes up or down according to the health of the national economy. Much of the data used in all these programs is stored in a massive computer system.

Various governors have tried different approaches to managing the Cabinet for Human Resources. Their appointees as top administrators have included former assistants to the governor, a medical doctor, and a public health specialist. Governor Ford tried to group all the activities under one department with highly centralized decision making, while Governor Brown decentralized the programs as three departments under a cabinet. At any rate, every governor must come to terms with the complex problems of human resources.

Managing Law Enforcement

Although he/she is not involved in law enforcement on a daily basis, the governor is a major actor in the process. He/she has at command a small army—the Kentucky National Guard, which is composed of weekend citizen soldiers stationed around the state in various armories. Much of their budget and all their equipment comes from the national government, and they are subject to call to active duty by the president. Some of the 7,000 troops have been used by governors in the past in times of emergency to protect property and save lives. Governor Nunn did not hesitate to bring in the guard during the Vietnam War demonstration at the University of Kentucky in 1970.

The state police are full-time sworn law enforcement officers carrying out many different types of police functions, especially in rural counties. Their force of 1,000 troopers is a formidable group, but they are scattered around the state in posts. Governor Wetherby used them to slow down large-scale illegal gambling activities in Newport in 1951. They are most noticeable when enforcing traffic laws on the state's highways.

Managing Public Regulation Activities

In business regulation activities, the governor operates largely through his/her appointees to various commissions and boards that deal with selected parts of the business community of the state. Governor Ford sought to group these functions together in a Public Protection and Regulation Cabinet, but they largely go their own way, and the turnover in cabinet secretaries has been high. For example, the alcoholic beverage control board supervises the licensing and operation of businesses in an unusual way, since it has both rule-making and law enforcement functions. But, the crucial appointments in the past decade of spiraling costs have been to the public service commission, which regulates telephone, water, gas, and electric rates. Governors have been hard pressed to find commission members who are willing to serve and survive its highly technical proceedings in the search for balance between industry and consumers.

Transportation Management

Ever since Governor Chandler built a new divided highway from his hometown, Versailles, to Lexington, it has been almost traditional for governors to build some sort of major road during their administrations. The public demanded better roads, and the federal government accommodated them with United States highways and the interstate system plus an Appalachian road system for eastern Kentucky.

Every governor since the early 1960s has had the privilege of supervising the laying out of an interstate corridor or tollroad and then cutting the ribbon to open it to traffic. Governor Combs supervised the building of the Mountain Parkway, and Governor

Nunn had the Cumberland Parkway built across the south central part of the state. Governor Carroll made sure that I-24 was finished in the far western part of Kentucky before he left office. Governor Brown initiated planning for an AA highway across northeastern Kentucky before he left office.

In addition, one of the governor's most crucial appointments has been the secretary of the Transportation Cabinet. Sometimes secretaries have been engineers, but one of the most successful, Henry Ward, was a politician/administrator. The secretary must deal with local officials, the federal highway administration, his/her own engineers, and contractors in the setting of priorities and the building of roads.

Reorganization

As government has grown bigger, governors have wrestled with reorganization, trying to make government more manageable and responsive to the public. Governor Chandler made major changes in 1936, but the most sweeping reorganization took place under Governor Ford in the 1970s, as departments and programs were grouped by cabinets whose secretaries were to form the governor's cabinet. Naturally, such major changes caused tension in both the bureaucracy and its various constituencies; that was most apparent in the vast human resources area. Governor Brown, on the other hand, made several changes that did not fit into an organization chart based on unity of purpose very easily: corrections was taken from justice and temporarily put under transportation. Every governor must determine how to blend the personalities of his/her appointees with organizational needs for unity of command and accountability. Needless to say, reorganization is still an inexact science.

Making the Budget

In the end, the best management tool the governor has at his/her command is the budget. The budget creation process in long, detailed, and full of compromise as departments battle to save what they have and promote what they think they need. The bargaining process becomes especially intense in the fall of the years just preceding the biennial visits of the legislature to Frankfort. Budget making in the human resources and transportation areas is especially complex, since estimates fluctuate with federal grant programs and the state of the economy.

An equally tough problem is determining the revenue estimate as specialists in the revenue cabinet juggle all the available data and unknown factors. A governor is often in the dark as to all the details, since estimating revenue requires the expertise of a certified public accountant and a good crystal ball to come up with a workable budget. The same problems exist in the legislature; the Appropriations and Revenue committee of the house of representatives goes over the same material. At any rate, the buck stops at the office of the governor on the first floor of the capitol building.

ANALYSIS

Everyone is agreed that the office of governor in Kentucky is a powerful position in both the political and economic life of the state, but there is disagreement about whether the existing power of the office should be further contained or increased to meet pressing needs.

The Benefits

In order to attract competent people to run for governor and not run the risk of corruption, salary and fringe benefits should be reasonable in terms of the work load and in comparison with other states and private business. There is some similarity between the responsibilities of the governor and those of a chief executive officer of a company with $5 billion in sales each year.

Governor Brown received a salary of $50,000 per year in his last two years in office; the figure was raised to $60,000 as of December 1983.[37] The salary of the state's highest public official should at least be the highest of all the programs for which he/she has major budget responsibility. At present, however, it is only among the top ten with the inclusion of higher education. The governor also gets fringe benefits such as air and automobile transportation, state police guards, tickets to all athletic contests of the University of Kentucky and the University of Louisville, some break on food costs, state life and health insurance, and an expense account. The most visible benefit is the use of the governor's mansion next to the capitol building in Frankfort.

Privacy

One of the major complaints of governors everywhere is the lack of privacy both for themselves and their families.[38] Even with the renovation, the mansion in Frankfort is an extension of the capitol building. The main floor is open for tourists to visit several days a week. The family of the governor is protected by state police, but they must be careful wherever they go. During Governor Brown's heart bypass operation, the press explored every detail of medicine and surgery with his doctors in daily news conferences.

Tenure Potential

Another problem is the amount of time a governor is allowed to remain in office. Kentucky's governors are presently limited by the constitution to one term at a time; only Governor Chandler has been elected to two separate terms in recent years. There are good arguments for this practice, since governors may become bound by pressure groups over a four-year span to the point that the larger public interest is lost within the system. Yet, Kentucky is one of only four states in the Union that do not allow their chief executive the opportunity to succeed themselves immediately.[39] The majority of states think a good governor ought to be able to face the voters again after four years in office and let them decide whether he/she should continue his/her work. Even the federal government allows the president to run for one additional term. However, the voters of Kentucky rejected such a proposal made by Governor Brown in 1981.

Succession in Office

There are further difficulties of interpretation of gubernatorial succession when a governor is not able to carry out his/her duties while still in office. In one situation, the Kentucky constitution provides that the lieutenant governor assumes the duties of governor if the governor is "from any cause, unable to discharge the duties of his office." During Governor Brown's serious heart operation and recovery in the summer of 1983, Lieutenant Governor Collins, on the advice of counsel, assumed the duties of governor for a short period when the governor was clearly incapacitated. The proposed 1966 revision of the constitution spelled out in some detail the procedure whereby the supreme court would handle such a situation.[40] Since that revision did not get the approval of the voters, confusion remains.

In another succession difficulty, a governor relinquishes his/her power temporarily to the lieutenant governor when out of the state. Several recent lieutenant governors have carried this too far: either calling special sessions of the legislature without consulting the governor or keeping the governor a virtual prisoner in Frankfort. Both of these situations need study and change.

Some Recommended Changes

Some changes must be considered to improve the office of governor:

1. Constitutional Amendments
   a. The portion of the oath of office that deals with dueling should be removed.
   b. The provision that power passes to the lieutenant governor when the governor is temporarily out of the state should be removed.
   c. The governor should be allowed to succeed himself/herself for one term by the vote of the people.
   d. The lesser constitutional executive officers should be removed from the constitution, and the general assembly should provide for the functions of those offices as needed.
   e. Candidates for governor and lieutenant governor should be required to run as teams.
   f. Specific responsibility for determining whether a governor is clearly incapacitated should be given to the supreme court.

2. Possible Changes in Statute Laws
   a. The governor should be paid a salary similar to that paid in surrounding states. The position should at least be the highest paid office in state government.
   b. The lieutenant governor should be nominated and elected on a slate with the governor and designated as the second-ranking state official in the administrative chain of command. The lieutenant governor should be paid a salary that is the second highest in state government.
   c. Severe restrictions should be put on political campaign finance, with more emphasis on matching funds to cut down the pressures that may encourage corruption and placement of people in positions for which they are not qualified.

Finally, the public should not be satisfied with mediocre or status quo strategies in the state's highest elected office in the face of very low ratings among the states in per capita income and educational attainment levels. The governor should be subject to the checks and balances of the normal legislative and legal processes, but he/she ought not to be unnecessarily hindered by conflicts with numerous boards and elected constitutional officers working in a nineteenth century model of government that was designed for a rural society. He/she should be paid a reasonable salary, and in turn, he/she should manage the affairs of state in a decisive manner rising above local pressures and interest groups. The recruitment process should balance political needs with management experience by incorporating the lieutenant governor into the management system before he/she runs for governor. In summary, the governor should be looked on as the only statewide officer who can assemble the political capital to deal with the major problems of the state as its citizens try to compete in an international economy. Kentucky deserves the best in its top political office.

FOOTNOTES

1. Larry Sabato, *Goodbye to Good-time Charlie: The American Governorship Transformed,* 2nd edition (Washington: The Congressional Quarterly, 1983) p. 2.
2. Joan Wells Coward, *Kentucky in the New Republic: The Process of Constitution Making* (Lexington: University Press of Kentucky, 1979) p. 29.
3. Thomas D. Clark, *A History of Kentucky* (Lexington: The John Bradford Press, 1960) p. 339.
4. The Kentucky Legislative Research Commission, *Constitution of the Commonwealth of Kentucky,* 9th edition, Informational Bulletin No. 136 (Frankfort: The Legislative Research Commission, 1980) p. 31.
5. Steven A. Channing, *Kentucky: A History* (New York: Norton and Co., 1977) pp. 173-175.
6. Bob Johnson, "In the Beginning: The 1935 Campaign, *Chandler v. Rhea,*" *The Louisville Courier-Journal,* May 8, 1983.
7. "Governor Albert B. Chandler," *The Register of the Kentucky Historical Society,* 34 (January, 1936) pp. 1-2.
8. Jasper B. Shannon, "Happy Chandler," in J.T. Salter, ed., *The American Politician* (Chapel Hill: The North Carolina U. Press, 1938) pp. 175-191.
9. Frederic D. Ogden, ed., *The Public Papers of Governor Keen Johnson, 1939-1945* (Lexington: University Press of Kentucky, 1982) p. 10.
10. Robert A. Powell, *Kentucky Governors* (Frankfort: Kentucky Images, 1976) pp. 94-95.
11. Simeon Willis, Governor. *1943 Your Kentucky Government 1947* (Frankfort, 1947) pp. 75-77.

12. "Clements, Earle C.," *Current Biography—1955* (New York: The H.W. Wilson Co., 1955) pp. 130-132.

13. Kleber, John E., ed., *The Public Papers of Governor Lawrence W. Wetherby, 1950-1955* (Lexington: University Press of Kentucky, 1983) p. 1.

14. "Chandler, Albert B.," *Current Biography—1956* (New York: The H.W. Wilson Co., 1956) p. 106.

15. George W. Robinson, ed., *The Public Papers of Governor Bert T. Combs, 1959-1963* (Lexington: University Press of Kentucky, 1979) Foreword.

16. "Breathitt, Edward T.," *Current Biography—1960* (New York: The H.W. Wilson Co., 1960) pp. 94-96.

17. Robert F. Sexton, ed., *The Public Papers of Governor Louie B. Nunn, 1967-1971* (Lexington: University Press of Kentucky, 1979) Appendix I, pp. 573-578.

18. W. Landis Jones, ed., *The Public Papers of Governor Wendell H. Ford, 1971-1974* (Lexington: University Press of Kentucky, 1979) Appendix I, pp. 653-657.

19. Powell, p. 112.

20. Ray Cohn, "Carroll Cites Accomplishments, Critics See Contradictions," *The Lexington Herald*, December 10, 1979.

21. "John Y. Brown, Jr.," *Register of the Kentucky Historical Society*, 78 (Spring, 1980) p. 95.

22. Articles by Livingston Taylor, Bob Johnson, and Ed Ryan in *The Louisville Courier-Journal*, December 4, 1983.

23. Ed Bean, "Collins Prides Herself on Hard Work," *The Lexington Herald*, May 8, 1983.

24. Ed Ryan, "Brown Strips Agriculture Department of Major Responsibilities," *The Louisville Courier-Journal*, January 18, 1981.

25. "Breshear Says His Consumer Advocacy Helped Public," *The Louisville Courier-Journal*, August 2, 1983.

26. Frank Ashley, "Expanded Auditor's Office is Exercising Its Newfound Clout," *The Louisville Courier-Journal*, September 23, 1979.

27. Kentucky Legislative Research Commission. *Text of Kentucky Constitutions of 1792, 1799, and 1850*. Informational Bulletin No. 41 (Frankfort: The Legislative Research Commission, 1965).

28. Frank Ashley, "Businessman, State Treasurer Want to Keep Kentucky's Records," *The Louisville Courier-Journal*, August 30, 1979.

29. Frank Ashley, "Instruction Superintendent's Power Has Eroded," *The Louisville Courier-Journal,* October 2, 1979.

30. Frank Ashley, "State Treasurer Holds the Key to Billions of Taxpayer Dollars," *The Louisville Courier-Journal,* August 21, 1979.

31. The Council of State Governments, *The Book of the States, 1982-1983* (Lexington: The Council of State Governments, 1982) p. 154.

32. Frank Ashley, "State's Next Lieutenant Governor May Have an Expanded Role," *The Louisville Courier-Journal,* October 10, 1979.

33. Fleming, James T. and John E. Reeves, *A Comparison: The Present, The Proposed Kentucky Constitution,* Informational Bulletin No. 52 (Frankfort: The Legislative Research Commission, 1966) p. 34.

34. Powell, the entire book.

35. Kentucky Legislative Research Commission, *General Assembly Action, Regular Session, 1968,* Informational Bulletin 67 (Frankfort: The Legislative Research Commission, 1968) Foreword.

36. Anne Pardue, "Executive Branch Wins Ruling in Suit on Legislative Power," *The Louisville Courier-Journal,* November 4, 1982.

37. Kentucky Revised Statutes 64.480.

38. The National Governors Association for Policy Research, *Governing the American States: A Handbook for New Governors* (Washington: Hall of the States, 1978) chapter sixteen.

39. Thad L. Beyle, "The Governors and the Executive Branch, 1980-1981," *The Book of the States, 1982-1983* (Lexington: The Council of State Government, 1982) p. 144.

40. Fleming, p. 29.

BIBLIOGRAPHY

Newspapers

The Lexington *Herald*

The Louisville *Courier-Journal*

Articles and Books

Beyle, Thad L. "The Governors and the Executive Branch, 1980-1981," *The Book of the States, 1982-1983.* Lexington: The Council of State Governments, 1982, 141-150.

"Breathitt, Edward T., Jr.," *Current Biography—1964.* New York: The H.W. Wilson Co., 1964, 49-51.

"Chandler, Albert B.," *Current Biography—1956.* New York: The H.W. Wilson Co., 1956, 106-108.

Channing, Steven A. *Kentucky: A History.* New York: Norton and Co., 1977.

Clark, Thomas D. *A History of Kentucky.* Lexington: The John Bradford Press, 1960.

"Clements, Earle C.," *Current Biography—1955.* New York: The H.W. Wilson Co., 1955, 130-132.

The Council of State Government. *The Book of the States, 1982-1983.* Lexington: The Council of State Governments, 1982.

Fleming, James T. and John E. Reeves. *A Comparison: The Present, The Proposed Kentucky Constitution.* Informational Bulletin No. 52. Frankfort: The Legislative Research Commission, 1966.

"Governor Albert Benjamin Chandler," *The Register of the Kentucky Historical Society,* 34 (Spring, 1936) 1.

Jones, W. Landis, ed. *The Public Papers of Governor Wendell H. Ford, 1971-1974.* Lexington: University Press of Kentucky, 1979.

Kentucky Legislative Research Commission. *Constitution of the Commonwealth of Kentucky,* 9th ed., Informational Bulletin No. 136. Frankfort: The Legislative Research Commission, 1980.

Kentucky Legislative Research Commission. *General Assembly Action, Regular Session, 1968,* Informational Bulletin No. 67. Frankfort: The Legislative Research Commission, 1968.

Kentucky Legislative Research Commission. *Texts of Kentucky Constitutions of 1792, 1799, and 1850,* Informational Bulletin No. 41. Frankfort: The Legislative Research Commission, 1965.

The Kentucky Revised Statutes.

Kleber, John E., ed. *The Public Papers of Governor Lawrence W. Wetherby, 1950-1955.* Lexington: University Press of Kentucky, 1983.

Ogden, Frederic, ed. *The Public Papers of Governor Keen Johnson, 1939-1945.* Lexington: University Press of Kentucky, 1982.

Powell, Robert. *Kentucky Governors*. Frankfort: Kentucky Images, 1976.

Robinson, George W., ed. *The Public Papers of Governor Bert T. Combs, 1959-1963*. Lexington: University Press of Kentucky, 1979.

Sabato, Larry. *Goodbye to Good-time Charlie: The American Governorship Transformed*, 2nd ed. Washington: The Congressional Quarterly, 1983.

Sexton, Robert F., ed. *The Public Papers of Governor Louie B. Nunn, 1967-1971*. Lexington: University Press of Kentucky, 1978.

Shannon, Jasper B. "Happy Chandler," in J.T. Salter, ed. *The American Politician*. Chapel Hill: North Carolina U. Press, 1938, 175-191.

Willis, Simeon, Governor. *1943 Kentucky 1947*. Frankfort, 1947.

Chapter 4

THE GENERAL ASSEMBLY

Malcolm E. Jewell, University of Kentucky
and
Gary Cox, Kentucky State University

The Kentucky General Assembly is in a period of transition. For many years the legislature was characterized by amateur, inexperienced members, very short sessions, and very little power, particularly in dealings with the governor. The legislature still plays a more limited role in government than is true in many states, but it has undergone fundamental changes in recent years that make it a more powerful partner in state government.

There is much less turnover in the membership of the legislature currently, and as a result, the members are more experienced and have more opportunity to become familiar with issues. The state constitution imposes more rigid limitations on the length of legislative sessions than is true in most states, but the legislature has developed a more flexible schedule for meetings during the session and has developed an extensive interim committee system between sessions, giving the members much more working time. The legislature is still less powerful and less independent than those in many states, but it has taken several steps to enhance its authority. The committee system has been streamlined and better staffed, and the interim committee system has made the members less dependent on the governor and interest groups for information and legislative initiatives. The interim committee system has also made possible a more thorough review of the budget and more extensive oversight of executive agencies.

Some questions remain about whether the legislature's new independent power rests on a solid foundation. In 1982 the legislature passed several laws designed to strengthen its oversight of executive agencies. These new laws were challenged in the courts by Governor John Y. Brown, and in January 1984 the state supreme court handed down an opinion, in *Legislative Research Commission v. Brown*, that invalidated most of them. The legislature benefitted from Governor Brown's decision not to attempt the domination of the legislature, which had been the practice of his predecessors. His successors are likely to work harder to reestablish influence over the legislature.

The most significant changes in the formal operation of the legislature result from a constitutional amendment adopted in 1979. The constitution had restricted the legislature to biennial sessions of only sixty days (excluding only Sundays and holidays). In 1969 and again in 1973 the voters rejected constitutional amendments that would have authorized annual sessions of the legislature. The 1979 amendment adopted by the voters retained the biennial sixty-day limit, but permitted the legislature to schedule those sixty days of meetings over the first three and one-half months of the year, with committees able to meet at other times.

The 1979 amendment also made an unusual change in the legislative elections schedule: beginning in 1984 legislators will be elected in even-numbered years even though the governor and other state officials are elected in odd-numbered years. The purpose of the change is to make the interim committee system work more effectively by having the committees meet before rather than after the regular session. Under the new schedule, for example, the legislature would be elected in 1984, hold a ten-day organization session in January 1985, schedule interim committee meetings during the rest of the year, and hold its regular session from the beginning of January to mid-April in 1986. One consequence of the new schedule is that the legislature will have been organized for a year when a new governor takes office, reducing the prospects for gubernatorial influence over choice of legislative leaders. The governor, of course, can call a special session and choose its agenda at any time; the legislature cannot call itself into special session.

The general assembly consists of a 38-member senate, with senators elected for four-year terms (half of them every two years), and a 100-member house of representatives, with members serving two-year terms. All members are elected from single-member districts, a practice that is common but not universal in other state legislatures. (Senators served five years and representatives three years during the transition from odd-numbered to even-numbered election years.)

It is impossible in a brief chapter to describe all of the characteristics of the legislature; the purpose here will be to emphasize the way in which the legislature has changed recently and the way it operates today. The chapter is divided into the following major sections: the selection of members, legislators and their constituents, political organization and legislative decision making, legislative committees, legislative oversight of the executive branch, the budgetary process, legislative management, and trends in the legislature.

SELECTION OF MEMBERS

One of the most important changes in the Kentucky legislature in recent years has been the decreasing turnover of membership. There are more experienced members and fewer freshmen than in the past. In the elections from 1947 through 1965 only one-third of the state senators and about 40 percent of the representatives were reelected. Over half of the senators and nearly half of the representatives retired (or sought other offices); the rest lost primaries or general elections. The proportion of freshmen in the Kentucky legislature was higher than in most states.

In recent years, as Table 4.1 shows, two-thirds of the senators and over three-fourths of the representatives have been reelected in each election. Only one-fifth of the senators and one-eighth of the representatives leave the legislature voluntarily in each election. Kentucky is now closer to the national average. The higher retirement rate for senators is understandable because they serve longer terms than do representatives. Table 4.1 shows that there are no partisan differences in the senate, but in the house Republicans are a little more likely to retire or seek other offices.

The most important reason for the drop in turnover is that fewer members leave the legislature voluntarily than used to be the case. One reason for this change is the end of rotation agreements. In the period before the mid-1960s, in many rural districts that included several counties and that were dominated by one party, agreements were made between the county party organizations that the seat should be rotated among the counties after one or two terms. During the period from 1947 to 1965, more than one-tenth of the legislators retired each term because of such agreements, which are no longer used.

The most important reason there are fewer retirements is that more members enter the legislature with the intention of serving an extended career in politics. Some stay in the legislature for many years, rising to positions of leadership. Others run for statewide or congressional office when the opportunity arises. A number of representatives also run for the state senate. In recent years the proportion of representatives serving in at least their fourth term has risen to over 40 percent; about half of the senators have served as many years, and about one-fourth have also served previously in the house.

TABLE 4.1
Electoral Fortunes of Kentucky Legislators
(in percentages)

| | Senate Elections | | | | House Elections | | | |
| | 1975–81 | | | 1947–65 | 1977–81 | | | 1947–65 |
	All	Democ.	Repub.	All	All	Democ.	Repub.	All
Proportion of All Incumbents:								
Elected	67	66	72	32	77	80	68	41
Defeated	11	12	6	16	10	9	14	15
Retired	22	22	22	52	12	11	17	44
(Number)	(76)	(58)	(18)	(171)	(300)	(231)	(69)	(900)
Proportion of Those Incumbents Who Ran:								
Elected	86	84	93	67	88	90	82	73
Lost Primary	10	13	0	31	8	7	12	20
Lost Gen. Elect.	3	4	7	2	3	3	5	7
(Number)	(59)	(45)	(14)	(82)	(263)	(206)	(57)	(504)

    The decline in turnover does not mean that there has been any increase in the proportion of seats safe for one party. The low proportion of general election defeats shown in Table 4.1 is about the same as in the past, indicating that most legislative districts continue to be dominated by one political party. Table 4.2 shows how few legislative districts are closely competitive in general elections. It shows what proportion of legislators were elected by various percentages in the four senate elections from 1975 to 1981 and the three house elections from 1977 to 1981. The most important finding is that half of the senate seats and over half of the house seats were won without partisan opposition. Most of the uncontested seats are won by Democratic candidates, particularly in the western part of

81

the state. But, there are a number of districts in the traditionally Republican counties of southeastern and south central Kentucky where no Democratic candidates run. In fact, one-sixth of all uncontested races are won by Republicans, and over one-third of Republicans who win have no Democratic opponent. At the other extreme, 16 percent of senate seats and 19 percent of house seats are won by narrow margins—no more than 60 percent, with Republicans more likely to win narrowly.

TABLE 4.2
Legislative Districts by Winning Percentages
in General Elections
(in percentages)

Winning Percentage	Senate Districts 1975–81 Elections			House Districts 1977–81 Elections		
	All	Democ.	Repub.	All	Democ.	Repub.
50 – 60	16	14	22	19	12	40
61 – 70	20	15	34	16	17	16
71 – 99	14	16	11	10	11	6
100	50	55	33	55	60	39
(Number)	(76)	(58)	(18)	(300)	(230)	(70)

Another way to show how little party competition exists in legislative races is to look at the pattern of voting in house districts over a longer time period—the five elections from 1973 through 1981. In forty-one of those districts the minority party either never ran a candidate or ran one no more than once in five elections; thirty-six were Democratic and five Republican safe districts. At the other extreme, there were only sixteen districts where any partisan turnover occurred in five elections, and half of these were in Jefferson county, where a large proportion of the most competitive districts are found and where both parties usually contest most districts. What this means is that in districts that are dominated by a single party, the minority party seldom makes an effort to run legislative candidates. Sometimes there is little competition even in counties where there is close two-party balance. An example occurred in 1979 in Fayette county, where there was no party competition for any of the legislative seats held by either party.

The decline in turnover of members is caused partly by an increase in the success of incumbents at being renominated in primaries. This is evident if we look at the part of Table 4.1 that shows primary defeats as a proportion of all races in which incumbents ran. In recent years only 10 percent of senators who ran and 8 percent of representatives who ran lost primaries. But, from 1947 to 1966 nearly one-third of the senators and one-fifth of the representatives who sought renomination were beaten in the primary.

It is obvious that state legislators are in a stronger position when they run for renomination than used to be the case. Because the legislature is more active and the members usually serve longer terms, they become better known to the voters. Their greater political strength discourages potentially strong opponents from running against them. During the elections from 1975 to 1981, almost half of the incumbent senators who sought renomination were unopposed; in the house elections from 1977 to 1981, slightly more than half of the representatives who ran again had no primary opposition. On the other hand, when the incumbent did not seek another term, there was a contested primary in the incumbent's party almost four-fifths of the time. In districts dominated by one party, it is not unusual for incumbents to be renominated without opposition in either the primary or the general election.

Because legislators are serving more terms and because legislative work takes more of their time than was the case previously, it is becoming more difficult to combine a legislative career with another profession or occupation. In occupational terms, Kentucky legislators are rather typical of those in other states, but they are not a very good cross section of state population. A recent legislative session included as the most common occupations thirty-eight attorneys, twenty-seven businesspersons, seventeen realtors, twelve farmers, eleven educators, ten other professional persons, nine members in management or sales, and nine skilled workers or labor union officials. In recent years there have been only about ten women in the legislature and no more than four black members, with most blacks and women coming from the largest counties.

LEGISLATORS AND THEIR CONSTITUENTS

Serving the needs of constituents is one of the most important legislative responsibilities, and in recent years it has become more significant—and time consuming—for Kentucky legislators. Legislators who have long-term career goals in politics are likely to devote more attention to constituency service. Moreover, as the members become more active and better known in the district, constituents are more likely to bring problems to them for solution.

A large part of the legislator's job is keeping in touch with constituents. Because senate districts have a little less than 100,000 population and house districts have about 37,000 people, it is possible for members to maintain personal contact with their constituents. Active legislators welcome opportunities to speak to local organizations; when controversies arise, they attend meetings on school problems or hearings on zoning changes, for example. In order to be visible and accessible to constituents, they attend many social functions, ranging from church suppers to athletic events and county fairs. One rural legislator finds that attending auctions is one of the best ways to meet constituents. Legislators find it easiest to maintain contacts in their own county, where they are well known and have frequent casual contacts with constituents. Legislators in rural Kentucky who represent more than one county find it more difficult to maintain contact outside their home county. Some schedule regular visits to the courthouse or other public places in other counties.

About one-third of Kentucky legislators make some use of public opinion polls to find out what their constituents are thinking. These may be printed in the local newspapers, or distributed door to door by volunteers or by the legislator, particularly during a reelection campaign. Some legislators mail polls to a list of a few hundred supporters or persons who have written to them. It is generally too expensive to mail polls to all constituents. Legislators generally recognize that polls are an imperfect way of measuring opinion, but it may be better than depending entirely on mail and personal contacts. Most mail is likely to come from organized groups, and it is important to members to know what the important groups in their districts are concerned about. They also want to know what other constituents think about issues, and this may be more difficult to judge without the aid of a poll. Of course, as legislators grow more experienced and more familiar with their district, they usually learn more about the range of constituent opinions and interests.

In order to make their own views and activities known to constituents, legislators must rely to a large extent on the media. In rural areas it is not difficult for a legislator to get coverage in the county newspaper for speeches or press releases. By contrast, in Fayette or particularly Jefferson County, it is more difficult to get press coverage because there are so many members representing one county. Some legislators, particularly in rural areas, write a regular column for a newspaper. As many as one-fourth of Kentucky legislators make some use of newsletters. Like the polls, these may be printed in the newspaper, distributed by volunteers, or mailed to a subgroup of constituents. This gives the member a chance to describe legislative accomplishments and emphasize services that are available to constituents. Polls are often included in newsletters, and results are published in them.

An increasing amount of a legislator's time is spent providing services for individual constituents. Legislators vary in the importance they attach to that work and in the number of requests they get in the district. Legislators are most likely to get requests from constituents if they publicize their willingness to provide constituency services. Members recognize the political advantages of serving needs, and many believe that this is a vital part of their job. As one Louisville representative describes it, "Just cutting through the bureaucratic red tape for your people—if you just do that you are doing 99 percent of what you are elected to do."

Constituents bring a wide variety of problems to their state legislators. They often have difficulty in understanding government regulations and in dealing with a variety of agencies. Those who think they are entitled to particular benefits from government— food stamps, workmen's compensation, or health care, for example— often seek help when their request has been turned down or unanswered. Kentucky legislators often are asked to help constituents get jobs in state government. The problems that are brought to state legislators often can only be solved by federal or local governments. In these cases the legislators work closely with congressmen or local officials to get the matters solved.

State legislators also play an important role in helping local governments in their district deal with state agencies. Among the most important problems are the repair and resurfacing of roads and highways, particularly in the coal-mining areas where heavy coal trucks have done so much damage. Legislators may help a local neighborhood get a traffic light installed. Local governments need help with flood control and drainage ditches, they need assistance in getting health facilities improved, and they want improvements in state park facilities in the area. In rural areas the legislator must try to negotiate with the governor and state agencies to get such help; in metropolitan areas more collective bargaining occurs. Members of legislative delegations in counties such as Jefferson and Fayette meet regularly with local officials to determine local needs and plan their tactics for seeking state help, as well as to discuss legislation that is needed to help the local government. Their success depends in large part on the ability of the county delegation to work together on projects and legislation. The Jefferson County delegation, with its diversity of constituent interests, has had some problems in recent years in agreeing on priorities and maintaining unity.

POLITICAL ORGANIZATION AND LEGISLATIVE DECISION MAKING

The organization of the Kentucky General Assembly is similar to that found in most state legislatures. The speaker of the house is the presiding officer and is also the leader of the majority party. As presiding officer he has considerable discretion in such matters as recognizing members to speak and make motions and ruling on parliamentary questions, and he plays a key role in committee assignments and assigning bills to committees. As party leader, he carries much of the responsibility for maximizing party unity in support of legislative programs, particularly when there is a Democratic governor.

The lieutenant governor is the presiding officer of the senate and actually presides over that body much of the time (unlike the role of the vice-president in the United States Senate). The top officer chosen by the senators is the president pro tem, who presides in the absence of the lieutenant governor. Much of the power exercised by the speaker in the house is divided between the lieutenant governor and the president pro tem in the senate.

The Democratic party has had a majority in both the senate and the house for more than sixty years. In recent years the Democratic majority has usually been between 70 and 80 percent in each house of the legislature, although during the 1960s the Republicans sometimes held more than one-third of the seats in one or both houses. Each party in each chamber chooses its own floor leaders, party whips, caucus chairmen, and other leaders.

For many years the Kentucky governor (when a Democrat) played a decisive role in the selection of the presiding officer and the other Democratic leaders in the legislature. The governor had no constitutional authority to choose legislative leaders but exercised his political influence at the beginning of his term, and the Democratic legislators accepted his suggestions. Normally, of course, the governor paid some attention to legislative preferences, but in the last analysis he made the effective choices. When John Y. Brown was elected governor in 1979, he announced that he would make no effort to influence the choice of leaders, and the contests for leadership positions were wide open. The 1979 legislative amendment provides for the election of leadership during the odd-numbered year organizational session, which offers some insulation from gubernatorial control.

One consequence of the governor's choosing legislative leaders was that these leaders normally held their positions for only four years. Another was that the leaders exercised less independent power because they were perceived as representing the governor. House Speaker William Kenton personified that new independence of the leadership. He had been picked as speaker by Governor Julian Carroll in the 1976 and 1978 sessions, and during his first two terms developed a reputation as a strong, skillful speaker. After John Y. Brown's election in 1979, Kenton won an unprecedented third term on his own, consolidated his power, and was assured of a fourth term when he died suddenly in November 1981.

One technique used by the Democratic leadership in the house and the senate is to maintain control of the legislative schedule, determining how bills will be assigned to committees and subsequently brought to the floor. Although the jurisdiction of committees is generally specified in the rules, the majority leadership has some flexibility in determining what bills go to which committees. After bills are reported by standing committees, they go to the Rules Committee, which is a bipartisan body but is dominated by the Democratic leadership. This committee may reassign a bill to a second committee in order to delay it or amend it, and it determines the order in which bills are brought to the floor. Late in the session, when the calendar is crowded, delay of a bill for a few days in the Rules Committee may assure its death.

When bills reach the floor, the majority leader has priority in getting recognition and may make motions that will facilitate amendments or that will cut off further debate and amendment if approved by the membership. Once the roll call begins on a bill, the leadership may delay completion of the roll call (by asking members to exercise their right to "explain their vote") while they round up absentees or persuade members to change their vote in order to pass a bill (or to defeat it). Skillful legislative leaders can use the control over the calendar and procedural tactics to maintain powerful influence over legislative decisions.

The Kentucky legislature is organized along party lines, and the Democratic party holds a majority on each committee approximating its majority in the senate or house. The leaders of each party in a chamber hold caucuses of all members from time to time. These caucuses have several purposes. They give the leadership and the sponsors of bills a chance to explain proposed legislation. They give members a chance to discuss bills and air their disagreements in private. Caucuses also give the leaders a chance to take unofficial straw votes on bills, which may guide them in decisions on seeking party cohesion on the floor. It is difficult to judge how effective the caucuses are; there is little evidence that members are often under serious pressure to go along with the majority viewpoint in the caucus.

Although the Democratic party clearly has a dominant position in the legislature, relatively few votes are taken that follow party lines. Actually if the Democratic majority were smaller, there might be more party line votes. Because the Democrats are so strong, their leaders do not need complete party unity to get bills passed. The Republican legislative party is so weak that it has little incentive to try to win legislative battles. In fact, the Republican members rarely try to develop a strong, cohesive party position on issues, a position that might attract public attention as the Republican alternative.

The Democrats do not vote as a bloc on most issues not only because their majority is so large but also because it is so diverse. The Democratic party represents the relatively conservative western part of the state, many of the coal-mining counties in eastern Kentucky, and most of the metropolitan districts of Jefferson and Fayette Counties. Democratic legislators represent constituencies with a wide variety of viewpoints and interests. It is not surprising that they often disagree on issues of taxation, strip mining, and major economic and social issues.

On some issues the most important voting blocs are not political parties but regional, rural, or metropolitan blocs, or coalitions mobilized by interest groups. For several years the Mountain Caucus has carried some weight on issues affecting the mountain counties, particularly bills allocating proceeds from the coal severance tax to local governments. Before the mid-1960s metropolitan counties such as Jefferson and Fayette were underrepresented in the legislature. Now these and other metropolitan counties are strong enough to force the legislature to confront issues of concern to them, but on controversial issues metropolitan legislators rarely vote as a bloc. In fact, the delegation from Jefferson county has been handicapped in getting legislation passed that specifically affects that county because of serious divisions among its own members, who represent quite different constituencies.

On some issues the only identifiable voting blocs are those put together by organized interests. Organized labor and business groups mobilize their supporters on opposite sides of some issues. A good example of that was the alignment that developed in the 1982 session over the issue of multicounty banking. There were no clear partisan or regional lines, but members largely responded to the views expressed by bankers in their own districts.

During the late 1950s and 1960s, when Democratic politics was dominated by factions, there was some evidence of factional alignments within the Democratic legislative party. The governor could count on the loyal support of a bloc of factional allies. Factional opposition to the governor among legislators was subdued, however, because the governor had so much power in bargaining with legislators. These types of stable factional alignments are no longer found among Democratic legislators, and no other factional alignments appear consistently in legislative voting.

Active support for legislation by the governor can still have an important impact on voting patterns in the legislature. The governor's powers of persuasion can be reinforced in a number of ways, such as helping a legislator to get a bill passed or supporting projects in the member's district. On bills that are part of the governor's program, the legislative leadership often builds a diverse supporting coalition. It is likely to include legislators who are loyal, or indebted, to the governor and those who are committed to the interest groups that support the bill. It is likely to be overwhelmingly Democratic, but Republican legislators sometimes join such coalitions, perhaps to get some help for their district.

In recent years legislators have tried in a variety of ways to assert their independence from the governor, but they often seek the governor's support for bills that they sponsor, and they bargain with the governor for support of bills of interest to the governor. The legislature has demonstrated its ability to override gubernatorial vetoes in recent years. In the past most bills reached the governor late in the session, and he vetoed some of them after the legislature had adjourned. The new flexibility in scheduling legislative sessions makes it possible for the legislature to take a recess after all bills have been submitted to the governor and to reconvene ten days later to vote on overriding gubernatorial vetoes. Some of the more ambitious efforts to assert legislative independence of the governor have resulted from the growth of the interim committee system, more thorough review of the budget, and more oversight of executive agencies, which are the topics discussed in following sections.

LEGISLATIVE COMMITTEES

Legislative committees are the organizational units that provide the required division of labor and issue specialization to consider and dispose of hundreds (about 1,400 bills are introduced in an average session) of bills introduced during each legislative session. The maturing of the Kentucky General Assembly, which resulted in the adoption of the 1979 constitutional amendment strengthening the legislative role, was preceded by the establishment of a meaningful committee system.

A functioning legislative committee system was initiated in 1968. In that year committees were reorganized into fourteen standing, comparable senate and house committees. Between 1890 and the committee reorganization of 1968, the senate consistently was organized into over twenty-five committees, the house into over thirty-five committees. There was, in effect, no issue-oriented committee structure.

The large number of committees that existed prior to 1968 belie the actual functioning committee structure in existence at that time. In the recent past, prior to 1968, three committees, Statutes I, II, and III, made up the functioning committee structure. Bills, regardless of subject, were assigned to these three committees, all of which were controlled by the governor. Statutes I received bills that were to be held or delayed, Statutes II received bills needing quick action, and Statutes III received bills that were destined for failure.

It was against this backdrop that the modern committee system was established in 1968. At that time fourteen parallel house and senate committees were organized by subject matter. Although the titles and precise jurisdictions of committees have varied somewhat from session to session, the concept of subject matter committees continues, with generally parallel jurisdiction in the two chambers. The committees cover such subject matter areas as appropriations and revenue, banking and insurance, education, the judiciary, local government, health and welfare, labor and industry, agriculture and natural resources, business organizations, energy, elections and constitutional amendments, transportation, and state government.

Upon adjournment of the 1968 session, the Legislative Research Commission (LRC), which will be discussed subsequently, merged the comparable house and senate sessional committees into subcommittees of the commission. These LRC subcommittees were called interim joint committees, and they were authorized to meet periodically during the twenty-one-month period between legislative sessions. Interim joint committees have continued to function and expand their role since the 1968 reorganization.

Since 1968, legislators have accepted a growing responsibility for committee work. Generally speaking, each house member serves on two or three committees, and senators serve on three committees. Interim responsibilities continue to increase, with committees being subdivided into several subcommittees; now almost continuous committee activity brings a legislator to the capitol for meetings several days each month.

The interim committee system offers an opportunity for legislators to prepare for the next session. During the interim period, issues can be discussed in detail, executive agency personnel can be questioned, state facilities can be visited, and prospective legislation can be drafted, considered, and recommended for passage in the next legislative session. Through this procedure, interim committees consider bill drafts without the pressures of time faced during a sixty-day biennial session. An interim committee or an individual member has the option of prefiling a bill, which means that the bill automatically will be introduced on the first day of the session. Committee prefiled bills usually carry an expression that "same should pass."

Special or select committees are also appointed during the interim period to concentrate on a particular issue or concern. These groups usually are established by resolution while the legislature is in session and are charged with considering or studying an issue and reporting to the general assembly at the next session. Such groups may be composed of legislators, interested or important citizens, and representatives of state agencies.

The reorganization of the legislature under the constitutional amendment mentioned previously further strengthens the committee system. As a result, the distinction between interim and sessional activity is decreasing. The 1983 general assembly organizational session began the new procedure and schedule of events preceding the regularly scheduled, even-year biennial session. The revised election schedule, with the primary and general elections being held in even-numbered years, also has a major impact. Under the new schedule, legislators are elected *before* the interim begins, allowing for legislative service on interim committees and continued service on those committees during the session. Previously, legislators stood for election (all house members and one-half the senate) every two years at the *end* of the interim period. Under that arrangement, committee assignments were not made until the session began. As a result, continuity was lost between interim and sessional activities because some legislators did not seek or did not win reelection, and others changed committee assignments at the beginning of the session.

The new arrangement results in a year of continuous and intense interim committee activity between the odd-year organizational session and the following-year regular session. Committee assignments are made in the organizational session, and legislative elections are held prior to the initiation of the organizational session. Consequently, interim committee activity now is in direct, uninterrupted preparation for the upcoming session.

The implementation of the 1979 legislative amendment represents the next logical step in increased legislative committee strength. Subject-matter, parallel house and senate committees have continued to expand their influence in the governmental process. Implementation of the legislative amendment removed several barriers to committee continuity. It also provided the opportunity, and expectation, that legislators specialize in subject-matter areas corresponding to their committee assignments.

LEGISLATIVE OVERSIGHT OF THE EXECUTIVE BRANCH

The general assembly has greatly expanded its role in executive oversight in recent years through the establishment of permanent legislative committees and the expansion of budget review activity. The move to develop special executive oversight committees began in 1972 with the naming of the Administrative Regulations Review Subcommittee of the Legislative Research Commission. Since 1972, the Personal Services Contract Review Subcommittee, the Legislative Program Review and Investigations Committee, and the Capital Construction and Equipment Purchase Oversight Committee have been formed. Each of these committees is directly involved in the oversight of some aspect of the executive management of state government.

Executive agencies often, by statute, are given authority to promulgate administrative regulations in implementing legislation. Administrative regulations are legally binding and are of interest and concern to many citizens. In 1972 the general assembly passed legislation making the procedure for promulgating administrative regulations more open to the public and subject to legislative review. Proposed regulations must be filed with the Legislative Research Commission for printing and public distribution. Concerned citizens have the opportunity to request a public hearing to voice their objections to a proposed regulation.

The Administrative Regulations Review Subcommittee meets monthly to review proposed regulations to determine whether the state agency proposing the regulation has the statutory authority to do so and whether the regulation is consistent with legislative intent. Unacceptable regulations are returned to the state agency for possible revision; however, the governor may issue an executive order promulgating a regulation for up to 120 days while the committee considers it.

The Personal Services Contract Review Subcommittee, established in 1978, receives proposed state agency contracts with firms and individuals outside state government. The committee reviews proposed contracts from three perspectives: does the need for the proposed service exist? can the service be performed by state personnel? and are the cost and duration of the proposed contract appropriate?

The Legislative Program Review and Investigations Committee, established in 1978, conducts performance reviews of state agency operations to gauge program effectiveness and expenditure appropriateness. Establishment of this committee signaled a direct legislative interest in reviewing executive agency operations in an organized, statutorily supported manner. For example, the committee has the power to subpoena witnesses and records and to require testimony under oath.

The Capital Construction and Equipment Purchase Oversight Committee, established in the 1979 special session, reviews records of the amounts expended and transferred for capital construction projects and equipment acquisitions and monitors the costs of such projects and acquisitions.

The establishing of the permanent committees and subcommittees listed reflects the desire of Kentucky legislators to take a more active role in all aspects of governmental operations. The biennial, even-numbered year legislative sessions historically have resulted in the governor's making many decisions when the legislature was not in session. Executive decision making flexibility has been reduced as a result of the oversight committee initiatives discussed here.

In 1982 the legislature passed a number of laws intended to strengthen its authority in several of these areas. For example, the Legislative Research Commission was given authority to block implementation of administrative regulations unless the governor declared that an emergency existed. The LRC was also given a veto power over federal block grant applications and over reorganizations of government agencies proposed by the administration. When these new laws were challenged in the courts, each was overruled by the Supreme Court in the case of *Legislative Research Commission v. Brown.* The Court also made it clear that the LRC could not exercise "legislative powers" between legislative sessions, but the Court left unchanged nearly all of the legislative oversight authority that had existed prior to 1982.

The 1979 constitutional amendment provided an additional encouragement for balancing power between the chief executive and the legislature—the veto session. Prior to 1979, the general assembly met in a continuous sixty-day session, which meant that adjournment was fixed in mid-March. Most bills passed in the last few days, allowing no real opportunity for legislative consideration and possible override of gubernatorial vetoes. Under the new arrangement, the legislature has until April 15 to conclude its business, allowing ample time for a veto session. Such an arrangement provides the general assembly the opportunity to review and override gubernatorial vetoes.

THE BUDGETARY PROCESS

In the not too distant past, the proposed budget submitted by the governor to the general assembly received virtually no legislative review prior to passage. Similarly, after passage, the governor had considerable flexibility in administering the budget. Through various statutory changes in recent years, the general assembly has limited the management flexibility afforded the governor in budget preparation and management.

The sessional and interim committee systems have provided an opportunity for greater legislative involvement in budget development, passage, and implementation. In recent years, the sessional Appropriations and Revenue Committees, and the merged interim joint committee, have taken an active part in the budget process. Topical budget oversight and review subcommittees have been formed to prepare the task of receiving the proposed executive budget drafted by the governor, of holding hearings, of considering amendments, and of taking final action. The topical subcommittee approach allows for legislator specialization and provides an organizational framework for legislative management and evaluation of the large quantity of data that constitute the budget request.

The budget review subcommittees are especially active in the months immediately preceding the legislative session. This early preparation precedes the rather extensive budget hearings that are conducted early in the regular session. The house and senate Appropriations and Revenue Committee conduct the hearings, either jointly or individually. Through this process of review of the executive budget request and consideration of amendments, an appropriations bill is prepared for legislative consideration and passage.

Between sessions, the budget subcommittees concentrate on agency oversight efforts. Agency expenditure patterns are reviewed, state agency heads are invited to meet with the group, and information is gathered in preparation for the next appropriations bill passage process.

In recent years the legislature has also dealt with the problem of revenue shortfalls that force changes in a budget that has already been enacted. It has required state agencies to develop plans for reduced spending in the event of cutbacks, has incorporated these in the budget bill, and, through its interim committees, has monitored compliance with these provisions. The Supreme Court has held that the legislature has authority to oversee implementation of the budget in this fashion.

LEGISLATIVE MANAGEMENT

The legislative branch is managed by certain constitutional and statutory provisions and by rules adopted by both chambers. The house and senate leadership forms a bipartisan agency known as the Legislative Research Commission, which serves as the primary source for legislative policy development and for the provision of legislative staff services. In addition, during the legislative session, several constitutional officers serve under the supervision of the house and senate clerks. The clerks employ part-time staffs during the session to manage the flow of proposed legislation properly, to maintain the journal, enroll legislation, and perform similar duties.

The growth and development of the general assembly have been paralleled by similar growth and development of the Legislative Research Commission. The Democratic and Republican leadership in both chambers makes up the commission, which makes policy and provides staff assistance. The president pro tem of the senate and the speaker of the house serve as co-chairmen of the commission by a change adopted in 1974. Prior to 1974, the lieutenant governor served on the commission and held the position as chairman.

The commission employs a full-time staff of professionals to meet the various needs of committees and the legislative membership. Except for small leadership staffs, all staff services are provided by the commission through its director, the chief staff officer of the general assembly.

The staff has grown in responsibility and in numbers over the last decade. Originally, the commission's major responsibility was to maintain the property of the legislature between sessions and to conduct research projects. Today the commission provides a wide range of services, including bill-drafting assistance for members, committee staffs of all types, research projects, facilities maintenance, some constituent service assistance, and public information services. Most legislators do not have personal staffs, however.

The part-time nature of the general assembly, the infrequency of legislative sessions, and the growing responsibilities and duties of the general assembly have increased the importance of legislative staff services. Legislators depend heavily on staff assistance provided by the commission to meet the varied demands of membership.

LEGISLATIVE TRENDS

The 1891 constitution that remains in effect today, with certain amendments, defined a very narrow role for the legislative branch of government. The general assembly was authorized to meet for sixty consecutive days every other year; only the governor could convene a special session, and the general assembly could consider only those subjects designated by the governor.

The general assembly began a transformation in the late 1960s that continues today. This transformation was further encouraged in 1979 with the adoption of the legislative amendment to the 1891 constitution. The amendment was not fully implemented until 1984; consequently, assessing its impact is speculative at best.

The increased demands on members' time likely will alter the type of individuals able to serve in the future. The demands of more traditional legislative service also have changed in recent years. Citizens who are able to give more time to the legislative process throughout the year, who are willing to accept additional constituent service responsibilities, and who are willing to specialize in subject matter areas are likely to be drawn to legislative service.

The 1979 amendment further alters the established pattern of election and service expectations. Previously, sessional activity was followed by an interim period in which momentum built toward the next session some twenty-one months away. The momentum was interrupted by primary and general elections the year preceding the session. The post-amendment procedure changes that schedule drastically. Legislators now run for reelection after the session. The interim period begins after the organizational session is completed in January of odd-numbered years. Several possible trends may result, including (1) an impact on legislative elections caused by legislators standing for reelection while issues from the previous session remain vivid in voters' minds, (2) a possible tendency for the governor to turn the organizational session into a special session since legislators will be in the state capital and available to meet, and (3) a strengthening of interim committee activity because continuity is maintained from organizational session to the opening of regular session.

Executive oversight will continue and is likely to become more effective, although the Court has made it clear that the legislature's authority to review executive decisions does not give it the power to veto them. The establishment of oversight committees and their resulting staffing have developed an expectation that the legislature will continually review executive decisions. The provision of constituent services builds familiarity with executive agency operations that promotes greater oversight.

In summary, these trends should result in the general assembly continuing to assert its independence and strengthening its position in comparison with the executive branch. The limited legislative role that was envisioned in the 1891 constitution will give way to a more balanced executive-legislative working relationship in the years to come.

Chapter 5

THE HISTORY AND STRUCTURE OF KENTUCKY'S COURT SYSTEM

Paul J. Weber and Delta S. Felts, University of Louisville

Kentucky's courts have not escaped the colorful, sometimes violent struggles that have enlivened state history.[1] If there is any theme or thread running through the history of the judiciary, it would be the struggle between the values if independence and responsiveness. Kentuckians have vacillated between wanting a judiciary adequately large and sufficiently free of legislative pressures to provide prompt justice and wanting a judiciary responsive to popular will, and therefore subservient to the legislature. The various reforms inaugurated from time to time have reflected that vacillation.

1792 TO 1799

During its first decades of exploration and settlement, Kentucky was governed for the most part as a portion of Virginia. What

The authors wish to thank the staff of the Administrative Office of the Courts' Public Information Office for their help in locating documents, charts, and maps, as well as checking the accuracy of statements. Much of the information in this chapter is drawn from their publications. Justice Charles Leibson of the Kentucky Supreme Court graciously took time from his court duties to read the manuscript and make suggestions from an insider's perspective. Professor Mary K. Tachau of the University of Louisville gave many helpful suggestions and directed the authors to several little known sources. Professor Weber adds an additional note of gratitude to Dr. Hall Carter of Grosse Ile, Michigan, who made his island home a winter haven in which to write critical portions of the manuscript.

rudimentary administration of justice existed came under that state's laws.[2] As a prerequisite of statehood Kentucky was required to develop its own constitution. As discussed elsewhere in this book, this task was completed by a convention of leading citizens assembled at Danville in 1792. The judicial structure established was closely patterned after Virginia's. The similarity allowed an orderly transfer of pending cases and provided a familiar system for the initiation of new suits.

At this point the structure of the courts was very simple. Judicial power was vested in a supreme court, which was called the court of appeals, and such inferior courts as the general assembly thought necessary. The constitution stated somewhat vaguely that a "competent number" of justices of the peace should be appointed in each county. The governor was given the power to appoint all judges. In practice these appointments were for life, although the judges could be removed for reasonable cause either by impeachment or upon a petition of the governor approved by two-thirds of each house of the general assembly.

As appropriate for a rural, frontier state in the process of settlement, land titles were the civil issue of paramount importance.[3] Evidence of the importance of settling land title disputes lies in the fact that the court of appeals had original jurisdiction in all title disputes, and its decisions were considered final.* As a safeguard against judicial tyranny, however, title disputes were to be tried before a jury unless both parties agreed to let the judges decide the issues.† The constitution did allow the appeals court judges some discretion in determining how land disputes could be brought to a hearing "so as to enable them to do right and justice to the parties, with as little delay and at as small an expense as the nature of the business will allow." At the same time, it also required that all complaints, defenses of the parties before the court, and all judicial opinions, including dissents, be put in writing to "perpetuate the testimony."

The seeds of later turmoil were sown by constitutional provisions that the general assembly could create inferior courts as it saw fit, and in all cases other than land titles, the court of appeals had

---

*The term *original jurisdiction* means that cases start in that court. A court with appellate jurisdiction is one that can hear cases on appeal from other (called "lower") courts. It was unusual for the supreme court to be given original jurisdiction; this indicates the importance attached to the settlement of land disputes.

†The role of a jury was to determine what the facts of a case are, e.g., whether a pioneer had indeed lived on the land as long as he claimed, whether he had paid the previous owner in full, etc. Once that was decided, the judges were to interpret and apply the law properly.

appellate jurisdiction over these courts subject to broad legislative power to make exceptions and impose regulations. The result was that successive legislatures created a variety of courts with often overlapping jurisdictions and administrative, as well as judicial, powers. For example, the first general assembly set up three different court systems, which had jurisdiction over the thirteen counties into which Kentucky was then divided. In each county a court of quarterly sessions handled primarily civil cases other than land titles, and a county court had authority over administrative matters. In addition, a statewide court of oyer and terminer was given jurisdiction over criminal cases.* Each quarterly session and county court was presided over by three justices of the peace, but the court of oyer and terminer had three justices with statwide jurisdiction.

This quickly proved to be unwieldly, and in 1795 the general assembly, with the acquiescence of the court of appeals, reorganized the system by allowing lower courts some jurisdiction over land cases (they were becoming too numerous) and by combining the court of oyer and terminer and quarter-sessions into a system of district courts with both civil and criminal jurisdiction. Curiously, however, the reorganization provided that all criminal cases had to be heard by the Franklin District Court in Frankfort. Recognizing that there was no one court to which the state itself could take its cases, the legislators also established a new general court, which was to meet periodically in Frankfort to decide cases "for and in behalf of the Commonwealth."

Before moving to the changes made by the next constitutional convention, it may be well to draw attention to some of the characteristics of Kentucky's first judicial system. The first feature is that the constitution gave enormous power to the governor. All judicial offices (with one exception) were to be appointed by the governor, and when the first general assembly provided for 125 justices of the peace to be spread over the thirteen counties, the governor was given enormous political leverage. Since professional qualifications were all but nonexistent, factional loyalty became the first prerequisite for appointment. Second, by allowing the general assembly to establish inferior courts as it saw fit, the constitution allowed matters of jurisdiction and organization to become the subject of legislative whim and political fortune. Third, it confused judicial, executive, and legislative functions and made power struggles between them inevitable. In this struggle the judiciary

---

*The terms *oyer* and *terminer* come from English common law. They simply mean a court that can "hear and determine" criminal cases.

started out by far the weakest branch. It had only two bases of power: judges were relatively difficult to remove once appointed, requiring the concurrence of the governor and a two-thirds majority in each house of the legislature. In one exception to the governor's power to appoint, the court of appeals could select its own clerk. While this may seem of small moment, clerks played a key role in the development of judicial power. The original clerk's office was responsible for establishing the docket, maintaining court records, and collecting costs for each case. Additionally, the clerk issued certificates of good standing and licenses to attorneys, in effect determining who could and could not practice law in Kentucky.

Finally, the decentralized nature of the court system assured that the administration of justice was neither uniform nor unified. There was little control over the quality of the decisions rendered by the justices of the peace, most courts kept few, if any records, and appeals were haphazard at best.

1799 TO 1850

When a second convention revamped the constitution in 1799, for the most part it left the judicial article intact. The major exception was giving constitutional status to county courts and expanding their administrative powers. Specifically, each county court was given authority to recommend by majority vote of the justices of the peace two persons to fill the offices of sheriff, surveyor, coroner, and justice of the peace. The governor could than choose one of the two recommended. An additional feature of the 1799 constitution enhanced the power of the court of appeals. While each court was allowed to appoint its own clerk, no one could be appointed unless he or she was certified by a majority of the judges on the court of appeals. The certificate attested that the clerk-to-be had been examined by the appeals court clerk and found qualified. Any appointed court clerk could be removed only for breach of good behavior, and then only by the court of appeals when two-thirds of its justices concurred. This provision added measurably to the power of the court of appeals since, as discussed previously, clerks possessed substantial power.

In 1802 the general assembly, recognizing a continuing growth in the number of cases, once again tinkered with the trial court system. This time the district courts were reorganized into a system of nine circuit courts with one judge chosen on a statewide basis to preside over each circuit. Two assistant judges from each circuit were appointed to serve with him. The change did little to reduce the case load, but the appointment of a presiding judge from a statewide pool of candidates provided a small step toward uniformity and independence from local interests.

The most interesting event to occur during this period was the "old court" versus "new court" controversy. Economic and population expansion after the War of 1812 gave such hope for prosperity that many small farmers and merchants borrowed heavily from Kentucky banks to finance their own economic growth. Banks loaned money far beyond the margin of safety, and when a recession hit in the late teens, creditors began to demand repayments the debtors could not make, and foreclosures began. Farmers sought relief from the legislature, which in 1821 passed the Replevin Act.* Among other things the act allowed for the postponement of debt repayment. In a famous case from Bourbon County, *William v. Blair*, Blair sued Williams for $219.67, a debt that he admitted owing but postponed under the Replevin Act. Judge James Clark of Clark County not only found for Blair but declared the Replevin Act unconstitutional. Clark was later upheld by the court of appeals.

The reaction of the general assembly was quick and severe but not immediately successful. Attempts to impeach Judge Clark and force the governor to remove the judges of the court of appeals barely missed reaching the necessary two-thirds majority vote required. The campaign of 1824 for legislative seats focused on the issue of abolishing the court of appeals. In the election the Relief party, representing the small farmers and merchants, swept both houses of the general assembly and immediately passed an act abolishing the old court of appeals and establishing a new court. The act was signed by the governor and became law on Christmas Eve of 1824. What happened then is reported in graphic detail by the editor of *Kentucky Bench and Bar*:

> The Old Court met January 28, and announced that no business would be translated until the autumn term. The Old Court gave no indication that it thought itself abolished.
>
> The New Court met in February, 1825, and promptly took the Old Court's furniture to the Senate Chamber and started business. Both the Old and the New Courts went to the public with protests and arguments. The New Court demanded of the Clerk of the Old Court for its records, which demand was refused. Francis P. Blair, Clerk of the New Court broke into the Chambers of the Old Court through a window and seized all the records he could find, but most of the important records had been hidden in

---

Replevin means a procedure to recover property unlawfully taken.

the vaults of the Bank of Kentucky, and some had been taken home by the three Judges of the Old Court.

Archilles Snead, Clerk of the Old Court, was held in contempt by the New Court but refused to release any records. The Old Court held Blair in contempt for seizing records.

Feelings ran high all over the State. Meetings were held in every county seat, either endorsing or condemning the Legislature. Grand Juries indicted members of the New Court and the Legislators who voted for the Reorganization Act. One of the New Court Judges openly stated that he wore two pistols even when he went to Prayer Meeting. Families were divided and friendships broken.

The bitterness of the controversy worsened the economic conditions in the State. Bank Notes were worth fifty cents on the dollar. Debts were uncollectible, and creditors were without judicial process. Law enforcement practically ceased. Respect for all Courts was shattered and a wave of crime resulted. Lawyers representing creditors tried to get their cases into the Old Court and those representing debtors tried to get their cases into the New Court. Some of the Circuit Judges recognized the New Court and some the Old Court, but most Circuit Judges "sat on the fence" and sent their appeals to both New and Old Courts.

Between December, 1824, and October, 1825, it was difficult to determine which was the law of the land. Apparently each Court considered itself in existence.

The election of August, 1825, was bitter. The Old Court Party won enough new members in the House to pass a repeal bill, but the New Court Party was able to block it in the Senate. Supported by a Resolution of the House the Old Court tried to recover the records seized by Clerk Blair of the New Court. Blair promptly armed his office and announced that anyone trying to seize these records would be fired upon.

All sorts of proposals were made to settle the controversy but with no results. The Legislature spent many days "investigating" Blair's armed forces. The capitol had been burned in November, 1824, and the Legislature of 1825 was sitting in a Church. Now the Church was burned and after six weeks of doing nothing the Legislature adjourned.

After another bitter election campaign the Old Court Party won the election in August, 1826. Promptly, when the Legislature convened in December, a bill was passed to repeal the Court Reorganization Act. The bill was vetoed by Governor Desha, but was repassed over his veto. The battle of the Courts was over.[4]

The wounds opened by the great court battle took decades to heal, but the victory of the old court faction in 1826 had been decisive, and with the return of prosperity, passions cooled, and the courts were able to conduct their business in relative tranquility. The most important outcome of the controversy was that the court system survived as an independent branch of government. Given the mood of the electorate just a few years earlier, that was no mean feat.

1850 TO 1890

The first major reorganization of Kentucky's courts was mandated by its third constitution, adopted in 1850. While the bitterness of the great struggle twenty-five years earlier had faded, the memories had not. The framers of the new constitution tried to incorporate two basic principles: independence of the judiciary from the general assembly and responsiveness of the judges to the electorate. As a first step all existing courts except the general court, whether created by the constitution or the legislature were given constitutional status and thus protection. The general court was simply abolished.

All judges were to be elected, those on the court of appeals for terms of eight years. In addition, for the first time the office of clerk of the court of appeals was made elective and therefore somewhat independent of the justices. The constitution further required that if the general assembly determined that court should be held in any of the judicial districts, voters of that district would elect their own clerk, provided only that he had the same qualifications as the clerk of the court of appeals and could get a certificate from either a judge of the court of appeals or a circuit court judge attesting to his qualifications.

The general assembly was not entirely frozen out, however. It retained the right to establish such other inferior courts as it deemed necessary, it could direct the court of appeals to hold its sessions in any one or more of the judicial districts, it could provide for a special judge to staff a court should any of the elected judges be disqualified, it could set the jurisdiction of the circuit courts, and it could change the rules for right of appeal from the circuit courts to the court of appeals.

In retrospect, the 1850 constitution had two serious flaws in its judicial article. With the general court abolished and the legislature in control of appeals, there was no central coordinating feature, and the circuit courts functioned as virtual fiefdoms. Furthermore, the general assembly could still create new inferior courts. The combination of these flaws triggered the next major controversy. In 1882 a well-intentioned general assembly, addressing the problem of a backlog of over a thousand cases on appeal, created a new, purportedly intermediate court, which it called the superior court. This three-judge court was given jurisdiction over "less significant" cases, i.e., those that did *not* involve the validity of statutes, property titles, felonies, or controversies where the amount at issue was over $3,000. While appeal from the superior court to the court of appeals continued to be a possibility, it rarely happened. Opponents immediately dubbed the two appellate level courts "The Rich Man's Court" and "The Poor Man's Court." While this time there were no buildings burned and no pistol-packing judges, a bitter debate raged for eight years and was settled only by another constitutional convention. Opponents of the superior court finally forced its disbanding. Fortunately, by the time the court closed its books, the backlog of cases had been disposed.

1890 TO 1975

In 1890 a constitutional convention once again tackled the judicial structure. What it produced could hardly be called a reform, and it established a system only in the most expansive sense of that word. But, if nothing else, the revision had the virtue of longevity, lasting eighty-four years. At the very least, this allowed many of the old animosities to die.

Basically the new constitution provided for a court of appeals to be staffed by seven judges elected from each of seven appellate districts. This court had general appellate jurisdiction except over a few clearly defined areas such as divorce and contempt rulings, some misdemeanors, and cases where the money in dispute was deemed too small to warrant review. The judicial article also divided the state into circuit court districts. While the districts increased over the years from thirty to fifty-six, there were always more counties than districts, and many judges literally rode the circuit to hear cases in each county of their district. The circuit courts had original jurisdiction over all cases not vested exclusively in some other court. They also had appellate jurisdiction to retry cases on appeal from lower courts.

Finally, in each county a group of lower courts was created, including the county court, quarterly court, police court, and magistrate or justice of the peace court. In one foolish bow to its authority, the state legislature was empowered to determine the jurisdictions of the county courts and the qualifications of its officers. The result over the years was a growing hodgepodge of overlapping or concurrent jurisdictions presided over by a mixture of lawyers and laypersons. Many of the justices of the peace were untrained part-timers paid only a percentage of the fines they collected. Even more shocking, by the late 1960s no one was even sure how many justices of the peace, magistrates, trial commissioners, or police courts there were in Kentucky.

The new system did solve one problem of legislative interference by prohibiting the creation of any court not specifically mandated by the constitution, and it did provide an intermediate appellate level for some cases in the circuit courts. In addition, the county-level courts were not required to keep detailed records, and as citizens became increasingly less tolerant of their haphazard administration of justice, the appellate system was overworked. The 1891 constitution's judicial provisions may have had a second virtue unforeseen by its authors, namely, that it became so irksome to so many different clientele of the courts that it assured an adequately broad coalition of interests to promote yet another reform. That occurred in 1975.

1975 TO PRESENT

The process leading to the constitutional amendment of 1975, creating a vastly different judicial system, is too complex to be fully detailed here, but a few highlights can be noted. As early as 1923, a commission studying state government efficiency recommended unification of the trial courts under the chief justice, but there was little popular support for such a reform, especially when it became clear that only a constitutional amendment could provide the legal foundation. Finally in 1968 the Kentucky Bar Association got behind an amendment proposal. A first draft died in the 1972 general assembly, but enough interest had been sparked that a number of traditional and ad hoc citizens groups took up the torch. The most important of the groups were the Kentucky Bar Association, the Kentucky Circuit Judges Association, the League of Women Voters, the Kentucky Citizens for Judicial Improvement, the Kentucky Judicial Conference, and the American Judicature Society.

Special notice should be given to the 1974 and 1976 sessions of the general assembly. A bill proposing the constitutional amendment passed both houses in 1974, probably only because enough legislators were confident it would be defeated at the polls. In fact, as a result of a careful and exhaustively thorough campaign by its advocates, the amendment passed by 54.6 percent of the votes in the 1975 general elections.* It was left to the 1976 general assembly to flesh out implementation procedures and details. Despite flashes of the old legislature versus courts animosity (one commentator observed that "asking the legislators to create an efficient court system is somewhat like asking thieves to design a jail"), members of the general assembly, the Office of Judicial Planning (later to become part of the Administrative Office of the Courts), and Governor Julian Carroll's office worked together remarkably well to create the new court system. In one swift step, Kentucky moved from the ranks of the nation's most outdated judicial systems to one of its most progressive.

CURRENT COURT SYSTEM

If one word could be used to describe the differences between the old and new court systems, it would have to be *unified*. The new judicial article of the constitution even refers to the court of justice in the singular. In fact, there are four levels of courts: the supreme court, the court of appeals, the circuit courts, and the district courts. The chief justice of the supreme court has executive and administrative authority over the entire system. Figure 5.1 shows the formal differences between the old and new systems.

An exclusive focus on the formal structure of the courts provides only a portion of the picture. The system is supported by an extensive administrative organization created by the general assembly and known as the Administrative Office of the Courts (AOC). The remainder of this section will provide a brief description of the formal court system and the administrative branch.

_____

*That may seem a substantial majority for most elections, but it is interesting to note that only thirty-four counties, including the ten urban ones, approved the amendment, while it was defeated in eighty-six mostly rural counties.

FIGURE 5.1

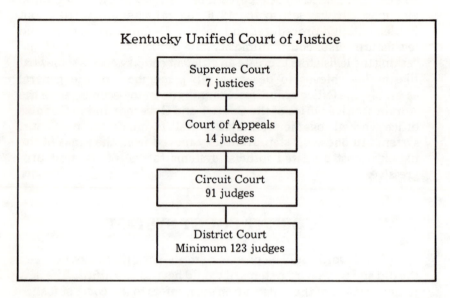

Kentucky Unified Court of Justice

Supreme Court
7 justices

Court of Appeals
14 judges

Circuit Court
91 judges

District Court
Minimum 123 judges

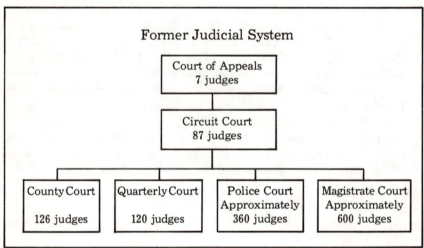

Former Judicial System

Court of Appeals
7 judges

Circuit Court
87 judges

County Court	Quarterly Court	Police Court	Magistrate Court
		Approximately	Approximately
126 judges	120 judges	360 judges	600 judges

STRUCTURING JUSTICE

The supreme court is composed of seven justices, one elected from each of the appellate districts. Terms of office for the justices are eight years, staggered among the districts so that no sudden political passion can ever instantly create a new court. The chief justice is elected for a four-year term by his fellow justices. The supreme court has appellate jurisdiction and ordinarily hears cases of constitutional or otherwise significant importance on discretionary review from the court of appeals. Circuit court decisions imposing the death penalty, life imprisonment, or more than twenty years in prison, however, are automatically reviewed by the supreme court as a matter of right. Traditionally, the supreme court has had the final word on the admission of attorneys to the Kentucky bar and can discipline them as well. The current court has a great deal of discretion in determing the rules of practice and procedure for the entire court system.

The court of appeals, an intermediate appellate court, is the one entirely new level in the system. It consists of fourteen judges, two elected from each appellate district for terms of eight years. Unlike the supreme court, which always sits *en banc* in Frankfort, the court of appeals may divide itself into panels of at least three judges and move to various locations in the state. Panels are chosen on a rotating basis so that every judge sits with every other judge at least annually. A chief judge of the court of appeals is elected by his or her peers for a term of four years. The chief judge's duties are primarily the assignment of judges and cases to the various panels. The court of appeals normally hears only cases from the circuit courts.

The workhorse of the system is the circuit court, which is the original trial court for all felonies, contested probate, and cases involving monetary values of more than $2,500. The circuit court also has jurisdiction over domestic relations and cases appealed from district court and administrative agencies. The ninety-one circuit judges are locally elected for terms of eight years from the fifty-six judicial circuits shown in Figure 5.2. This means some judges serve up to four counties, others serve in one judge-one county districts, and in the urban counties there are multijudge circuits. By law, circuit court must be held in each county, so some of the judges travel from county to county to hold court. There is no overall chief judge at the circuit court level. Rather, each district has a chief judge. If it is a one-judge circuit, he or she is automatically designated chief; if there are two or more judges, one is elected for a two-year term. Circuits are arranged into regional administrative units under a circuit judge appointed by the chief justice. The only

FIGURE 5.2

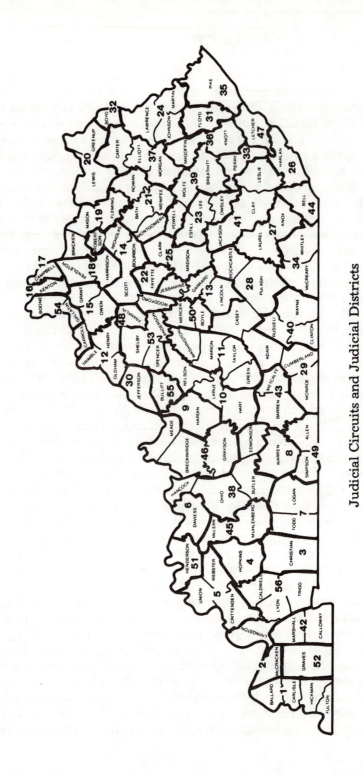

Judicial Circuits and Judicial Districts

statewide organization at this level is the Kentucky Circuit Court Judges' Association, which elects a president but has no formal judicial function.

District court rounds out the formal structure of the Kentucky system, and it is the lowest court having limited jurisdiction over felony preliminary hearings, mental inquest warrants, probate, misdemeanors, including traffic violations, juvenile matters, and civil cases where the amount is less than $2,500. Since the bulk of routine cases begin and end in district court, it also has the most judges. Currently there are 123 judges serving in judicial districts contiguous to those of circuit court. One interesting feature is that in counties where no district judge resides, a trial commissioner must be appointed to handle routine legal matters. District court judges are elected for four-year terms. In multijudge districts one judge is elected chief for a two-year term as is the circuit court chief judge. The only statewide organization is the District Judges' Association, a voluntary organization. Figure 5.3 provides a brief summary of the organization and jurisdiction of the new court system as compared with the former system.

Although not shown in Figure 5.3, an increasingly important part of district court is the small claims division. With an office in each county, small claims court settles disputes involving money or property valued at $1,000 or less. Court procedures are purposely kept informal so that citizens can file a claim or defend themselves without the expense of an attorney. Not unlike the procedure on the popular television show, "People's Court," the parties involved tell their stories to a judge, who may ask questions to clarify the facts then make a decision based on the applicable law. No juries are used in small claims court.

No description of the formal court system would be complete without some mention of the clerks of court. An elective office since 1850 and source of independent political power, the position of supreme court clerk was last filled by Martha Layne Collins, who later became Kentucky's first woman governor. The 1975 constitutional amendment, passed in the same election that gave Ms. Collins the office, provided that future supreme court clerks would be appointed and serve at the pleasure of that court. Clerks of the circuit court, who also serve as clerks of the district courts, however, continue to be elective offices. There is one circuit court clerk for each of Kentucky's 120 counties, and each is elected for a six-year term.

Finally, the 1976 general assembly legislated that judges should be elected from a nonpartisan ballot, the theory being that judges should be above party politics. Since judicial candidates are

111

FIGURE 5.3

FORMER SYSTEM	NEW SYSTEM
Court of Appeals 7 Judges Direct appeal from circuit	**Supreme Court** 7 Justices Appeals mainly from Court of Appeals except death penalty and 20 years or more imprisonment where appeal is from circuit court
None	**Court of Appeals** Direct appeal from circuit court Possibility of direct appeal from state administrative agencies Meets in panels of 3 judges throughout the state
Circuit Court 56 Judicial Circuits 87 Judges Court of general jurisdiction Continuous session & term courts Lower limit civil jurisdiction $500 (50 concurrent) Lower limit criminal jurisdiction $500 Concurrent criminal jurisdiction with lower courts down to $20 Equity matters Land title matters Contested Probate De novo appeals from lower courts Appeals from administrative agencies	**Circuit Court** 56 Judicial Circuits 91 Judges Court of general jurisdiction Continuous session Lower limit civil jurisdiction $2,500 Criminal jurisdiction for capital offenses & felonies only Equity matters Land title matters Contested probate On the record appeals from district court Appeals from administrative agencies

County/Quarterly/Justice Court
120 Courts
120 Judges,? Magistrates, JP's,? Trial Commissioners
Civil jurisdiction $50 (exclusive) $500 (concurrent)
Criminal jurisdiction
    Fine $20 (exclusive) $500 (concurrent)
    Imprisonment 12 months
    Uncontested probate
Juvenile matters
	District Court
	56 Judicial Districts
	123 Judges
	60 Trial Commissioners*
	Civil jurisdiction $500
	Small claims division $1,000
	Criminal jurisdiction
	    Felony Preliminaries
	All misdemeanors, violations, local ordinances
	Uncontested probate
	Mental Health
	Juvenile matters
	May be authorized to adjudicate local administrative cases

Police Court ?Courts ?Judges, Trial Commissioners Civil jurisdiction, same as county court (4th, 5th, 6th class cities only) Criminal jurisdiction, same as county court	

*Trial commissioner numbers are approximate. The number varies according to what new judges have been elected and what county they're from.

Prepared by
Administrative Office of the Courts

prohibited by the code of judicial ethics from discussing most substantive issues, judicial races have tended to become exercises in image building and name recognition.[5] As a result, polls of attorneys belonging to local bar associations, which rate the judicial candidates, have had a significant impact on the outcome of at least some judicial races. Whether such polls accurately reflect who would be better judges or who would simply be better for attorneys is still a matter of some dispute.[6]

ADMINISTERING JUSTICE

Like any large system, the courts are far more complex than on-line organizational charts can show. Yet, because they affect many lives so significantly and function for the purpose of administering justice, an ideal that goes to the heart of citizens' willingness to relate to others in society according to set rules, courts can tolerate very little ignorance, few errors, and less corruption within the system without destroying their own legitimacy in the eyes of the public. In addition, a court system that is too expensive will provide justice only for the wealthy, and one that is too slow will deny justice altogether. "Justice delayed is justice denied" is an old American adage. To minimize these five evils, the court of justice is supported by the Administrative Office of the Courts and a number of commissions, committees, and services. Figure 5.4 shows the relationship of the various components to the formal courts.

A discussion of the various judicial organizations follows.

The Judicial Council. The judicial council is an advisory group that reports directly to the supreme court. Its function is to serve as a continuous forum for study of the court system and to make recommendations for improvements. It serves as an informal focal point for various interests directly concerned with the courts, and its membership reflects this variety. *Ex officio* members are the chief justice of the supreme court, the chief judge of the court of appeals, the president of the Association of Circuit Court Clerks and the chairpersons of the judiciary committees of the general assembly. In addition, the chief justice appoints four circuit judges, four district judges, and three members of the Kentucky Bar Association for four-year terms. The director of the Administrative Office of the Courts serves as the council's general secretary.

The Judicial Nominating Commission. Although all judgeships in Kentucky are elective offices, the constitution provides that in the

FIGURE 5.4

**JUDICIAL AND ADMINISTRATIVE ORGANIZATION
KENTUCKY COURT OF JUSTICE**

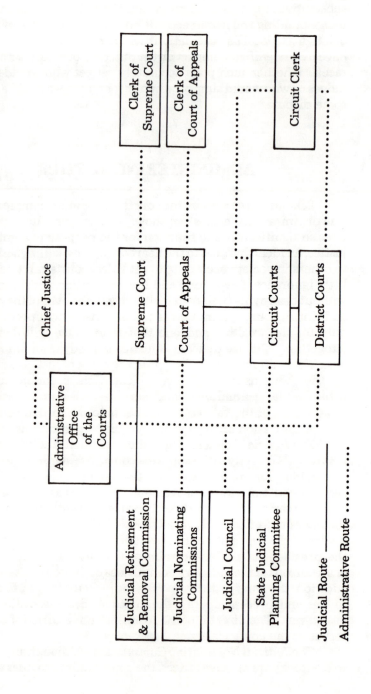

event of vacancies through death, disability, or retirement, the governor shall appoint a judge from a list of three names presented by a nominating commission. Each justice or judge so appointed must run for the office at the next regularly scheduled general election. There is one nominating commission for the supreme court and court of appeals and one for each circuit and district court jurisdiction, fifty-seven commissions in all. Each commission has seven members. The chief justice chairs all commissions, two commissioners are elected by the bar association of the jurisdiction in which the vacancy has occurred, and four are appointed by the governor, two from each of the two largest political parties. With the exception of the chief justice, all members serve four-year terms without compensation.

While this may seem a rather burdensome bureaucratic structure to fill vacancies between elections, nominating commissions can have an important impact on the court of justice. Between elections the number of appointed judges can approach 10 percent. For example, between January 1979 and May 1980, the governor appointed 20 of the 235 judges, and the 1983 circuit court elections left 23 vacancies in district courts that had to be filled by appointment. The commissions are one way to balance local and partisan control with nonpartisan concern for judicial competence.

The Judicial Retirement and Removal Commission. When elections, the appointive process, or sometimes nature fails to provide a high level of judicial competence, the judicial retirement and removal commission may step in. It is a watchdog with teeth. The commission has seven members and includes one judge of the court of appeals, one circuit judge, and one district judge, each elected by peers, one member of the bar association appointed by its governing body, and two persons not members of the bench or bar, appointed by the governor.

Traditionally, judges have been removed from office only by impeachment or, in Kentucky, by defeat at the polls. Both are cumbersome, expensive, and ineffective. The commission has the authority to order a temporary or permanent retirement of any judge who has a physical or mental disability so serious that it interferes with the normal performance of judicial duties, to reprimand in private or in public any judge who is guilty of serious misconduct, and to remove that judge if appropriate. Finally, the commission can remove any judge who was elected but did not have the proper qualifications.

The Judicial Planning Committee. The judicial planning committee was originally established as the result of a federal Law Enforcement Assistance Administration (LEAA) act in 1976. Its function is to plan for the use of federal funds that may be available for specific projects of the court of justice. Since federal funding has decreased dramatically, the role of the planning committee has been somewhat curtailed.

Administrative Office of the Courts

As mentioned earlier, ignorance, error, corruption, cost, and delay are the five evils any judicial system must constantly battle. If the four layers of formal courts are the backbone of the system, the AOC provides the arteries. Figure 5.5 shows the functional chart of this staffing organization. For the most part, it performs the duties of any governmental agency: budgeting, managing personnel and facilities, record keeping, auditing, planning judicial education, and informing the public. One unique and pioneering division of the AOC is Pretrial Services, which operates through fifty-seven field offices of various sizes. Pertrial Services has two major tasks: (1) it provides objective information to the courts about persons arrested to insure court appearance if they are released on their own recognizance, i.e., without posting bond (Kentucky is the only state that has outlawed commercial bail bonding), and (2) it operates dispute mediation programs in five local communities. These programs resolve conflicts that might result in misdemeanor charges if pursued in district courts through voluntary mediation between the disputants at considerable savings in time and money.

Pretrial Services has made a significant impact on case loads of the urban district courts that it serves. For example, for the period from July 1, 1980, to June 30, 1982, 65,021 complaints were received. Of these, 25,815 resulted in further warrants or summons. This means that 39,206 potential cases were kept out of formal court proceedings. Kentucky remains one of the most innovative states in the nation in finding more efficient ways to handle minor disputes.

CONCLUSION

This chapter has discussed the history and structure of the Kentucky court system. The history has been colorful on occasion, and one thing is clear: the courts reflect the interests, aspirations, politics, and divisions of the people of the state. A common theme through the years has been the struggle between an independent

116

FIGURE 5.5

FUNCTIONAL ORGANIZATION
ADMINISTRATIVE OFFICE OF THE COURTS

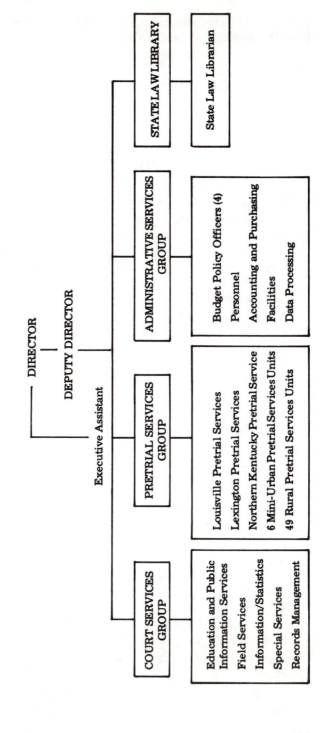

judiciary and a responsible one. Insofar as it has been resolved, it has been through the professionalization of the system. While it is hoped that the reforms following the constitutional amendment of 1975 will ensure the quality of justice Kentuckians have long sought, it is too early to tell whether or not citizens will continue to tinker with the system as they have so often in the past.

FOOTNOTES

1. Materials for this article have been gathered from numerous sources. For the early period, see Arthur K. Moore, *The Frontier Mind: A Cultural Analysis of the Kentucky Frontiersman*, Lexington, Ky.: University of Kentucky Press, 1957. For the constitutional period, see Joan Wells Coward, *Kentucky in the New Republic: The Process of Constitution Making*, Lexington, Ky.: University of Kentucky Press, 1979. For the early nineteenth century period, see Sandra VanBuakleo, "Desperate Deeds, Desperate Motives: Legal Politics in Kentucky," in W. Phillips Shively (ed.), *The Research Process in Political Science*, Itasca, Ill., L.E. Peacock Publishers (in press). For recent years see the annual reports of the Administrative Office of the Courts of the Commonwealth of Kentucky.

2. It should be pointed out that there was another court of justice functioning in Kentucky from 1789, two and one-half years before statehood was achieved. That was a federal district court, established as a result of the Federal Judiciary Act of 1789. The court had a much different, although still highly political, history. For a superb account, see Mary K. Tachau, *Federal Courts in the Early Republic, Kentucky 1789-1816*, Princeton, Princeton University Press, 1978.

3. The difficulty over land titles arose for several reasons. Surveying was primitive and incomplete, the state of Virginia was in the habit of paying debts and rewarding military officers by granting deeds to large tracts of western lands with ill-defined boundaries, Virginia and Kentucky too often granted conflicting titles to the same land, and squatters continually took up residence on lands that were left untended. It took decades to end the confusion.

4. Charles Landrum, Jr., "Old Court v. New Court," *Kentucky Bench and Bar*, Vol. 40, No. 1 (January 1976), p. 18.

5. Clause 7 of the American Bar Association Code of Judicial Conduct in Section B (1)(C) limits a judicial candidate from

making "pledges or promises of conduct in office other than the faithful and impartial performance of the duties of the office." Candidates are also forbidden to express their "views on disputed legal or political issues."

6. One judge who received a low rating claimed he had earned the enmity of several influential attorneys by refusing to allow them to collect what he considered "exorbitant" fees. For a general discussion of bar polls in Kentucky, see Joel Goldstein, "Do Bar Poll Ratings Influence Judicial Elections," *Judicature*, Vol. 63, No. 8, p. 376 (March, 1980).

Chapter 6

CIVIL LIBERTIES

Dennis O'Keefe, Northern Kentucky University

Under the United States and Kentucky Constitutions, the rights of individuals are protected from arbitrary and unreasonable actions by government. Guarantees of freedom of speech, press, and religion, as well as procedural protections, such as the right against self-incrimination in criminal cases, are some of these rights. The inclusion of these protections in the basic documents establishing the national and state governments reflected a fundamental fear of unbridled governmental power, which American colonists experienced under British rule. The newly independent states and those later added to the Union made sure to put restrictions against governmental power in their state constitutions, and the first Congress of the United States approved the Bill of Rights limiting federal power. The meaning and scope of these rights have been subject to controversy, often within the context of legal cases where defendants and plaintiffs have claimed that government officials have infringed upon them. These parties have looked to judges, particularly those on appeals courts, to render opinions supportive of their claims. Conversely, government attorneys have usually sought to persuade courts to make restrictive rulings limiting individual freedom.

The justices of the United States Supreme Court have the ultimate responsibility of interpreting the federal Constitution, and the Kentucky supreme court does the same in respect to the Kentucky constitution. State judges are constrained to follow United States Supreme Court decisions interpreting the Fourteenth Amendment, which prohibits any state from denying a person life, liberty, or property without due process of law or the equal protection of the laws. Most Supreme Court cases on individual rights or racial discrimination were initiated at the state level and appealed to the high court. Over the years, the Supreme Court has required states through the Fourteenth Amendment to meet nearly all of the standards of fairness applicable to the national government under the Bill of Rights.

The Kentucky bill of rights appears at the very beginning of the state constitution and contains twenty-six sections, many of which are similar to federal guarantees. For example, Kentucky's section one protects freedom of speech, peaceful assembly, and religion. In criminal prosecutions the commonwealth is required to follow procedures set down in both the federal and state constitutions to insure that a defendant is treated fairly. Some of the requirements of fairness include the right to be tried by an impartial judge and jury, the right against unreasonable searches and seizures, the right to counsel, and the right to be protected against self-incrimination. Although both conservatives and liberals generally agree on the need for these protections, disagreement arises over their application in particular cases. Criminal cases seldom raise issues of flagrant abuse of defendants' rights by law officers since the prosecutor would not likely seek indictments, or if he did, the trial judge would normally insure that due process requirements were followed. However, if errors are made at trial or if novel issues are presented, the losing party may appeal to the next highest level, which in the Kentucky system is the court of appeals.[1] Final appeal could be made to the state supreme court and beyond that to the United States Supreme Court if there were a federal constitutional question at stake.

This chapter will examine how the courts, particularly the Kentucky supreme court, have interpreted certain constitutional rights. The discussion will begin with due process in criminal law, move to freedom of religion, speech, and the press, and conclude with equal protection.

SEARCHES AND SEIZURES

One of the most frequently raised issues in criminal cases is the validity of searches and seizure of evidence. The Fourth Amendment of the United States Constitution and Section Ten of the Kentucky constitution prohibit unreasonable searches and seizures. This means that before police can act, they must obtain a warrant issued by a judge specifying the place and articles to be taken, as well as the name of the person who controls the premises. Exception to this requirement occurs when a crime is committed in the presence of an officer, who then may arrest and search the suspect and the area immediately under his control. A corollary to this exception is the plain view doctrine, which holds that if police have a legitimate reason for being present in a place and see in plain view illegal or stolen property, an arrest may be effected and the material confiscated.[2]

When an automobile driver is stopped by police for a traffic offense, a search may be made of the person, and if evidence of another crime is discovered, the individual may be charged with that offense as well. Yet, if the original charge results in a finding of not guilty, then the evidence discovered in the search is not admissible in a trial for the second offense.[3] The reason is that a search without a warrant can be made only incidental to a lawful arrest, and if there has been an acquittal on the original charge, the arrest is considered to be unlawful.[4]

Warrantless searches of automobiles is a vexing problem for the courts, as shown by the lack of uniformity between federal and Kentucky holdings. Federal rules permit law officers to stop and conduct a warrantless search of a car that they believe is being used in the commission of a crime.[5] The rationale is that the automobile may be driven away before police can obtain a warrant. However, in Kentucky even if police have probable cause to believe that the vehicle is being used in connection with a felony, they may not stop and search it without getting a warrant.[6]

JURY TRIAL

In criminal felony cases the accused is guaranteed trial by jury, but most criminal charges never reach the jury stage for a number of reasons. Commonwealth prosecutors must first decide whether the evidence warrants presentation to a grand jury, which is composed of twelve citizens drawn at random from the local community. A prosecutor may deem a case too weak to go to a grand jury and therefore will drop the charges. Second, the jury may decide not to indict the suspect after hearing witnesses and weighing the evidence. In most instances, however, it does indict since it finds the prosecutor's arguments convincing.[7]

The next step is to schedule a trial. While awaiting trial, a criminal defendant may negotiate through his attorney a guilty plea bargain with the prosecutor and thereby waive a jury trial. For the defendant who knows that the state has a solid case against him, pleading guilty may be more attractive than going to trial. The prosecutor is usually willing to drop some charges in a multicount indictment in return for a guilty plea on the remaining charge. Moreover, the defendant will likely receive a lighter sentence than would be the case if a trial were held. If there is no plea bargain, the accused felon will be tried before a twelve-member jury unless he agrees to a smaller number of jurors.[8]

Misdemeanors, such as disturbing the peace, are minor offenses not punishable by death or confinement in the penitentiary and are triable before either a judge or a six-person jury.[9] Before the adoption of the Judicial Reform Amendment, police and quarterly courts had jurisdiction over such violations, and the presiding judges did not have to be lawyers. The lack of legal training and knowledge on the part of lay judges was the basis for a petition for a writ of habeas corpus seeking the release of Lonnie North, who had been tried before C.B. Russell and convicted for driving while intoxicated. The suit was based on the argument that North could not have received due process of law by being tried before a nonlawyer judge. Both the Kentucky and United State Supreme Courts rejected North's claim, noting that under state law he had the right to appeal his conviction to a circuit court headed by a lawyer judge where a new trial could be held.[10] Presently, as a result of the reform amendment, all judges in the commonwealth must be lawyers, and misdemeanants are tried in the state's district courts.

RIGHT TO COUNSEL

Defendants have the constitutional right to employ counsel to represent them in criminal cases. If a person is indigent, the court must appoint an attorney who is either a public defender or a member of the local bar selected on a rotating basis.[11] Under the *Miranda* decision an accused must be informed by the police of his right to consult an attorney after his arrest and before police begin to question him about the crime.[12] The right to be represented by counsel assumes that a lawyer will have adequate time to prepare the case, including the following: full consultation with the accused, interviews with witnesses, and time to study the facts and law and to plan trial strategy.[13]

RIGHT AGAINST SELF-INCRIMINATION

An important protection afforded an accused under both the Kentucky and United States Constitutions is the right not to answer questions that are incriminating. This privilege applies to trial and grand jury proceedings, as well as to questioning a suspect by police after arrest. Exception to this protection occurs when a motorist, suspected of drunken driving, is arrested and refuses to take a breath analysis test. The courts have upheld the state's power to take away a driver's license for such refusal on the basis that operating a vehicle is a privilege granted by the state under certain conditions. The requirement of taking a breath analysis test for anyone arrested for drunken driving is a reasonable condition for holding an operator's license and does not violate the constitutional protection against giving evidence against oneself. Similarly, the courts have treated the taking of finger prints and blood samples in criminal cases as a search of the individual for evidence rather than as self-incriminating testimony.[14]

DOUBLE JEOPARDY

Section 13 of the state constitution prohibits the common-wealth from trying a person twice for the same offense. However, if a crime is punishable by both federal and state governments, then an individual can be tried for the same crime in both jurisdictions.[15] Within the Kentucky court system, the prosecution may not take a single act, which may constitute more than one offense, and try the person separately on each offense. Thus, a man charged and tried for rape could not be subsequently tried for the crime of detaining a woman against her will.[16]

The protection against double jeopardy does not apply to a conviction appealed by a defendant to a higher court, which finds error in the trial proceedings and remands the case to the lower court for a new trial. If found guilty, the accused may receive a more severe sentence than was meted out in his first trial. In the event of a hung jury or a mistrial, the state is also free to obtain another indictment and retry the accused without violating the ban against double jeopardy.[17]

PROHIBITION AGAINST CRUEL PUNISHMENT

Both the United States and Kentucky Constitutions prohibit government from imposing cruel punishment on those convicted of crime. Since neither document specifies what is cruel, judges have been asked to make that determination. The judicial response has been in almost all cases to defer to legislative will in setting the minimum and maximum penalties for each offense. Judges are very reluctant to substitute their views for legislative policy on what is the appropriate punishment for a particular crime. Nor will appellate courts overrule a trial judge's sentence of a convict who claims that it is disproportionate to sentences that others have received for the same offense, as long as the sentence is within statutory limits. For example, capital punishment was not only authorized for conviction of murder but at one time was also a sentence that could be imposed for burglary, robbery and rape as well.[18] Despite the rarity of such sentences, the Kentucky supreme court held that the death penalty for such offenses was not unconstitutional, since under common law there were many crimes that were punishable by execution.[19]

Today only murderers are subject to the maximum penalty, but such punishment cannot be mandatory in every murder case.[20] Judges or juries must consider aggravating and mitigating circumstances stipulated by the legislature to eliminate arbitrariness or capriciousness.[21] Included among aggravating circumstances are previous convictions for a capital offense, the commission of another felony in taking someone's life, murder for hire, and killing a police officer. Mitigating circumstances include in part acting under the influence of extreme mental or emotional disturbance, acting in a minor way as an accomplice to a killer, acting while intoxicated, and being of young age. If a death sentence is imposed, the judge or jury must put in writing the aggravating circumstance(s) found beyond a reasonable doubt.[22]

FREEDOM OF RELIGION

Like its federal counterpart, the Kentucky constitution protects an individual's freedom of worship and prohibits the state from establishing or aiding religion. These provisions were designed to prevent government from getting embroiled in religious controversy by favoring one religion against another or by establishing an official orthodoxy that all citizens would have to support. Separation of church and state was necessary to reduce the possibility of civil strife.

The Right to Worship

Throughout American history the value of religious liberty has been strongly held and widely exercised, as witnessed by the numerous religions found in this land. Rarely have either the state or national governments hindered groups from proclaiming and practicing their religious beliefs; however, when religions have engaged in conduct harmful to public morality, safety, or national unity, government has sometimes attempted to restrict such practices. Thus, the Mormons were prosecuted by federal authorities in the 1870s for engaging in polygamy ordained by their religion. Similarly, Jehovah's Witness children were suspended from public school because of their failure to salute the flag during World War II, and in the 1960s Amish were charged with violating compulsory school attendance laws. In all of these cases, the sect's beliefs ran counter to society's rules governing morality or civic virtue.[23]

The courts have tried to balance competing societal and individual claims as shown in the snake handling case. The general assembly had enacted a statute forbidding this practice in religious ceremonies. In upholding the law, the Kentucky supreme court said that the value of protecting people's lives outweighed the claim by snake worshippers of religious freedom. Since the handling of poisonous snakes is inherently dangerous, government is justified in prohibiting such worship.[24] The state's interest in public health was also the basis for the high court's upholding a law requiring compulsory vaccination of school children despite the objections of some parents on religious grounds.[25]

Parents have the right to enroll their children in religious schools under Section Five of the constitution, which states that no man shall be compelled to send his child to any school to which he is conscientiously opposed. A few sectarian schools have contended that this clause insulates them from being reviewed by state education officials to determine whether they are meeting minimum standards regarding teacher certification, textbooks, and curriculum. They have argued that if the standards were enforced, they would have to close the schools; consequently, their religious freedom would be infringed. A test case raising this issue was brought before the state supreme court in 1979. The court held that the commonwealth may only monitor the performance of private schools and not impose minimum standards. Kentucky may not move to close any of these schools unless student performance on nationally standardized examinations shows that the institution failed to accomplish its avowed purpose of educating.[26] It is clear from this case that Section Five requires the commonwealth to keep its hands off church-run schools and allow practically complete freedom for parents and sect leaders to operate them as they wish.

The No Preference Clause

The no preference clause of Section Five prohibits the commonwealth from giving support to any religious denomination. The separation of church and state did not become an important legal issue in Kentucky or the rest of the nation until the 1940s, when some states began to subsidize bus transportation for parochial school students. A Kentucky law providing this kind of aid was challenged on the ground that it violated the no preference clause, as well as Section 189 of the constitution, which prohibits taxes earmarked for education from being spent for any church school. The state supreme court held the statute unconstitutional and in so doing rejected the child benefit theory announced by the United States Supreme Court in a Louisiana case. The nation's highest court had said that Louisiana's purchase of textbooks for parochial school children did not breach the wall of separation between church and state because the program helped the student, not the religious institution.[27] However, in the Bluegrass State, the state supreme court did not find the bus subsidy law as aiding children in general but only those attending schools. If some of these schools are religious, then the program fails to meet the constitutional standard.[28]

The general assembly reacted to this decision by passing a carefully worded statute seeking to avoid the obstacle presented by Section 189. Instead of permitting local school boards to use educational levies to pay the cost of transportation, the legislature authorized county fiscal courts to provide the service financed from general revenue funds to which Section 189 did not apply. Nevertheless, a test case was brought alleging that this new scheme still violated the no preference clause. This time the supreme court upheld the law, ruling that the expenditure was for a public purpose, i.e., the protection of the health and safety of school children on their way to school. The fact that sectarian schools were indirectly benefited was not sufficient to defeat the declared secular purpose and the practical and wholesome effect of the law.[29] Two years after this decision, the United States Supreme Court ruled that a New Jersey law permitting local school boards to pay the cost of bus transportation for parochial school students did not violate the national First Amendment.[30]

Over the next thirty years there were many cases throughout the country contesting the validity of state aid to sectarian schools, as well as the teaching of religion or the observance of religious practices in public education. In Kentucky a lawsuit was brought by Americans United for the Separation of Church and State against school boards in six central counties for employing Roman Catholic nuns as teachers in public schools and for renting buildings from church officials for public instruction. These arrangements were subsequently upheld by the state supreme court on the grounds that the nuns were not teaching religion or attempting to force their religious views on the students. Nor did the nun's mode of dress, the traditional habit, constitute a violation, since there was no state law prescribing what teachers shall wear. Therefore, their attire was merely a personal matter that carried no secular endorsement. The rental of church school buildings also did not violate the no preference clause, since the church in no way attempted to influence or control what was taught.[31]

Two religious practices followed in public school systems were held unconstitutional by the United States Supreme Court in the early 1960s. These were recitation of prayers and readings from the Bible. The Court reasoned that under the First Amendment establishment clause the state of New York had no business drafting an official prayer to be said at the start of each school day. Even though the prayer did not favor any denomination and students were not required to say it, the fact that government composed and initiated it clearly made it aid in behalf of religion.[32] In the Bible-reading case, the Court said that the purpose and primary effect of this practice was to advance religion.[33]

Although the Supreme Court had spoken clearly on these matters, many public school districts did not accept the decisions and continued their traditional routines. For example, a study of Tennessee school boards found that only 1 out of 120 were in full compliance with the Bible-reading decision.[34] In Kentucky there were still statutes on the books requiring daily recitation of biblical passages and the Lord's Prayer. It was not until 1979 that the state attorney general issued a strongly worded opinion that readings from the Bible were unconstitutional and that school officials and teachers would risk being sued by any student for violation of rights if the practice continued.[35]

Reciting the Lord's Prayer was made voluntary by the legislature to lessen the possibility of legal attack. School officials were also supposed to inform students that the prayer was not meant to influence anyone's personal religious beliefs. The general assembly proclaimed that the purpose of the statute was secular: to have students "learn of our great freedoms including the freedom of religion symbolized by the recitation of the Lord's Prayer.[36] Yet, despite the effort of the legislature to give the prayer secular significance, it is doubtful that the law is constitutional.

When the general assembly enacted a bill permitting the posting of the Ten Commandments in public school classrooms, it also employed the secular purpose argument. The legislators affirmed that the commandments were one of the sources of common law and contemporary legal codes in western democratic governments. In an effort to thwart the charge that the act violated the establishment clause, the legislature provided that the printing costs be borne by private parties and not school boards. Nevertheless, the law was tested in the courts, and on appeal to the United States Supreme Court the statute was declared invalid. The high court found that the intention of the legislature was to give official support to religion and that the avowed secular purpose, was a thinly veiled rationalization.[37]

As we assess the field of church-state relations today, we find that state and local authorities must abide by three Supreme Court guidelines for determining whether a governmental policy violates the separation principle. Two of these were discussed earlier in the Bible-reading case: that the purpose be secular and that the primary effect of the program neither aid nor inhibit religion. A third guideline is no excessive entanglement between government and religion in the administration of the program. If any of these standards is breached, the program in question will be deemed a violation of the First Amendment establishment clause.[38]

FREEDOM OF SPEECH AND PRESS

Freedom of Speech

Sedition. Freedom to express and communicate information and opinions is considered one of the basic elements of an open and democratic society. It is not surprising to find that the United States and Kentucky Constitutions contain clear statements that no law shall be enacted that limits this freedom. However, American history is dotted with examples of radical critics being harassed and punished for expressing their views, particularly when the security of the nation was perceived to be endangered.

Kentucky was no exception to this point. Like many states during and after World War I, the commonwealth passed a criminal sedition law making it unlawful to advocate, publish, or counsel the desirability of overthrowing government by violent means. There have not been many prosecutions under this act, however. For the most part Kentuckians are politically conservative and have not been attracted to radical causes. Yet, the Bluegrass State has not been completely insulated from the unsettling winds of political and social change.

The eastern Kentucky coal fields were a battleground in the 1930s between miners and coal operators. Events in Harlan County raised serious questions of collusion between local law enforcement officers and mine owners to intimidate union organizers and strikers in order to break the labor movement. There was bloodshed in the Battle of Evarts in 1931, and miners were arrested on charges of murder and sedition. Novelist Theodore Dreiser organized a committee of nationally known literary, legal, and educational figures to investigate and report on the situation. They found that unionists had been arrested on the basis of flimsy evidence and that they had been denied due process of law, including biased selection of grand jurors, warrantless searches, and setting of unreasonable bond.[39] Only the murder indictments were tried and a jury found the defendants innocent.[40]

State sedition laws suffered a lethal blow in 1956 when the United States Supreme Court ruled in *Pennsylvania v. Nelson* that the federal Smith Act, making the advocacy of overthrow of government a crime, had preempted the field of subversion so that state laws on the subject were null and void.[41] This case had a bearing on the sedition conviction of Carl Braden of Louisville, a director of the Southern Conference Educational Fund, an organization dedicated to racial and economic equality. He appealed his conviction to the Kentucky supreme court, which reversed on the basis of *Nelson*.[42] Despite the holding, the sedition law was not repealed by the legislature until 1974, and during the interval there were arrests of political activists for violating the statute.[43]

In Louisville, civil rights demonstrators raised the question of the sedition law's constitutionality on First Amendment grounds. They were protesting racial-discrimination in housing and sought injunctive relief against city officials who invoked the sedition act, as well as other laws, to arrest the protestors. Relying on United States Supreme Court precedents that state laws prescribing membership in subversive groups were unconstitutionally vague and overly broad in restricting speech, a federal district court ruled that the Kentucky statute was similarly handicapped. Overbreadth meant that a statute made punishable both the expression of abstract doctrine, which was protected by the First Amendment, and advocacy designed to bring about violent action, which was not. Vagueness in defining criminal conduct was impermissible because the lack of certainty over what constituted criminal behavior violated basic concepts of due process. Besides the sedition law, the court threw out for vagueness and overbreadth a conspiracy statute making it a crime for two or more persons to join together to intimidate, alarm, disturb, or injure another. The application of other statutes and ordinances covering vagrancy, disorderly conduct, loitering, and the issuance of parade permits were also invalidated as too restrictive of political expression.[44]

Obscenity. Certain types of speech or writing, such as obscenity, are not protected by the First Amendment or by the Kentucky bill of rights. The critical question facing lawmakers in prohibiting sexually explicit books, magazines, or films from being sold or exhibited has been the definition of obscenity. At one time laws governing obscenity were vague, permitting police to seize almost any work that contained sexually descriptive accounts or photographs. In Kentucky one obscenity statute prohibited the selling of obscene material but did not define the word *obscene.* In reviewing the obscenity conviction of a Newport newsstand vendor in 1950, the Kentucky supreme court supplied a definition then current in legal circles. Obscenity was anything offensive to morality or chastity, indecent, or nasty. These words in themselves were sufficient to describe what was proscribed, being words in common usage and readily understood by persons of ordinary intelligence. The court also said that if the work tended to deprave and corrupt the morals of those whose minds were open to such influence and into whose hands the publication might fall, then a jury applying community standards could find it obscene.[45]

In response to a growing number of cases in the 1950s testing whether obscenity laws violated freedom of speech, the United States Supreme Court ruled that a work was obscene if is was utterly without redeeming social value and if the dominant theme, taken as a whole, appealed to prurient interest. These tests were to be applied by the average person using contemporary community standards.[46] In 1965 a Paducah bookseller was charged under the Kentucky obscenity law with selling two allegedly obscene magazines, *High Heels* and *Spree.* Convicted at trial, he eventually appealed to the United States Supreme Court, which reversed because the state failed to meet these tests.[47]

In 1966, the general assembly revised the obscenity statute by adopting the prurient interest test but not the redeeming social value test. The failure to include the latter provision was the basis of an appeal of an obscenity conviction by James Smith, a Hardin

County grocer, who had sold a hard-core pornographic magazine called *After Hours*. In upholding his conviction, the Kentucky supreme court said that the absence of the redeeming social value test did not invalidate the statute, since it was implied within the law. Moreover, the court asserted that the prosecution did not have to prove that the magazine in question was utterly without redeeming social value but simply show that it was on its face.[48]

The same law was also sustained by the court in a case involving one of the more infamous pornographic movies of the 1970s, *Deep Throat*. The court noted that the film contained repeated scenes of sexual intercourse, anal sodomy, fellatio, and cunnilingus and that the plot consisted entirely of the sexual exploits of actress Linda Lovelace. The judges concluded that the film was without any serious literary, artistic, political, or scientific value and was therefore obscene.[49] This test, plus the requirements that the matter depicted or described sexual conduct in a patently offensive way and appealed to prurient interest, is currently used in obscenity prosecutions. Within this framework, a judge or jury employing contemporary community standards may determine that the material is obscene.

Freedom of the Press

Courts have found vagueness to be a problem with the common law crime of libel, defined as false and malicious writing intended to degrade a person's reputation and to disrupt the public peace and morals. A criminal libel action was brought against Steve Ashton, a college student from Ohio, who had gone to eastern Kentucky to support the efforts of striking miners. He printed a pamphlet on the injustices inflicted on the miners by coal operators and local governmental officials in Hazard. The pamphlet contained several inaccuracies, for which he was indicted and tried for the common law crime of libel. The jury found that Ashton's allegations were maliciously false and defamatory toward the chief of police, the sheriff, and the publisher of a local newspaper. He appealed his conviction to the Kentucky supreme court, which upheld the trial court's verdict. A four-judge majority rejected Ashton's argument that the definition of criminal libel was so vague and inconclusive as to violate freedom of speech and due process rights.[50] On appeal, a unanimous United States Supreme Court reversed on the grounds that the law was too sweeping in its coverage and indefinite in meaning to withstand First Amendment challenge.[51]

In attempting to insure criminal defendants fair trials, judges have had to consider the problem of juror bias resulting from extensive press coverage of serious and heinous offenses prior to trial. The trial judge faces a dilemma of trying to insure that there will be unbiased jurors while meeting press demands that all pretrial hearings be open. One way of solving the problem is to put a gag order on media coverage of the preliminary proceedings with the prospect that the press will challenge it. This was exactly what happened in a murder case in Ashland. A local newspaper appealed the restriction to the court of appeals, which decided that pretrial hearings may be closed only after the trial judge had (1) heard the press in court on the issue and (2) found that the defendant's rights would be irreparably damaged if reporters were present. Additionally, since a free press is a preferred freedom, the judge needed to consider means less drastic than excluding the press to protect the rights of the accused. The appeals court found that the trial judge had failed to meet these conditions and removed the gag order.[52]

Press coverage of trials themselves is guaranteed by Section Eleven of the constitution, which states that criminal defendants shall have speedy and public trials. Judges have interpreted this as not only a guarantee for the defendant from being railroaded to justice but also a protection for the general public so that they may see if the laws are being impartially applied. Newspapers are usually very willing to assert the right of public access if a judge tries to close a trial. In a Lexington case a judge had prohibited newspapers from publishing the names of ten boys who were victims of a sodomist to reduce their suffering embarrassment and emotional trauma. The Lexington *Herald-Leader* appealed the ban to the state supreme court, which reversed on the ground that the trying of sexual offenses inevitably resulted in some embarrassment and emotional strain but that these were not sufficient to overcome the constitutional requirement of open and public trials.[53]

Kentucky has been in the vanguard of states that have tried to protect the identities of confidential informants used by reporters. The state shield law gave journalists immunity from testifying about their sources before grand or petit juries, administrative agencies, or legislative committees. Yet, the Kentucky judiciary has chosen to construe this protection very narrowly, as shown in the case of Paul Branzburg, a writer for the Louisville *Courier-Journal.* Branzburg had observed and written a story about the production of hashish and was called before the Jefferson County grand jury to answer questions about the article. He refused to identify the men whom he had seen making the hash and was threatened with a contempt citation if he persisted in his refusal. Relying on the shield law, he appealed to the state supreme court to stop the grand jury from compelling his testimony. The court held against Branzburg, distinguishing between the source of information for the story, which is protected, and the reporter's personal observation of criminal behavior, which is not. It did not matter whether the people who committed the crime were probably the same one who informed Branzburg since only their informant role was protected, not their criminal one. Therefore, Branzburg, like any other citizen who witnesses a crime, was required to respond to questions.[54]

The decision was appealed to the United States Supreme Court and was joined by two other cases from Massachusetts and California, raising the issue of whether freedom of the press under the First Amendment afforded reporters protection against revealing their sources. In a notable decision, the Court rejected the newspaper's contention that the right of free press clothed journalists with such immunity. The Court adopted a balancing approach, finding that the public interest in law enforcement outweighed the uncertain harm done to reporters in their efforts to gather news. Nor did requiring disclosure threaten the vast bulk of confidential relationships between reporters and their sources. Finally, the impact on the press was slight, since it was not being forced to publish names or to disclose them indiscriminately.[55] In conclusion, shield laws give reporters protection from revealing their sources to official agencies as long as the journalists themselves do not witness the informants engaging in criminal activity.

EQUAL PROTECTION

The equal protection clause of the Fourteenth Amendment prohibits a state from arbitrarily discriminating against persons. Racial discrimination is particularly suspect because of past enslavement of blacks and racial segregation in the use of public facilities. Despite the intentions of the drafters of the Fourteenth Amendment to require state governments to treat blacks equally, the Supreme Court upheld racial segregation in *Plessy v. Ferguson* (1896).[56] Although the system of segregation purported to offer equal facilities to blacks and whites, it was in design and practice an institutionalization of racial inequality. Public schools in the South, including Kentucky, were segregated. Even private schools were forced to comply with segregation policy.[57] The policy of separate but equal facilities remained in effect until 1954, when the Supreme Court ruled in *Brown v. Board of Education* that racial segregation in public education violated the equal protection clause. The Court asserted that separate but equal was inherently unequal because it imposed a stamp of inferiority on black children that they would have to bear the rest of their lives.[58]

Implementation of desegregation was to proceed with all deliberate speed. Kentucky, unlike states in the deep South, did not oppose the efforts of local school boards to comply voluntarily or to carry out court-ordered integration. For the most part, the process of desegregating Kentucky schools occurred without overt opposition at the local level. In 1956 Louisville peacefully implemented a desegregation plan covering fifty-four schools.[59] In contrast to Louisville's nonviolent transition, there was some trouble in Sturgis and Clay in western Kentucky, but Governor Chandler ordered national guard units to the area to prevent crowds of whites from interfering with the admission of blacks to the formerly all-white schools.[60]

Progress in eliminating racially identifiable schools continued in Louisville between 1957 and 1966 as the percentage of such schools declined from 78 to 55 percent of all schools in the district. But beginning in the fall of 1966, the trend reversed as migration of whites to the suburbs increased.[61] An inner-city schools became overwhelmingly black and outer-city and suburban schools retained their predominantly white enrollments, a de facto system of segregation emerged. This trend held true in major cities throughout the country, and inevitably suits were filed to have the courts resolve the problem. The response of the United States Supreme Court in the *Swann* case was to order busing as a means of eliminating the dual school system and of achieving racial balance in each school within the district. The decision applied only to those districts which had previously enforced a policy of *de jure* (official) segregation.[62] Because Louisville and Jefferson County fell into this category, suits were pressed by black plaintiffs to require the merger of the city and county systems and the use of busing to achieve racial balance in each school within the consolidated district. In their brief, plaintiffs noted that three of the six Louisville high schools were 94 to 100 percent black, and two others were 97 percent white. These figures, as well as past city-county cooperation in maintaining *de jure* segregation, led the Sixth Circuit Federal Court of Appeals to conclude that busing was needed to end the dual system.[63] It remanded the case to federal district court in Louisville, which approved a plan for busing 22,000 students in a new metropolitan district. Each school would have at least 12 percent minority enrollment, with no more than 40 percent black in any school.[64] Although there were angry demonstrations against busing, police and national guardsmen insured compliance with the court decree.

Protests subsided in ensuing years, but lower birthrates among whites compared to blacks and continued migration of whites to counties beyond Jefferson have helped to push the percentage of black pupils in 1983 beyond the limits imposed by the court. Although no school exceeded 50 percent black enrollment, there were twenty-five schools (19.4% of the total) that failed to stay within the range of court guidelines.[65]

Although the federal courts have played the biggest role in setting the direction of school desegregation policy, the legislative and executive branches at both national and state levels have also taken steps to eliminate racial discrimination. In 1960, the Kentucky General Assembly created a human rights commission to encourage understanding and respect among the races, to investigate complaints of discrimination, and, if persuasion failed, to issue cease and desist orders against violators. The commission has jurisdiction over complaints of discrimination on the basis of race, color, religion, or national origin in employment, public accomodations, and housing. Sex and age discrimination are also forbidden in employment.[66]

Racial discrimination in housing has been the area most resistant to change. At one time Louisville even enforced a zoning ordinance prohibiting blacks from living in certain neighborhoods, but this law was held to violate the due process clause of the Fourteenth Amendment as unreasonable interference with the right of private property.[67] Lately, there have been improvements in reducing racial bias in the housing market in Jefferson and Fayette counties, but real estate agents still deliberately steer clients to homes and apartments on the basis of race.[68]

There was also a pattern of segregation in public housing projects throughout the commonwealth. In the middle 1970s, Owensboro and Hazard maintained totally segregated facilities, and ten other cities, including Louisville, had segregation index scores of more than 71 on a scale of 0 (no segregation) to 100 (total segregation).[69] The reaction of the commission was to bring a complaint against the Middlesboro Housing Authority, seeking to have the agency follow a racial quota system for filling vacancies to insure that the apartments would become racially mixed. The Kentucky court of appeals endorsed the commission's quota order in principle, but only as a last resort if less drastic means failed to reduce the level of segregated units.[70] Nevertheless, this case did indicate that the Human Rights Commission was serious in its efforts to reduce discrimination in public housing, and as a result, the index of segregation in such housing throughout the state declined from 42.5 to 32.2 between 1980 and 1982.[71]

CONCLUSION

We have seen that Kentucky appellate courts normally do fulfill the role of protecting the rights of criminal defendants and religious dissidents, but they are not as protective of the rights of political dissidents or sellers of pornography. Freedom of worship has received strong judicial endorsement, but in regard to state support of religious practices, such as displaying the Ten Commandments in classrooms, Kentucky courts took an accommodationist stance and were overruled by the United States Supreme Court.

As might be expected from a body that is popularly elected, the Kentucky supreme court has not been vigorous in protecting the rights of political dissidents and dealers in allegedly obscene materials. The United States Supreme Court has reversed Kentucky decisions against radicals in some cases and provided clear precedents for state courts to follow in others. In regard to journalistic access to courtroom proceedings, the state supreme court has favored newspapers, but in interpreting the shield law, it has narrowly construed the right of reporters to protect the confidentiality of their news sources. Finally, in the area of equal protection, the federal judiciary has played the dominant role in requiring desegregation of public schools.

FOOTNOTES

1. The present court of appeals is a new appellate court created by the Judicial Reform Amendment of 1975. Prior to the amendment, the only appellate court in Kentucky was the old court of appeals, which is now the supreme court. To avoid confusion, the old court of appeals will be referred to as the supreme court throughout this chapter, whether or not the discussion deals with pre- or post-1975 cases.
2. Caine v. Commonwealth, 491 S.W.2d 824 (1973).
3. Commonwealth v. Vaughn, 296 S.W.2d 220 (1956).
4. Commonwealth v. Robey, 337 S.W.2d 36 (1960).
5. Carroll v. U.S., 267 US 132 (1925).
6. Commonwealth v. Chaplin, 211 S.W.2d 36 (1948).
7. At least nine jurors must agree to the accusation. KY CONST § 248.
8. Short v. Commonwealth, 519 S.W.2d 828 (1975).

9. Ky Const § 248.

10. North v. Russell, 427 U.S. 328 (1976).

11. Nelson v. Commonwealth, 175 S.W.2d 132 (1943).

12. Miranda v. Arizona, 384 U.S. 436 (1966).

13. Fugate v. Commonwealth, 72 S.W.2d 47 (1934).

14. Newman v. Stinson, 489 S.W.2d 826 (1972).

15. Hall v. Commonwealth, 246 S.W. 441 (1923). *See Also* Bartkus v. Illinois, 359 US I21 (1959).

16. Davis v. Commonwealth, 561 S.W.2d 91 (1978).

17. Cornwell v. Commonwealth, 497 S.W.2d 226 (1973).

18. Bradley v. Commonwealth, 156 S.W.2d 469 (1941).

19. Gibson v. Commonwealth, 265 S.W. 339 (1924).

20. Boyd v. Commonwealth, 550 S.W.2d 507 (1977).

21. Gregg v. Georgia, 428 U.S. 153 (1976).

22. Kentucky Revised Statutes 532.025.

23. THe Mormons lost their case, but the Jehovah's Witnesses and Amish were successful in their appeals before the U.S. Supreme Court. *See* Reynolds v. U.S. 98 US 145 (1878); West Virginia v. Barnette 319 U.S. 624 (1943); Wisconsin v. Yoder 406 U.S. 205 (1972).

24. Lawson v. Commonwealth, 164 S.W.2d 972 (1942).

25. Mosier v. Barren County Board of Health, 308 KY 829 (1948). The General Assembly has since provided a religious exemption to compulsory vaccination. Kentucky Revised Statutes 214.036.

26. Kentucky State Board of Public Instruction v. Rudasill, 589 S.W.2d 877 (1979).

27. Cochran v. Louisiana State Board of Education 218 U.S. 370 (1930).

28. Sherrard v. Jefferson County Board of Education 171 S.W.2d 963 (1942).

29. Nichols v. Henry 191 S.W.2d 939 (1945).

30. Everson v. Board of Education, 330 U.S. 1 (1947).

31. Rawlings v. Butler, 290 S.W.2d 801 (1956).

32. Engel v. Vitale, 370 U.S. 471 (1962).

33. School District of Abington Township v. Schempp, 374 U.S. 203 (1963).

34. Robert H. Birkby, "The Supreme Court and the Bible Belt: Tennessee Reaction to the *Schempp* Decision," *Midwest Journal of Political Science,* 10 (August, 1966) 304-315.

35. Kentucky, Office of Attorney General, *Opinion,* 79-463.

36. Kentucky Revised Statutes 158.175.

37. Stone v. Graham, 449 U.S. 39 (1980).

38. Lemon v. Kurtzman, 403 U.S. 602 (1971). For an example of the three-pronged test applied to a Kentucky case *see* Americans United v. Board of Education of the Beechwood Independent School District, 367 F.Supp. 1059 (1974).

39. National Committee for the Defense of Political Prisoners, *Harlan Miners Speak,* (New York: DaCapo Press, 1970 reprint of 1932 edition) p. 59.

40. E. J. Costello, *The Shame That Is Kentucky's* (Huntington, West Virginia: Appalachian Movement Press, 1972) p. 16.

41. 350 U.S. 497 (1956).

42. Braden v. Commonwealth, 291 S.W.2d 843 (1956).

43. *See* Richard Harris, *Freedom Spent* (Boston: Little, Brown, 1976) pp. 123-312 for a gripping account of the arrest of two antipoverty volunteers, Margaret and Alan McSurely, in Pike County in 1967.

44. Baker v. Binder, 274 F.Supp. 658 (1967).

45. King v. Commonwealth, 233 S.W.2d 522 (1950).

46. Roth v. U.S., 354 U.S. 476 (1957).

47. Austin v. Kentucky, 386 U.S. 767 (1967).

48. Smith v. Commonwealth, 465 S.W.2d 918 (1971).

49. Western Corp. v. Commonwealth, 558 S.W.2d 605 (1977). In Miller v. California, 413 U.S. 5 (1973), the U.S. Supreme Court had replaced the "utterly without redeeming social value" test with the following: "the work taken as a whole lacked serious literary, artistic, political or scientific value." The general assembly adopted this test in 1974 when it revised the obscenity law. Kentucky Revised Statutes 531.000.

50. Ashton v. Commonwealth, 405 S.W.2d 562 (1965).

51. Ashton v. Kentucky, 384 U.S. 195 (1966).

52. Ashland Publishing Company v. Asbury, 612 S.W.2d 749 (1980).

53. Lexington *Herald-Leader* v. Tackett, 601 S.W.2d 905 (1980).

54. Branzburg v. Pound, 461 S.W.2d 345 (1970).

55. Branzburg v. Hayes, 408 U.S. 665 (1972).

56. 163 U.S. 537.

57. In Berea College v. Kentucky, 211 U.S. 45 (1908), the U.S. Supreme Court upheld a Kentucky law prohibiting a private school from enrolling both white and black students.

58. 347 U.S. 483.

59. *New York Times,* September 10, 1956, p. 1.

60. *Ibid.,* September 7 and 11, 1956.

61. Gary Orfield, *Must We Bus?: Segregated Schools and National Policy* (Washington, D.C., Brookings, 1978), p. 396.

62. Swann v. Charlotte-Mecklenburg County Board of Education, 402 U.S. 1 (1971). In contrast to *Swann,* the Supreme Court held in Milliken v. Bradley, 418 U.S. 717 (1974), that in the absence of state-imposed *de jure* segregation or of complicity of suburban school boards to segregate, the existence of racial segregation in Detroit schools was the responsibility of Detroit alone to remedy and that there would be no metropolitan-wide busing. The *Milliken* decision relieved northern school districts of any legal obligation to embark on interdistrict busing.

63. Newburg Area Council v. Board of Education 489 F.2d 925 (1973).

64. *New York Times,* July 31, 1975, p. 12.

65. Kentucky Commission on Human Rights, *Jefferson County School Resegregation Increases* 1982-83, (1983) p. 1.

66. Kentucky Revised Statutes 344.040, 344.120, 344.360.

67. Buchanan v. Warley, 245 U.S. 60 (1917).

68. KCHR, *Apartment Discrimination Declines by Half in Fayette County, But Occurs to One Out of Four Apartment Seekers,* (1982) p. 1.

69. KCHR, *Public Housing Authorities in Kentucky Are Slow to Desegregate* (Frankfort, Kentucky, n.d.) p. 17.

70. Middlesboro Housing Authority v. Kentucky Commission on Human Rights, 553 S.W.2d 57 (1977).

71. KCHR, *Over Half of Kentucky's Public Housing Authorities Cut Segregation* (Frankfort, Kentucky, 1983) p. 1.

Chapter 7

POLITICAL PARTIES AND ELECTIONS

Paul Blanchard, Eastern Kentucky University

POLITICAL PARTIES IN KENTUCKY

Introduction

What are political parties? In the United States, defining a political party is sometimes difficult and is the source of much scholarly discussion and controversy. Political parties mean many different things to different people, and definitions vary according to one's own perspective, position, or level of involvement.

According to Robert L. Lineberry, an American political party can be defined in a number of different ways:

1. A symbol (a donkey, an elephant, a rooster) and a name on a voting machine ballot
2. A loyalty or psychological attachment, as when we say, "I am a Republican" or "I am a Democrat"
3. A group of national convention delegates meeting every four years to nominate a presidential candidate
4. A group of legislators or Congressmen sitting together and sharing a particular set of leaders
5. A national or state office with a chairperson, staff, and office space
6. A loosely defined coalition of interests
7. A legal entity empowered by state law to play a role in selecting candidates for office.[1]

Most students of American political parties agree that the one essential characteristic of all political parties is that they attempt to

141

win elections. This is certainly true of Kentucky's two major political parties, the Democrats and Republicans, and this perspective will provide the focus for much of the discussion that follows. In addition, it is often argued that three other important functions of political parties are (1) to stimulate interest and participation in politics, (2) to clarify issues and educate the voters, and (3) to take the responsibility for governing, in the case of the majority party, or to point out weaknesses or criticisms of the party in power, in the case of the opposition or minority party. In later sections, Kentucky's political parties will be examined according to how well they seem to perform these functions.

Perhaps the easy way to define Kentucky political parties is to cite the legal definition found in Kentucky Revised Statutes (KRS). According to KRS 118.015, a political party in Kentucky is

> an affiliation or organization of electors representing a political policy and having a constituted authority for its government and regulation, and which cast at least twenty percent (20%) of the total vote cast at the last preceding election at which presidential electors were voted for.

This definition, particularly the 20 percent provision, has proven to be a restrictive one, resulting in two major parties. Only the Democratic and the Republican parties have been able to meet this criteria in recent times, although George Wallace's American Independent party came very close in 1968, receiving more than 18 percent of the presidential vote in that election. Generally speaking, achieving political party status legally results in various privileges, responsibilities, and regulations, as well as an assured place on all partisan election ballots.[2]

Kentucky statutes also define *political organizations* or what most observers would call minor political parties. KRS 118.325 allows any political party that casts 2 percent of the presidential vote to nominate candidates for public office by either primaries or conventions for the next four years. Even the 2 percent standard has been difficult to achieve in Kentucky. For example, John Anderson's Coalition party received just over 2 percent of the vote in the 1980 election, but other minor parties that year, including Respect for Life, Socialist, Communist, Libertarian, and Citizen parties, received far less than 2 percent. The Libertarian party was the most successful of these, receiving less than .005 of the total presidential vote. In 1976, no minor party received even 1 percent of the total. Lacking legal status as a political organization requires nomination by petition for ballot access (KRS 118.315), a more difficult and time-consuming procedure.

Historical Background

No exhaustive history of Kentucky political parties is necessary or appropriate here, since this information is available elsewhere.[3] Only a few general observations will be made to provide a historical context for the discussion that follows. Perhaps the most important observation is the stability of Kentucky partisanship, what Jewell and Cunningham have called "the influence of tradition." Democratic and Republican fortunes and loyalties have remained remarkably consistent for more than 100 years throughout much of the state. Jewell and Cunningham ascribed much of this consistency to the lingering impact of the Civil War.[4]

In the early part of the twentieth century, until around 1928, the two major political parties were closely competitve. Democratic dominance was more evident in the 1930s and 1940s, as a result of the New Deal, and the presence of factionalism emerged as a significant factor in Kentucky politics. Factionalism, or intraparty competition, occurs as a by-product of one-party dominance and serves as a substitute, albeit an unsatisfactory one, for two-party competition.

Factionalism within the dominant Democratic party achieved some degree of continuity beginning in the late thirties, and for the next twenty-five or thirty years, two identifiable factions within the party were important. These two factions resulted from the impact of two powerful Democratic leaders in the state, A.B. Chandler and Earle Clements, whose influence over the party continued throughout most of this period. The Chandler faction was most evident in Governor Chandler's successful gubernatorial campaigns in 1935 and 1955, as well as his unsuccessful campaign in 1963, but was also an important factor in other statewide races, particularly those involving Governor Keen Johnson and Lieutenant Governor Harry Lee Waterfield. From the Clements faction emerged the successful gubernatorial candidacies of Clements (1947), Lawrence Wetherby (1951), Bert Combs (1959), and Edward Breathitt (1963), along with a few unsuccessful candidates.[5]

Kentucky factionalism differed from the more classic form of bifactionalism (two factions) found most notably in Louisiana around the same period, in that it was difficult to find any clear issue or policy differences between the two factions. Moreover, there were no consistent socioeconomic (e.g., rich-poor, urban-rural, religious, racial) alignments associated with the two factions, nor were there any clear regional or geographic differences. Besides the two dominant political personalities, other major reasons for the factionalism that occurred in Kentucky were the weakness of the Republican party, already mentioned, and the Kentucky electoral laws, which do not provide for a runoff primary. The latter factor has apparently forced political leaders in the state to narrow their preferences to the two strongest condidates in most elections. This, of course, has not been true of more recent gubernatorial elections, and the risk involved in not doing so was illustrated in both the 1979 and 1983 primaries. In 1983, a Sloane-Stumbo alliance would almost certainly have prevailed over Martha Layne Collins, who received less than 35 percent of the total Democratic vote. Similarly, in 1979, John Y. Brown, Jr., received less than 30 percent of the total Democratic vote and could have been defeated had two or three of his opponents made an alliance before the primary.

Democratic party dominance diminished in the 1950s and 1960s, as the Republicans were able to capture their share of statewide races, particularly those involving national races for president, United States Senate, and the United States House of Representatives. Republican strength reached its peak from 1967 to 1968, at which time Republicans held the governor's office, two United States Senate seats, and chief executive posts in Louisville and Jefferson County, as well as carrying the state for President Nixon in 1968. At the same time, the old bifactional pattern began to fade, as a natural consequence of a stronger Republican party and the dissipating influence of Clements and Chandler, who by this time were in their seventies and were well past their political prime. This fact was reflected in the 1971 primary, in which both major Democratic gubernatorial candidates, Bert Combs and Wendell Ford, were products of the old Clements faction. Although Democratic primaries have continued to be quite competitive (with the exception of 1975), factional continuity has all but disappeared.

Party Organization

In Kentucky, as in most other states, there is a difference between the formal party organization and the informal power structure within the party.[6] Often the latter group, which sometimes contains key elected officials from the party, is more influential than the former in making decisions about party matters. In spite of this, party leaders are significant not only because of the prestige and recognition they receive but also because, under state law, they have important responsibilities, such as filling vacancies for nominations and recommending the party's members for state and local election boards. In addition, they are often consulted about important political appointments and may serve as the channel through which patronage or other forms of political favors are distributed.

144

Kentucky parties are organized in what might be characterized as a hierarchy, with individuals and committees chosen for leadership responsibilities at the state level, the congressional district level, the county level, and the precinct level. The final authority for each party is the state party convention, which meets during presidential election years.[7] In this section, each level of party organization will be briefly described.

The State Central Committee. The chief governing body for each party is the *state central committee.* The powers, duties, and responsibilities of the two committees are similar and are defined in the *ByLaws of the Kentucky Democratic Party* (Article VIII, Section A) and the *Official Rules: Republican Party of Kentucky* (Rule 1:03).[8] One excerpt from the Republican rules will serve to illustrate:

> This authority shall include the managing and directing of Party affairs in all parts of the Commonwealth including the collection and disbursement of Party funds; the promotion and supervision of campaigns of Republican candidates at the national, state and local levels; and exercising such other duties, authorities, or privileges as imposed or granted either by State or Federal law and the rules of the Republican National Party.

As of late 1983, the Democratic state central committee (DSCC) contained fifty-five voting members and seven *ex officio* members.[9] The Republican state central committee (RSCC) was much larger, containing approximately eighty members. The exact number was difficult to determine because of unfilled positions and overlapping appointments. Each state central committee selects its members in a variety of ways, with some members elected at the state convention, some elected at congressional district meetings, and some appointed by virtue of holding other party or elected offices. For example, the DSCC contains the president of the Kentucky Democratic Women plus four members of the legislature. The RSCC, which has many members selected in this way, includes the president and seven district governors of the Kentucky Federation of Republican Women, the chaiman and seven district chairmen of the Kentucky Young Republican Federation, the president of the College Republican Federation, and the chairman of the Teenage Republicans.

Each state central committee elects officers, the most important of which is the *state chairman.*[10] The state chairman serves as the chief executive officer of the state party organization and, as such, has the authority to call meetings of the state central committee, to preside over these meetings, and to appoint special committees of the party and to name members to these committees.[11]

The state chairman may be called upon to be a spokesperson for the party when significant issues emerge on the state's political agenda. However, this will vary from chairman to chairman and from party to party. The most important variable is whether or not the party controls the governor's office. If it does, obviously the governor will usually serve as the party spokesman, leaving the chairman to handle strictly organizational matters, including fund raising, staffing the state headquarters, and similar activities.

The state chairman for the party not controlling the governor's office—in Kentucky this is usually the Republican party—will ordinarily be a more visible spokesperson. The Republican party's current chairman (as of late 1983), Liz Thomas, has been quite active in this regard. Besides speaking on behalf of the party around the state, she has been actively involved in recruiting Republican candidates for offices at both local and state levels, a function that is more appropriate for a minority party rather than a majority party.

In the Democratic party, besides deferring to the governor in articulating the party positions, the state chairman is nearly always actually chosen by the governor or the gubernatorial nominee, whose choice is readily accepted by the state central committee. Governor John Y. Brown, Jr., was responsible for selecting four party chairmen during his tenure as governor, Larry Townsend, Robert Cobb, Tracy Farmer, and Paul Patton. Each of these individuals was selected primarily due to fund raising ability and organizational ability and because they were men in whom Governor Brown had confidence. After the 1983 Democratic primary, the Democratic nominee, Martha Layne Collins, was allowed to name her choice as Democratic chairman, in preparation for the fall campaign. She named Senator Joe Prather, president *pro tem* of the senate, who had been her campaign chairman, not coincidentally the same role that Townsend had played in Brown's campaign four years earlier.

Both major parties in Kentucky also provide for a vice-chairman, who is to be of the opposite sex from the chairman. In addition, both parties' state central committees select a secretary, a treasurer, and a legal counsel. Also, Republicans provide for a state finance chairman.

Congressional District Committees. Both the Democratic and Republican parties hold congressional district conventions shortly before the state conventions.[12] The major item of business at these conventions is the selection of congressional district representatives to the state central committees, four from each district for the Democrats and three from each district for the Republicans, and the election of party delegates to the national conventions. In addition, each party selects some of its (electoral college) presidential electors at these meetings. Republican members also fill congressional

146

district offices, chairman, vice-chairman, and finance chairman. Republican rules call for the congressional district committee to meet semiannually in February and September. These committees consist of the three officers plus district representatives of auxiliary organizations (Republican Women, Young Republicans, etc.). According to Democratic bylaws, the Democratic congressional district committee meets only at the district convention every four years.

County Committees. Both parties provide for a county organization in every Kentucky county. Party leaders are selected in both parties at a county or legislative district (LD) convention held in the spring, every two years (even-numbered years) by the Republicans and every four years (presidential election year) by the Democrats. There are some significant differences between the two parties at this level. The Republicans appear to give greater attention to precinct level representation, and the Democrats more often use the state legislative district to organize larger counties.

As a result of recent changes in Democratic party rules, beginning in 1984, all registered Democrats are allowed to participate and vote in county or LD conventions.[13] County conventions are held in every county except Fayette and Jefferson, where conventions are held in each legislative district. At the county conventions, Democrats nominate and elect a *county executive committee,* consisting of not more than fifteen nor less than five members. All members of the executive committee must be registered Democrats residing in that county, and the committee must include at least one woman and one person age thirty or under. The members of the executive committee meet immediately after their election and elect a chairman and vice-chairman (one male, one female).[14] The county executive committee serves as the governing body for the county organization, and the county chairman acts as its chief executive officer, with power comparable to the state central committee and the state chairman.

In Fayette and Jefferson Counties the county organization consists of officers selected by the legislative district (LD) conventions. In Fayette, which contains less than six legislative districts,[15] the county executive committee includes the LD chairman and vice-chairman from each legislative district. In Jefferson, which contains more than five districts, the county executive committee consists of the chairman of each legislative district, with the vice-chairman elegible to serve only in the absence of the chairman. The county chairman and vice-chairman in Fayette and Jefferson are chosen in the same manner as the officers in other counties, i.e., by the membership of the county executive committee.

Besides electing county party leaders, the Democratic county and LD conventions elect delegates to the state and congressional district conventions. Delegates are apportioned among the counties based generally on the number of Democrats registered in the county or LD and the number of Democratic votes cast in the county or LD in the two most recent presidential elections.[16]

The Republican procedures are similar to those of the Democrats in that the county convention is open to all registered Republicans and that one major item of business is to elect delegates to the congressional district and state party conventions. Republican rules call for a county committee, which consists of all precinct officers (see following section), and it is this relatively large committee that elects county officers: chairman, vice-chairman, secretary, treasurer, and youth chairman. Republican party rules also permit, but do not require, the election of an executive committee consisting of not less than nine members, and these persons need not be precinct officers.[17]

One minor difference in the Republican county organization is that the LD organizational component only applies to Jefferson County. In other matters, including the powers and duties of the county chairman, the two parties have very similar provisions.

Precinct Committees. The precinct traditionally has been the basic, or grass roots, organizational component for American political parties, so it is not surprising that both Kentucky parties provide for committees and a leadership structure at this level. As suggested previously, the Republican party seems to give greater emphasis to the precinct level than do the Democrats in that precinct officers automatically serve on the county committee. Republican rules explicitly define the precinct as the basic organizational unit of the party in Kentucky.[18]

Both parties provide for a precinct convention. As at the county level, Republicans meet every two years, Democrats every four. In both parties, the precinct committee consists of three officers with similar titles and responsibilities. The Democrats call their precinct officers committeeman, committeewoman, and committee youth person, while the Republicans use the titles precinct captain, precinct co-captain (of the opposite sex), and youth captain. Democrats define their youth component as age thirty or younger, but the Republicans use age thirty-five to define the end of youth. Neither party provides in its official rules much information about the duties or responsibilities of its precinct leaders.[19]

Party Competition

As of mid-1983, there were 1,264,593 registered Democrats in Kentucky compared with 514,508 registered Republicans.[20] This Democratic advantage of nearly two and one-half to one may be somewhat misleading because it conceals an unknown number of Kentuckians' true party preference, given that substantial numbers of persons may well register with a particular party for reasons other than party loyalty. For example, a Republican loyalist might logically register as a Democrat in a strong Democratic county in order to vote in primary elections, where most county officials are, in fact, chosen in most elections. Since there are many more strong Democratic counties (see later discussion on counties) than Republican ones, we might reasonably conclude that the figures given previously may overstate Democratic strength in Kentucky.

Nevertheless, when we combine voter registration figures with election results and other related data, we must inevitably conclude that the Democratic party is dominant in Kentucky in the mid-1980s. This section will examine this dominance, particularly as it is reflected in partisan patterns at the state and county levels, and will suggest some reasons it is so pervasive. Later sections of the chapter will explore possible trends in the direction of a more competitive two-party process in the state.

In Table 7.1 data are presented from statewide elections for the period from 1952 to 1980.[21] From these data, which report *Republican* percentages of the two-party vote for each election, we can chart the rise and fall of party fortunes at the state level over the past thirty years. An analysis of Table 7.1 suggests three major conclusions. The first would be that when one considers this *entire* period, there is a striking degree of two-party competition. Of the twenty-eight presidential, United States senatorial, and gubernatorial elections that have been held in Kentucky since 1952, thirteen of them have resulted in Republican victories, and in fifteen the Democrats were victorious. However, this overview does conceal two other patterns that suggest a less competitive picture.

One is that the Republicans have had much better success in national elections, while the Democrats have been stronger in state-level (gubernatorial) elections. Since 1952, the Republicans have carried the state in five of eight presidential elections and have won seven of twelve senatorial elections. In these elections the average percentage for the Republicans has been very near 50 percent for the entire period. Democrats, on the other hand, have won six of the seven gubernatorial elections during this period, with an average of slightly over 50 percent of the vote. Other evidence, not presented,

149

TABLE 7.1

Republican Percentage of Two-Party Vote in Statewide Elections, 1952 to 1980

Year	President	U.S. Senator	Governor
1952	49.96	51.5	
1954		45.5	
1955			41.7
1956	54.6	50.3 (Morton)	
		53.2 (Cooper)	
1959			39.4
1960	53.6	59.1	
1962		52.1	
1963			49.3
1964	35.7		
1966		64.3	
1967			51.6
1968	53.8*	51.9	
1971			46.6
1972	64.6	48.3	
1974		45.1	
1975			37.2
1976	46.3		
1978		37.7	
1979			40.6
1980	50.7	34.9	
Average	51.2	49.5	43.8

*Nixon received 43.9 percent of the three-candidate total, including Wallace votes.

indicates that Democratic strength in state-level elections extends to elections for the state legislature, where the Democratic party is even more dominant. For example, in the 1984 general assembly, Republicans made up only 23 percent (23 of 100) of the house and 26 percent (10 of 38) of the senate.

Why have the Republicans been more successful in national elections and the Democrats more successful in state-level elections? In observing this phenomenon for an earlier period, Jewell and Cunningham suggested five possible reasons:

1. Off-year elections for governor
2. Presidential voting more volatile—state-level voting based more on habit and tradition
3. The presence of "national Republicans"
4. The personal popularity of some Republicans, particularly former Senator John Sherman Cooper.
5. The difficulty of raising funds for Republican candidates in state elections
6. A stronger state Democratic organization[22]

As Jewell and Cunningham point out, each of these ideas helps to explain this phenomenon, except the presence of "national Republicans." National Republicans are voters who, it is believed, vote for Republicans in national elections and for Democrats in state elections. Observers of southern voting since the 1950s have sometimes argued that there must be a sizable bloc of these voters because of the voting patterns that we have noted in Kentucky. However, Jewell and Cunningham find no evidence of a significant number of these "national" voters, nor does our analysis lend support to this idea. A more logical explanation is that different *groups* of people will vote in elections at different levels. Thus, the off-year electoral structure emphasizes these different voting habits and tends to perpetuate the traditional state-level voting.[23] In addition, it is clear from more recent experiences that the Democratic advantages in organizational and fund raising capabilities observed by Jewell and Cunningham in the 1960s have continued into the 1980s.[24]

Another obvious pattern in the results reported in Table 7.1 is the decline in Republican fortunes beginning in the late 1960s and early 1970s. As noted earlier, Republican success seemed to peak in the 1967 to 1968 period. It may be noted (in Table 7.1) that as of November 1968, the Republicans controlled the governor's office and both United States Senate seats and had carried the state for President Nixon in that year. Although Republicans did not control the state legislature at that time, they did control two important local offices, mayor of Louisville and Jefferson County judge, which gave additional evidence of Republican strength and competitiveness. Control of these two positions, as well as the governor's office, gave the Republicans a significant resource they had not often had—control of hundreds, perhaps thousands, of jobs they could distribute as patronage rewards to their supporters along with the opportunity to grant substantial state and local contracts, which could be distributed to similar advantage. Presumably, this should have allowed the party to solidify and extend its influence and thus remain in a strongly competitive position.

Unfortunately for the Republicans, these hopes for continued power and competitiveness were dashed by a string of Democratic victories beginning with the loss of Louisville and Jefferson County in 1969. While Nixon carried the state overwhelmingly in 1972, this was to be the only statewide Republican victory for the rest of the decade. The Democrats regained the governor's office in 1971, one Senate seat the following year, and the other Senate seat in 1974. Democratic dominance was confirmed by Julian Carroll's election as governor in 1975 by an overwhelming 63 to 37 margin, the most decisive gubernatorial victory for the entire period. Democratic victories continued in 1976, 1978, and 1979, all with impressive margins. The Democratic string was broken when President Reagan carried the state in 1980, but any Republican optimism over this victory was offset by Wendell Ford's overwhelming senatorial margin the same year. The only two bright spots for the Republicans during the 1970s, amid a succession of defeats, were Larry Hopkins's congressional victory in the usually Democrat-dominated sixth district and the recapture of the county judge-executive position in Jefferson County by Mitch McConnell. Thus, Democratic dominance has been characteristic of Kentucky politics at the state level, with few exceptions, for the past fifteen years.

What about party competition at the county level, which has not yet been considered except for a brief reference to Jefferson? Throughout this period it is important to note that patterns of two-party competition are not distributed evenly throughout the state. Even in times of extreme Democratic dominance, a number of counties nearly always vote Republican and a few counties have intense party competition in which each party has a relatively equal chance of success. Obviously, a large proportion of counties are nearly always carried by the Democrats, however. Tables 7.2 and 7.3 and Figure 7.1 provide information about two-party competition at the county level in Kentucky.

Table 7.2 represents a summary of county-level data for the thirteen statewide elections (for president, United States Senator, and governor) that have occurred during the 1967 to 1980 period. Counties were classified on the basis of how many times they had been carried by a particular party and, to some extent, by the size of the victory margin.[25] For example, strong Republican counties were those the Republicans carried in at least ten of the thirteen elections with an average percentage of at least 60 percent. Using this classification system, the ten most Republican counties in Kentucky were (in order) Jackson, Clinton, Casey, Monroe, Rockcastle,

McCreary, Owsley, Cumberland, Butler, and Leslie. With one exception (Butler), these counties are all in the Fifth Congressional District and are geographically clustered in south central and southeastern Kentucky. This tends to be true of most of the twenty-seven counties classified as Republican or strong Republican.[26] In addition, traditionally Republican counties generally tend to be among the poorest, most rural, and least populated counties in the state.[27]

TABLE 7.2

Partisan Classifications for Kentucky Counties
1967 to 1980

	Number of Counties
Strong Democrat	53
Democrat	17
Democrat Inclined	5
Marginal	12
Republican Inclined	6
Republican	12
Strong Republican	15
TOTAL	120

Note: Classifications are based on county-level data in thirteen statewide elections for president, U.S. Senator, and governor during this period. See note 25 for information on how classifications were made.

Traditionally Democratic counties, those in the strong Democrat or Democrat categories in Table 7.2, share some similarities to the traditionally Republican counties. They also tend to be poorer and less populous than average, although they are not nearly as geographically clustered as the Republican counties, at least in part because there are so many more of them—a total of seventy in the two top categories in Table 7.2. This classification revealed that the following are the ten most Democratic counties in the state (in order): Ballard, Breathitt, Knott, Owen, Carroll, Franklin, Daviess, Fleming, Elliot, and Carlisle. Even in this list, we find counties distributed in every congressional district except the strong Republican Fifth District and the Third District, which includes only the urban part of Jefferson County.

In Table 7.3, which is also projected geographically in Figure 7.1, Kentucky counties are presented according to party registration. Democratic dominance is again demonstrated by the fact that in more than one-third of Kentucky's counties (N=46), less than 10 percent of the registered voters are registered Republican when percentages are calculated on the basis of the two-party total. Exactly half of Kentucky's counties have a Republican registration of less than 20 percent, and only thirty Kentucky counties, or 25 percent of the total, have a Republican registration of more than 50 percent. From Figure 7.1 it is clear that counties with an overwhelming majority of Democratic registrants are distributed widely across the state. Again, in each congressional district except the third and fifth, there are several counties with less than 10 percent Republican registration (i.e., counties designated with a 0 on the map). Similarly, counties with larger numbers, indicating Republican majorities in registration, are concentrated in the Fifth Congressional District.

While the Republican counties in particular illustrate the close correlation between electoral success (the basis for the categories in Table 7.2) and registration advantage, the correlation is not as strong at the Democratic end of the spectrum. On the Republican side, for example, of the fifteen counties in Table 7.3 with more than 70 percent registered Republicans, thirteen are classified strong Republican, and two are classified as Republican, suggesting consistent electoral success for the Republican party in those counties. Considering counties with sizable Democratic registration majorities, there are a number of cases in which competitive two-party politics occurs. For example, among the twenty-nine counties in Table 7.3 where the Democrats had registration percentages of 70 to 90 percent, there were at least ten counties where two-party competition was the norm rather than the exception. While three of these were classified as Democrat inclined, five were classified as marginal (the most competitive category), and two were actually classified as Republican inclined.[28]

TABLE 7.3

Party Registration by County
Republican Percentage of Two-Party Total, 1981
(Rank-Ordered within Categories)

80% or more (6)	30% to 39.9% (9)	5% to 9.9% (30)
Jackson	Boyd	Bullitt
Owsley	Hart	McCracken
Martin	Magoffin	Hopkins
Monroe	Metcalfe	Scott
Clay	Hancock	Bourbon
Leslie	Greenup	Robertson
	Campbell	Shelby
70% to 79.9% (9)	Harlan	Montgomery
Rockcastle	Jefferson	Grant
Casey		Bath
Clinton	**20% to 29.9% (15)**	Wolfe
Whitley	Oldham	Floyd
McCreary	Perry	Henderson
Laurel	Fayette	Menifee
Butler	Rowan	Bracken
Cumberland	Boone	Logan
Lewis	Barren	Meade
	Madison	Nelson
	Washington	Livingston
60% to 69.9% (7)	Kenton	Simpson
Edmonson	Pike	Trigg
Pulaski	Fleming	Calloway
Russell	Letcher	Harrison
Knox	Muhlenburg	Marshall
Johnson	Powell	Lyon
Adair	Mason	Gallatin
Grayson		Spencer
		Franklin
50% to 59.9% (8)	**10% to 19.9% (14)**	Nicholas
Allen	Caldwell	Morgan
Ohio	McLean	
Wayne	Daviess	**0% to 4.9% (16)**
Garrard	Hardin	Webster
Estill	Jessamine	Henry
Green	Warren	Trimble
Lee	Boyle	Fulton
Bell	Mercer	Breathitt
	Anderson	Owen
40% to 49.9% (6)	Clark	Marion
Crittenden	Pendleton	Union
Lincoln	Woodford	Graves
Taylor	Christian	Ballard
Carter	Larue	Carroll
Lawrence		Hickman
Breckenridge		Todd
		Carlisle
		Elliot
		Knott

FIGURE 7.1

Party Registration by County, October 1981

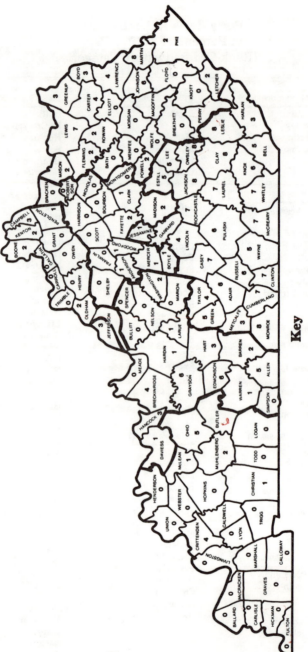

Key

Republican Percentage of 2-Party Total:

0 = 0—9.9%	2 = 20—29.9%
1 = 10—19.9%	3 = 30—39.9%, Etc.

The latter findings reinforce observations made earlier in this chapter about the need to be cautious in interpreting party registration data. The ten counties referred to serve as empirical examples of a behavior long believed to exist in Kentucky, behavior that is exhibited by persons who register Democrat because that is the predominant pattern in their home county and yet vote Republican more often than not. This is surely one signal that there is some potential for greater two-party competition in a state like Kentucky, which is so clearly Democratic in many respects. The next section examines other forces that may move Kentucky in a more competitive direction.

Prospects for Greater Two-Party Competition: The Urban Triangle

When Senator Jim Bunning began his unsuccessful campaign for governor in 1983, political insiders suggested that his only real chance for victory would be to combine a better-than-usual showing in the traditional Republican stronghold, the Fifth District, with sizable majorities in the so-called urban triangle, that portion of the state formed by a line drawn roughly from Louisville to Lexington to the northern Kentucky counties of Kenton and Campbell and back to Louisville. While Bunning did not do well enough in the urban triangle to win the gubernatorial election, losing by about 97,000 votes, the Republican strategy to concentrate on this area of Kentucky was a sound one for at least two reasons. The most obvious is that this is where a substantial proportion of Kentucky voters live. Just four counties—Jefferson, Fayette, Kenton, and Campbell—include about 27 percent of the registered voters in the state, while the entire area includes close to half of all Kentucky voters.

The second and more important reason, for this discussion, is that Republican candidates have tended to fare better in this part of the state, particularly in the four populous counties mentioned, than in most other parts of Kentucky. For example, in the thirteen statewide election contests held from 1967 to 1980, the Republicans carried Fayette County nine times, Jefferson County eight times, Campbell seven times, and Kenton six times. It will be recalled from earlier discussions that these Republican successes were occurring during a period when the party's fortunes were declining statewide; Republicans won only four of those thirteen contests throughout the state in spite of their success in the four large counties.

It might be argued that the Kentucky Republican party is evolving from a rural party into an urban-suburban party. As of the early 1980s, most of the prominent Republican officials represent urban-suburban constituencies. Examples would include Larry

157

Hopkins, Mitch McConnell, Jim Bunning, and, to some extent, Gene Snyder. It is significant that Hopkins, McConnell, and Bunning represent the three points of the urban triangle. Congressman Hopkins parlayed his strength in Fayette County to win a victory in the traditionally Democratic Sixth Congressional District. Judge McConnell received a substantial urban and suburban vote to win two terms as Jefferson County judge-executive, and from this base he may provide a strong challenge to United States Senator Walter Huddleston in 1984. Bunning's failure in 1983 stemmed not so much from his failure to attract urban and suburban voters as it did from his late start, his relative inexperience in state politics, a fairly united Democratic party, a Democratic candidate with strong ties to several communities in the urban triangle, and some evidence of lack of unity in his own party.

Congressman Snyder, whose Fourth Congressional District corresponds roughly to the Louisville–northern Kentucky side of the triangle, emerged in 1983 as perhaps the most influential person in the new Republican party, although much of his influence occurred behind the scenes. He apparently was influential in the selection of Bunning as the Republican gubernatorial nominee, and he was alleged to have much influence over the party's organizational apparatus as well, through his close association with State Chairman Liz Thomas, another northern Kentuckian who serves on his paid staff. Snyder was apparently the source of some significant intra-party friction that emerged during the 1983 gubernatorial campaign. His influence over the party was both resisted and resented by some of the rural elements of the party, most notably former governor Louie Nunn and his brother Lee, a former state party chairman.

This intraparty conflict in the Republican party suggests both the problems and the potential for future Republican success in Kentucky and indeed for a more competitive party process. If the Republicans can find a way to resolve the conflict between its rural and urban-suburban elements and combine its traditional strength in the Fifth Congressional District with its emerging strength in the urban triangle, it is likely to become a formidable force in future political races. Reconciliation is unlikely to come easily, and it is not likely to occur until the rural wing of the party realizes that the party's success is dependent upon appealing to urban and suburban interests. Whether or not this occurs, increasing urbanization and suburbanization in Kentucky are likely to enhance the prospects for a stronger Republican party and for greater two-party competition. As other parts of the state become more like the metropolitan counties of Jefferson, Fayette, Kenton, and Campbell, and it seems inevitable that they will in the long run, the result will be a stronger and more competitive two-party system.

The Future of Job-Oriented Politics

Before turning to a discussion of voting in Kentucky, it is appropriate to evaluate party politics in this state by posing a question mentioned very early in this chapter: How well do Kentucky's political parties perform the classic functions political parties are supposed to perform? How well do Kentucky political parties—

1. stimulate interest and participation in politics?
2. clarify issues and educate the voters?
3. take the responsibility for governing (majority party function)?
4. point out weaknesses or criticisms of the party in power (minority party function)?

To answer these questions, one final aspect of state political parties must be recognized. According to John Fenton and other scholars, state political party systems can be classified into two general categories, depending on whether they tend to be job oriented or issue oriented. In an issue-oriented state, political parties tend to focus on issues and policies, and party competition usually corresponds to the public's response to the issues and the parties' positions on them. Nearby states that are issue oriented are Michigan, Wisconsin, and Minnesota.[29] By contrast, job-oriented states tend to de-emphasize issues and to focus on patronage-related elements of politics, such as jobs and contracts. Fenton has classified Kentucky—along with other adjacent states of Ohio, Indiana, and Illinois—as being a classic job-oriented state. Other job-oriented party characteristics Fenton found in Kentucky included the following:

1. There is substantial interest in politics by individual citizens, but this interest is focused not on issues but upon personalities and jobs.
2. The electorate is rarely provided much information about or solutions to the problems faced by the state.
3. Because of this, the voters find it difficult to make electoral decisions based upon their own economic self-interest; instead their attention is diverted from issues to personalities, appearance, family and ethnic background, etc.

4. Even with two-party competition, there tends to be little responsiveness of government to the wishes of the electorate.

5. Government actions tend to maintain the *status quo*.[30]

While Fenton described Kentucky in these terms in a book published nearly twenty years ago, most observers would acknowledge that they remain accurate in the mid-1980s. To the extent they still do describe Kentucky, one could conclude that Kentucky's political parties fall short in performing most of the classic functions of political parties. While interest and participation is stimulated to some extent, issues are often not clarified, and voters are usually not provided information upon which to make educated political choices. The majority party cannot govern effectively, nor can the minority party criticize because of the issueless basis of political discussion. The result, as Fenton pointed out, is a status quo government. For evidence of this, readers are encouraged to consider other chapters in this book and to determine how many significant changes have occurred in Kentucky's government in the recent past that were the result of deliberate decisions of political leaders. While there have been some, they have been the exception, not the rule.

Are any changes occurring in Kentucky in this regard? Is there any movement in the direction of a more issue-oriented politics? There are few indications that this is the case. According to Malcolm Jewell, who knows Kentucky politics as well as any scholar, Kentucky in the 1980s remains less issue-oriented than any state in this country.[31] Evidence from the 1983 elections, both primary and general, certainly supports this view. While Senator Bunning took a few specific issue positions, Democratic candidates were very difficult to pin down on most important issues. Even Senator Bunning tended to "waffle" on the issues as election day approached.[32] Both parties in Kentucky seemed to cluster around what Jewell has called the "mushy middle"—neither clearly liberal or conservative.[33]

National politics in the United States, on the other hand, has moved clearly and steadily toward a more issue-oriented perspective during the past two decades. This suggests that the average American voter is becoming more interested in and responsive to coherent policy positions. For this reason, one may assume that in the long-term future Kentucky politics also will be drawn inevitably in this direction.

VOTING AND ELECTIONS

This relatively brief section of the chapter continues and concludes the discussion of political participation in Kentucky by examining several aspects of voting and elections in this state. Topics will include voter qualifications, problems associated with the frequency of elections and the long ballot, voter turnout, and suggested reforms in Kentucky's electoral system.

Qualifications for Voting

As a result of decisions made at the national level, particularly the passage of the Fifteenth, Nineteenth, Twenty-fourth, and Twenty-sixth Amendments to the United States Constitution, most requirements for voting are uniform throughout the nation. All United States citizens, including Kentuckians, are entitled to vote if they are eighteen years old, residents of their communities for at least thirty days, and properly registered.[34] It is interesting to note that Kentucky anticipated the Twenty-sixth Amendment several years before it was ratified, in allowing eighteen-year-olds to vote in 1955.

The basic unit of the electoral structure in Kentucky is the precinct, and a polling place is provided in each precinct. According to KRS 117.105, each county must provide voting machines for use in each precinct in each election. Voters may vote by absentee ballot if they are unable to get to the polling place due to age, infirmity, or illness or if they are absent from their home county on election day. Absentee ballots must be applied for no later than seven days before the election.[35]

Registration procedures are administered in Kentucky by the state board of elections. Citizens may register by filling out a simple form and returning it to the county clerk no later than thirty days prior to an election. Forms are available from each county clerk, but voters may also be registered by political parties, civic organizations, or individuals, assuming proper procedures and forms are used.

Frequency of Elections and the Long Ballot

Some observers argue that voter fatigue is a problem in Kentucky, due both to the frequency of elections and the number of officials who are elected. Elections are held twice every year, primary elections in May and general elections in November. Over a four-year cycle, Kentuckians must in one year (e.g., 1983) select their governor, other statewide officers, circuit judges (every eight years), and a number of city officials. The following year, elections are held for president, the United States Senate, Congressional seats, state

161

legislative seats, school board seats, and some judicial offices. The following year are elections for major county offices, some city offices, and district judgeships. Finally, in the fourth year of the cycle (e.g., 1986) are Congressional and Senatorial elections, state legislative races, school board elections, and at least one supreme court race. In addition to all of these, chances are high that in each year some sort of referendum will be submitted to the voters of certain constituencies. Besides constitutional amendments, referenda may be submitted to the voters regarding local liquor sales, bond issues, millage rates, and several other issues.[36]

Besides the frequency of election, a related but separate problem in Kentucky is the number of offices to be filled in any given election. The term often applied to the practice of electing a large number of officials is the *long ballot*, and few if any states have a longer ballot than Kentucky.[37] This is particularly true during odd-year elections, which alternate between state and county contests. In state-level elections, voters must choose among candidates for *eight* major constitutional offices plus railroad commissioner, in addition to other contests and questions that may be on the ballot that year. This situation is aggravated in the primary, where the Democratic dominance in state elections usually encourages several Democratic candidates to file for each statewide office. As a result, a Democratic voter in the primary will ordinarily be faced with a list of twenty-five or thirty candidates from which to choose in a single election.

Two years later, in the county elections, a similar situation occurs, as voters must elect at least six county officials. Again, the primary will ordinarily attract three times as many candidates as positions from the dominant party in a given county.

Defenders of the long ballot argue that it is consistent with democratic practices to elect as many officials as possible in order to insure responsibility and responsiveness and to keep government close to the people. This sentiment is shared by a majority of Kentuckians in that no serious attempt has been made to eliminate a number of these offices from elective politics. Critics of the long ballot argue that this system inhibits responsible decision making. The average voter is unable to make intelligent voting choices because of the difficulty in obtaining sufficient information about all the candidates who are running. In addition, because executive and administrative decisions are shared by so many officials it is difficult for the voter to hold a single decision maker responsible for a particular policy or set of policies, a situation which is aggravated by the constitutional prohibition against reelecting the governor and other statewide officials. While reforms have been suggested for confronting this problem, they have met with little success.[38]

Voter Turnout

Jewell and Cunningham have pointed out that voter turnout in Kentucky has been below the national average since the 1920s.[39] They attribute this to the relative lack of meaningful competition in the state during this period. Although it is beyond the scope of this chapter to provide extensive data comparing Kentucky's and national voter turnout, a few observations can be made that are supported by the available voting data.

First, at any given time, between one-fourth and one-third of all eligible Kentuckians are not registered to vote. In 1976, for example, about 72 percent of the voting-age population in Kentucky were registered, but that was up about 6 percent from four years previously.

Second, the number of registered voters is greater than the number who actually vote. In presidential elections, around 70 percent of the registered voters ordinarily vote, although this figure varies 3 or 4 percent from one election to another. For the last three presidential elections (1972, 1976, 1980), the percentages have been 73, 68, and 71 percent.

Considering these two observations together, it is clear that in a typical election, a large proportion of Kentuckians of voting age will not be voting. Table 7.4 provides information on this question for the 1960 to 1976 period.[40] During the 1970s, the percentage of voting-age Kentuckians who actually voted in presidential elections dropped below 50 percent. This figure had been over 80 percent in four elections during the early part of the twentieth century but has steadily declined since the 1920s, dropping below 60 percent for the first time in 1936[41]

As is indicated in Table 7.4, even fewer Kentuckians participate in nonpresidential elections, with United States Senatorial and gubernatorial elections lagging behind by about 10 percent and Congressional elections attracting even fewer voters in nonpresidential election years.[42] Kentucky's voter turnout levels have generally been below the corresponding turnout throughout the nation over the past several decades, but the gap has actually narrowed in recent years, as voter turnout has actually been declining at a faster rate nationally than it has in Kentucky.

Because of this, low voter turnout must be considered both a national trend, or problem, as well as a concern in Kentucky. Although many reasons have been suggested for why fewer and fewer Americans decide to vote, two major reasons seem to be the decline of political parties in the United States and an increasing apathy and/or loss of confidence in political institutions.[43] Thus,

remedies or actions to deal with these more general problems will
need to be national in scope.

TABLE 7.4

Percent of Kentucky Voting Age Population Casting Votes
1960 to 1976

Year	President [†]	United States Senator [‡]	United States Representative [†]	Governor [‡]
1960	57.6	55.8	46.8	
1962		42.0	32.9	
1963				45.3
1964	53.3		48.6	
1966			33.9	
1967				43.7
1968	51.2	45.7	41.9	
1970			22.2	
1971				42.9
1972	48.4	47.2	44.7	
1974		32.7	29.6	
1975				32.1
1976	49.2		41.7	

Source:
[†]U.S. Census Bureau, Population Reports; U.S. Census Bureau, Statistical Abstract, 1975.
[‡]Kentucky State Board of Elections, Compiled by Legislative Research Commission.

Voting Reforms in Kentucky

Most of the election reforms in Kentucky involve the long
ballot which was discussed earlier. One reform does however, relate
to low voter turnout just discussed. While nonvoting is a national
problem, Kentucky does restrict voting in one unusual way: the
length of the voting day extends from 6 A.M. to 6 P.M. Only a handful
of other states close the polls this early on election day, and this
practice appears to place an undue burden upon the average working
Kentuckian. Since voting machines are used throughout the state,
allowing for a relatively quick and easy compilation and reporting of
voting results, there are few, if any, apparent reasons for closing the

polls as early as 6 P.M. If Kentuckians view encouraging voter turnout as a desirable goal, serious consideration should be given to extending the voting hours at least one hour in the evening.

While various reforms that would shorten Kentucky's ballot have been made over the past two decades, two that have been suggested recently deserve some attention. House Speaker Bobby Richardson's suggestion that the office of lieutenant governor be abolished had just been made as this chapter was being written, but his proposal was never introduced as legislation during the 1984 general assembly. Some observers and editorials, in supporting Richardson's recommendations, pointed out that his arguments about the lieutenant governor's position—that it was not needed and was a waste of tax dollars—applied to other elected offices as well, e.g., secretary of state, state treasurer, and commissioner of agriculture. Others have pointed out for a long time that the office of superintendent of public instruction should be appointive rather than elective, and this recommendation was supported in 1983 by both major candidates for that office. While several bills were introduced in the 1984 general assembly to effect these changes, it appeared late in the session that no constitutional amendment involving statewide elective offices would be proposed to the voters in 1984.

Another recently suggested reform was advocated by former State Democratic Chairman Paul Patton. In his final address as state chairman in June 1983, he focused on another aspect of the long ballot, the problem of nuisance candidates, particularly in the primary. Nuisance candidates are individuals who, though virtually unknown to all Kentuckians, can be placed on the ballot for the state's highest offices by paying a token fee and presenting a petition signed by as few as two persons (see KRS 118.125, 118.255). Patton advocated the provision of more rigorous, yet reasonable, standards for access to the ballot. His proposals seem certain to receive serious consideration in the near future, given his influence in the Democratic party and at the local level as a well-known county judge-executive.

Conclusion

Voting in Kentucky provides a significant opportunity for political participation, but it is not as meaningful as more intense participation in campaigns and political parties. To a great extent, voter turnout is a reflection of these other political activities and events. The more active and competitive political parties are, and the livelier and more visible a campaign is, the more likely a higher

165

voter turnout will result. The likelihood that an individual will register and vote depends upon complex political patterns in his community, in the state, and across the nation. More important, it also depends upon how that individual *perceives* those patterns. In an era when one-party dominance is the rule in most areas of Kentucky in both local and state elections, it should be no surprise that many persons choose not to vote.

Readers are urged to consider the problem of nonvoting in Kentucky, to compare Kentucky to other states, and to consider what reforms might be suggested to political decision makers in this state. Consider not only what laws could be changed but how political parties might be made more responsible and responsive to individual voters and what actions, both formal and informal, could be taken to encourage greater political participation.

FOOTNOTES

1. Robert L. Lineberry, *Government in America*, 2nd ed. (Boston: Little, Brown, 1983) pp. 200-201.
2. For examples of privileges and responsibilities of major parties in Kentucky, see KRS 117.015 and 117.035 (membership in state and county boards of elections) and KRS 118.760 (authority to nominate candidates for special elections). Parties are strictly regulated by various state laws regarding primaries, conduct of elections, and campaign financing, as well as by many recent federal laws.
3. See, for example, Malcolm E. Jewell and Everett W. Cunningham, *Kentucky Politics* (Lexington: University Press of Kentucky, 1968), particularly Chapters 1, 4, and 5; Thomas D. Clark, *A History of Kentucky* (Lexington: John Bradford Press, 1960).
4. Jewell and Cunningham, pp. 179-182.
5. Ibid., Chapter 4.
6. Ibid., p. 26.
7. In 1984, the Democratic state convention was held on June 2 while the Republican state convention met on May 12.
8. These governing documents of the two major parties in Kentucky are included in the state publication *Kentucky Election Laws* (Commonwealth of Kentucky, State Board of Elections, 1982) and are current as of July 1982. Any changes made in party rules in 1984 are not included in this discussion.

9. In various places in the Democratic bylaws, the DSCC is also referred to as State Central Executive Committee.

10. Both parties as of 1982 use the term *chairman* rather than *chairperson* to describe leadership roles at various levels.

11. The authority to name special committees is explicit in the Republican *Rules* (see 2:04) and implicit in the Democratic *Bylaws*.

12. Actually, in 1984, the Democrats held *two* sets of organizational meetings at various levels—one set (in March and April) leading to the selection of delegates to the national convention and the other set (April and June) to reorganize the state party. Most of the discussion in this chapter refers to the latter series of meetings.

13. Prior to 1984, Democratic county conventions allowed only precinct officers to serve as voting members.

14. See the Democratic *Bylaws*, Article IV, Section B.

15. Ibid., Article IV, Section B2, 3. The bylaws provide for two different procedures, one for counties with between three and five LDs, one for counties with more than five LDs. Currently these provisions apply only to Fayette and Jefferson Counties.

16. See Ibid., Article II, Section L, for the specific formula.

17. *Official Rules*, 4:01, 4:02, 4:03, 4:06.

18. Ibid., 5:01.

19. See Democratic *Bylaws*, Article V and Republican *Rules*, Section 5.

20. The data were provided by the State Board of Elections in a printout dated May 9, 1983. At that time, 59,470 Kentuckians registered Independent ("no preference"), and 796 were registered with minor parties.

21. This is an updated and revised version of Table 5.1 in Jewell and Cunningham, *Kentucky Politics*, p. 183. This table and some of this discussion have been previously presented in Paul D. Blanchard, "Continuity and Change in Kentucky Voting Behavior," a paper presented at the annual meeting of the Kentucky Political Science Association, Northern Kentucky University, February 1982.

22. Jewell and Cunningham, pp. 209-214.

23. Beginning in 1984, Kentucky state legislators will be elected in even-numbered years. One of the least-discussed implications of this change is that legislators will be elected when national officials are being selected. Based on the analysis presented

here, this could enhance Republican chances in state legislative races.

24. Martha Layne Collins in 1983 had strong campaign organizations in virtually every Kentucky county while Jim Bunning's late start and other difficulties discussed later in this chapter prevented him from establishing effective organizations in many areas of the state. While final campaign expenditure data for 1983 were not available as this is written, preliminary reports examined at the Kentucky Registry of Election Finance indicate that Governor Collins outspent Senator Bunning by nearly three to one if both primary and general election campaigns are included. She spent well over $4 million, while he spent only about $1.5 million. While her spending advantage in the general election was substantially less (about $1.8 million to $1.4 million), she ended the general election campaign with an unprecedented *surplus* of over $250,000, most of which was donated to the state Democratic party.

25. The seven categories were used by Jewell and Cunningham to classify counties for an earlier period (1920 to 1966). Their classification scheme, explained on p. 187 of their book, was followed as closely as possible. To be precise, a county was classified as strong Democrat or Republican if the party carried the county in at least ten elections and had a median percentage of at least 60 percent. To be classified as Democrat or Republican required at least nine electoral victories and a median of at least 55 percent. To be classified as Democrat or Republican inclined required that the party carry at least eight of the thirteen elections; in almost every case, the median percentage was less than 55 percent for these counties. Marginal counties were those where neither party carried more than seven of the thirteen elections during the period.

26. For a complete list of counties and how they are classified, see Blanchard, "Continuity and Change," Table 1.

27. This conclusion is supported by a recent study where it was reported that Kentucky's Fifth Congressional District was the fourth poorest in the nation in terms of per capita income and ranked tenth nationally in the percentage of families living in poverty (24.9%). See *U.S. News and World Report,* September 26, 1983, as reported in the Lexington *Herald-Leader,* September 26, 1983.

28. These ten counties were Madison, Powell, and LaRue—classified as Democrat inclined—Oldham, Boone, Barren, Kenton, and

Fleming—classified as marginal—and Fayette and Jessamine—classified as Republican inclined.

29. John H. Fenton, *Midwest Politics* (New York: Holt, Rinehart, and Winston, 1966).

30. See Fenton, *People and Parties in Politics* (Glenview, IL: Scott, Foresman, 1966), particularly Chapter 4.

31. Malcolm E. Jewell, "Two-Party Politics in Kentucky," a lecture presented at the Robert A. Taft Seminar, Eastern Kentucky University, June 1982.

32. For example, Bunning became less supportive of a right-to-work law in Kentucky in the latter weeks of the fall campaign. See the Lexington *Herald-Leader,* September 29, 1983.

33. For a discussion of a "mushiness index" for American voters, see Robert Lineberry, *op. cit,* p. 186.

34. Exceptions to the rule include convicted felons, those in prison, persons declared mentally incompetent, and nonresident persons on active military duty in Kentucky.

35. Much of the information in this section was taken from *The Kentucky Ballot,* Kentucky Legislative Research Commission (Frankfort: LRC Research Report #140, 1977).

36. For a list of statutes relating to various ballot questions, see ibid., pp. 5-6.

37. See ibid., especially Table 7 and Tables 9 to 15.

38. *The Kentucky Ballot,* pp. 16-21.

39. Jewell and Cunningham, pp. 8-9.

40. Reproduced from *The Kentucky Ballot,* Table 2.

41. Jewell and Cunningham, p. 8.

42. In the 1983 general election for governor, only about 55 percent of the registered voters voted in the governor's race. The percentage was even lower in the races for other statewide offices. In the governor's race, Martha Layne Collins received 561,674 votes, Jim Bunning received 464,650 votes, and third-party candidate Nicholas McCubbin received 14,347 votes.

43. See, for example, Arthur T. Hadley, *The Empty Polling Booth* (Englewood Cliffs, N.J.: Prentice-Hall, 1978).

44. Early accounts were reported in the *Courier-Journal,* October 6, 1983.

Chapter 8

POLITICAL FINANCE IN KENTUCKY

Joel Goldstein, University of Louisville

INTRODUCTION

Most, if not all, of the concerns that have been raised over the last fifteen years in the national arena about campaign finance have surfaced as issues in Kentucky politics. Questions have been raised about nearly every dimension of campaign finance: the amount of money raised, the way it is expended, the impact of public financing, and the consequences for public policy formation that results from this process.

The most basic concern with campaign finance, at all levels, is over the amount of money that is raised and spent to elect individuals to public office. At least $275 million were spent in 1980 to influence the selection of a president.[1] The costs associated with electing a governor in Kentucky in 1983 exceeded $10 million.[2]

Reformers claim that the quality of the government's performance may be compromised in order to raise the money necessary to be competitive in politics. Ambassadorships or cabinet positions may be allocated on the basis of campaign contributions or fund-raising capabilities of the aspirant rather than their job qualifications. Elizabeth Drew, for example, reported that Ray Donovan was selected secretary of labor by President Reagan because "he was virtually the only heavy hitter in the northeast money raising for Reagan between 1978 and 1980.[3] Eleven weeks before the 1983 governor's election, the *Courier-Journal* reported that Dr. Floyd Poore was available to serve in a potential Collins

170

administration. Dr. Poore estimated that he had a hand in raising up to $900,000 across the state for the lieutenant Governor.[4]

Some critics assert that campaign contributions are able to influence the allocation of state contracts. The controversy that surrounded Mr. William H. May's contributions to Democratic gubernatorial candidates and to the continuation of profitable contracts to inspect Kentucky toll roads, surfaced in the spring of 1983.[5] This was just one example of a perennial problem.

Reformers are concerned about the ability of campaign contributions to influence not only who does work for the state ("to the victor belongs the spoils") but also what work gets done.

> Believers in coincidence will accept denials that there is the faintest connection between $10,000 in contributions to Governor Brown's campaign fund and five entrances to a shopping mall near Paducah that were approved four days later. Fans of the tooth fairy may believe that members of the Youngstown, Ohio, developer's family donated the money as a civic duty solely to assist the rise of a new star on the national political scene.[6]

Finally, critics of the system of private or semipublic financing of politics argue that it is possible for a wealthy individual to buy an election for a major office. John Y. Brown, Jr., for example, lent his primary campaign for governor over $1¼ million in 1979. Dr. Harvey Sloane, a relative newcomer to Louisville and its politics, spent $140,000 of his own money to win the 1973 Democratic mayoral nomination. His total expenditures for that campaign were $189,492, and his principal opponent spent only $110,951.[7]

HISTORICAL BACKGROUND

Questions raised by the large amounts of money spent by politicians and their supporters to win elections in Kentucky and concerns over the potential effects on the efficiency and effectiveness of state government of these contributions are not new. Kentucky adopted a comprehensive Corrupt Practices Statute in 1916 (section 1565b-1 to 10; KRS 123.010 to 123.990).[8] This legislation was revised and strengthened in 1966. This law regulating campaign finance has been amended several times since then.

The 1916 statute sought to limit the total expenditure of candidates and to regulate the sources of campaign contributions. New York was the first state to regulate campaign finance through public disclosure in 1890. Comparable federal legislation was adopted in 1910 and 1911.[9]

Candidates and their campaign committees were required to file public statements outlining the contributions and expenditures of their campaigns. In addition, the 1916 statute sought to limit the amount of money that could be spent by candidates and their supporters in both the primary and general elections. These limits were as follows:

Governor	$10,000
Other statewide offices	5,000
Court of Appeals	3,000
State Senate	1,000
State Representative	750
County Office (with 1st Class city).	2,500
County Office (with 2nd City)	2,000
County Office (with 3rd City)	1,500
County (other)	1,000
City Office—1st Class city	5,000
Other	500[10]

Unlike the expenditure limits associated with the presidential campaign, these limits were not indexed to inflation. The statute did not have any public financing provisions; consequently, the expenditure limits would have been declared unconstitutional by the United States Supreme Court's holding in *Buckley v. Valeo*.[11]

The statute also sought to enumerate the purposes for which campaign expenditures may legally be made. Any purpose not listed was forbidden. The allowable expenditures were for the following reasons:

employing clerks and stenographers
printing and advertising
securing suitable halls for public speaking
suitable headquarters
stationery and stamps
actual traveling expenses[12]

Finally, the statute forbade contributions from individuals to candidates who in their official capacity were "required by law to perform any duties peculiar to such person not common to the general public, to supervise, regulate or control in any manner the affairs of such person or to perform any duty in assessing the property of such person for taxation."[13]

However, the 1916 Corrupt Practices Act was not an effective regulator of campaign finance in Kentucky. It did not control the level of campaign expenditures. "Newspapermen estimated that about $2,000,000 went into the 1959 contest for the Kentucky

Democratic gubernatorial nomination between Bert T. Combs and Harry Lee Waterfield."[14] Nor did it effectively control the use of campaign funds. A Legislative Research Commission report issued in 1965 stated that "the outright buying of votes has allegedly been common practice in certain Kentucky counties for decades.[15]

The 1916 Corrupt Practices Act failed because it did not delegate to any agency the responsibility and the resources to enforce it. In addition, the expenditure limitations were extremely low, and the penalties associated with the statute were too severe to insure adequate enforcement. The reporting provisions were vague, allowing independent committees and special interest groups to fall outside the legal limitations.[15]

The old statute did have some impact on politics in Kentucky. The limits on individual candidate expenditure encouraged campaign fund raising and expenditures by the political party organizations on the county level. The parties worked for their whole slate of candidates, thereby strengthening their position in the political system.[16] It is interesting to note that the power of the famed Jefferson County party organizations of both the Republicans and Democrats withered, and the open primary was introduced soon after the adoption of the campaign finance reforms of 1966.

REGULATION OF CAMPAIGN CONTRIBUTIONS

The current laws regulating campaign contributions in Kentucky vary depending upon the type of election (public issue or public office), the level of office (federal or state), and the type of donor.

Type of Elections

Contributions to committees seeking to influence voters for or against public issues that appear on the ballot, such as referenda or constitutional amendments, are not as regulated as contributions to individuals seeking public office. Corporations, for example, are not allowed to aid individuals seeking public office but can provide funds to support or oppose public issue campaigns. Citizens Fidelity Corporation, First National Bank of Louisville, First Boston Corporation, Humana, Maybe Coal Company of Corbin, and Phillip Morris Incorporated are just a few of the many corporations that gave money to the committee supporting the adoption of the Succession Amendment in 1981. Several churches contributed to the United

173

Dry Forces of Ashland, while the Ashland Oil Company gave $135,000 to the Citizens for a Progressive Community.

There is a limit on how much money an individual can contribute to a candidate for public office, but there is no limit on what can be given to a public issue campaign. L. Roger Wells, Jr., of Glasgow contributed $5,000 to the pro-succession amendment committee. Tracy Farmer, Ron Geary, Edward Glasscock, Frank Metts, and William Sturgill each guaranteed loans of $34,355 for the pro-succession amendment committee. These actions would have been illegal if they were done on behalf of an individual candidate for public office.

The Kentucky General Assembly amended KRS 121.035 to allow corporate contributions to campaigns on public issues in 1980. This action was in response to *First National Bank of Boston v. Bellotti*, 435 U.S. 765 (1978), which held that a state cannot restrict a corporation from exercising its First Amendment rights in the debate over public issues, including those which appear on the ballot. As a result, the corporate sector was extremely active in the Jefferson County reorganization referenda as well as the 1982 school tax levy question. Corporate contributions have also been present in campaigns to legalize the sale of alcoholic beverages across Kentucky.

Level of Office

The rules regulating campaign contributions vary according to the level of office sought. Candidates for the United States House of Representatives or the Senate must abide by the standards outlines by the Federal Election Campaign Act of 1971, as amended in 1974, 1976, and 1979. Candidates for local and state office must comply with the standards adopted by the general assembly.

In federal elections, individuals can contribute only $1,000 per candidate per election. Primary and general elections are considered separate elections, so that an individual can contribute $2,000 during each election cycle. Consequently, a husband and wife can contribute as much as $4,000 in each election cycle. The $2,000 limit also applies for each member of the family (children, for example) who had an independent source of income. An individual can also spend an additional $1,000 in voluntary expenses in support of a candidate for federal office. Political Action Committees (PACs) can contribute as much as $5,000 per candidate per election. In addition, PACs can expend an unlimited amount of money seeking to influence an election, as long as the activity is done without consultation with the candidate and is reported to the Federal Election Commission (if the amount involved is greater than $250.00).

Political Party Committees on the federal and state level can contribute $5,000 each per candidate for national office per election. In addition, these committees can each expend $14,720 (1980 dollars) for each house candidate and over $75,000 (1980 dollars) for a Kentucky senate seat for "coordinated" campaign activities. The party committees, for example, can purchase the campaign's polling or television time.

Type of Donor

The millions of dollars raised each year to finance primary and general election campaigns in Kentucky come from three types of donors: (1) individuals, (2) groups or political action committees, and (3) political parties. State law deals differently with each source of campaign funds, although individuals probably gave the money to the political action groups and political parties.

Individuals. Kentucky law restricts the amount an individual can contribute to a candidate for state or local office to $3,000 per election. The 1966 general assembly created the Kentucky Registry of Election Finance; however, the contribution limits were not added to the statute until 1974. Like the federal restrictions on contributions, this limit is *not* indexed to inflation. Consequently, increases in the cost of living has consistently eroded the buying power of these maximum political contributions. (See later section for a full discussion of the increasing costs of conducting political campaigns in Kentucky.)

The individual contribution limit applies to loans made to a candidate, as well as to outright gifts to the campaign. The total contribution and loan can not exceed $3,000 per election. Consequently, an individual can give as much as $6,000 in a year ($3,000 in the primary and another $3,000 in the general election). Spouses and children with independent sources of wealth are also able to give up to the legal limit in each campaign.

These limits do not apply to a candidate for public office. Candidates can give or loan to their campaigns as much money as they wish and can afford. John Y. Brown, Jr., for example, was legally able to loan his 1979 primary campaign for governor $1,265,000 (about half was repaid during the campaign). Harvey Sloane loaned and guaranteed loans of $363,500 during his 1979 campaign for governor.

Corporations, PACs, and Political Parties. Corporations are prohibited from making contributions to candidates for public office. Section 150 of the 1891 Kentucky constitution prohibits corporations from making contributions to candidates for public office.

Political action committees can be established by individuals in management positions within a corporation, by the membership of a labor union, by the members of a professional or trade association, or by any group of citizens with a special interest. PACs aggregate the contributions of these like-minded individuals. The leaders of the PACs direct the flow of these funds to candidates in order to maximize the group's political influence. State law does not regulate how much money a PAC can contribute to an individual candidate for public office, nor is there a limit on how much money an individual can give to a PAC (the money cannot, however, be given to a PAC for the purpose of aiding a specific candidate).

KEPAC (the Educators Public Affairs Council, an arm of the Kentucky Education Association), for example, gave $53,400 to the general campaign of Governor John Y. Brown in 1979. The contribution was dated December 13, 1979, a full month *after* the election. It is important to remember that Kentucky statutes do not limit when an individual or a group can make a political contribution. The auto workers Union gave over $12,000 to Governor Brown (also after the election). Candidates of both parties benefit from PAC gifts. Jim Bunning in his 1979 campaign for state senate, received $5,000 from the Kentucky Business PAC. The Kentucky Bankers Committee for State Government gave $3,000 each to John Y. Brown and Louie Nunn, his Republican opponent, in 1979 and $1,000 each to Martha Layne Collins and Hal Rogers, the opposing candidates for lieutenant governor.

Large PAC contributions were also made during the 1983 gubernatorial campaign. The Teamsters Union PAC in Washington and the United Steelworkers of America PAC in Pittsburgh gave $15,000 gifts to the Collins campaign. Ten thousand dollars was given by the United Autoworkers PAC in Indianapolis. The Liberty United Bancorp Pact of Louisville gave $4,000, while the Refuse Collectors PAC of Louisville gave $5,000.[17]

Political parties are also not restricted in the amount of money they can contribute to candidates for public office. In addition to direct financial contributions, the political parties can provide in-kind contributions of services such as surveys or direct mail campaigns (political parties are eligible for reduced postal rates). The Republican party of Kentucky, for example, gave $25,000 to support their gubernatorial candidate in the 1983 campaign.[18]

PUBLIC FINANCING

Kentucky is one of nineteen states that have adopted legislation providing for the partial public financing of politics.[19] The general assembly in 1976 established a dollar checkoff on the state income tax form, the proceeds of which would be used by the state central committee of the two major parties. The individual taxpayer must designate which political party is to receive the money be checking a box labeled Democratic or Republican on the face of the tax form.

The 1982 general assembly amended the law to increase the amount to be distributed to the parties to $1.50 in 1983 (tax year 1982), $1.75 in 1984, and $2.00 in 1985 and thereafter. Fifty cents of the increased allocation will be distributed to the county party organization.[19]

Table 8.1 provides the taxpayer participation rates for the Kentucky checkoff. The average participation rate for the first six years of the program was 14.0 percent. This rate does not compare very favorably with the average participation rate for the presidential election campaign fund, which was 27.5 percent for the five years 1976 to 1980.[20] The significantly lower participation rate for Kentucky's system may be caused by the partisan nature of the checkoff. Taxpayers may not be eager to reveal to the state revenue department the party they support.

TABLE 8.1

Taxpayer Participation—Kentucky Political Party Income Tax Checkoff

Tax Year	Total Amount Checked Off	Total ± of Taxpayers	Participation Rates (by %)	Amount Distributed to Democrats	Republicans
1976	$175,387	1,412,123	12.4	$128,967	$46,420
1977	244,865	1,484,179	16.5	180,127	64,738
1978	223,169	1,520,825	14.7	160,039	63,130
1979	228,450	1,584,351	14.4	166,521	61,929
1980	214,447	1,585,715	13.5	143,222	71,225
1981	194,739	1,585,468	12.3	134,411	60,328
1982	171,738	1,598,967	10.7	118,908 (State)	54,373.50
				58,169.50 (County)	26,157

Source: Herbert E. Alexander and Jennifer W. Frutig, *Public Financing of State Elections,* Los Angeles: Citizens' Research Foundation, 1982, p. 64. The data for 1981 and 1982 were provided by the Department of Revenue, Commonwealth of Kentucky.

The Democrats received 68.7 percent of the revenue generated by the checkoff in tax year 1982, and the Republicans obtained the remaining 31.3 percent. This split closely parallels the division in voter registration between the two parties. Consequently, one cannot attribute the lower response rate to specific partisan fears.

In fact, the Republican share of the tax checkoff pool increased from 27.1 percent in tax year 1979 to a high of 33.2 percent in 1980. In 1981 and 1982 the GOP's share dropped a little to 31.0 and 31.3 respectively.

The number of taxpayers utilizing the checkoff has been declining over the last six years (tax years 1977 to 1982). In tax year 1977, 16.5 percent of the taxpayers availed themselves of the opportunity to give a dollar of the state's money to their favorite party, while only 10.7 percent opted to do so in tax year 1982. This decline in participation is especially interesting in light of the slight increase in the participation rate among taxpayers opting in favor of the presidential checkoff (25.4 percent in 1978, 27.4 percent in 1979, and 28.7 percent in 1980).[21]

The continued decline in participation vote in the tax checkoff continued in 1982 after the inclusion of the county party organizations. Some political leaders thought that the sharing of this governmental largess with the local organizations would encourage the promotion of the checkoff. The continued decline is perhaps another indicator of the weaknesses of the political party organizations on the county level in Kentucky.

The ways the parties can use this money are restricted by statute. It can be used only for the administrative costs of maintaining a political party headquarters and for the general election support of the party's candidates.[22]

Expenditures

Politics is a multimillion-dollar industry in Kentucky. Nearly $15 million were expended by candidates in partisan races, in nonpartisan local and judicial races, and in support of and opposition to various ballot questions in 1981, an off year in Kentucky politics. Over $10 million were spent in 1983 contesting the primary and general elections for governor alone.

Table 8.2 details the expenditures made on behalf of candidates and political issues in Kentucky since 1967. The data include contests in primary, special, and general elections. The figures reported by the Kentucky Registry of Election Finance are approximations. They are slightly inflated because money transferred among campaign committees is counted at least twice. On the other

TABLE 8.2

Total Political Expenditures—Kentucky 1967 to 1982

Year	Primary				General			
	Republican	Democratic	Other	Judicial	Republican	Democratic	Other	Judicial
1967	338,529	1,028,221			671,667	909,175	11,542	
1968*	139,041	283,903			650,721	206,686	2,428	
1969	568,129	1,054,043	67		1,513,125	762,150	23,339	
1970	14,983	38,959			403,611	260,655	3,091	
1971	354,782	1,806,081			1,483,630	1,190,878	8,069	17,491
1972*	473,891	163,101	227	17,795	1,601,018	1,190,878	65,179	94,820
1973	517,331	1,474,591	149,563		450,410	765,948	345,385	
1974	190,404	526,003	228,671	48,162	501,366	1,014,903	219,785	23,774
1975	359,532	3,881,631	357,176	217,000	584,985	1,627,114	430,118	117,344
1976†	16,919	54,034	542,112		18,032	45,768	751,498	165,979
1977	910,955	2,983,248	665,805	172,947	1,197,165	748,461	416,457	
1978†	206,132	421,481	732,742	16,335	224,986	353,227	912,681	24,030
1979	922,205	9,009,043	622,958		2,329,286	3,205,417	1,023,624	
1980†	151,793	339,939	416,746	15,903	249,441	533,589	631,957	38,551
1981	1,810,859	4,761,837	751,045	178,737	2,580,823	2,645,431	1,736,082	472,895
1982†	123,874	498,627	305,673	208,672	188,700	471,215	1,229,808	192,865

*excludes funds spent on the presidential election

† excludes funds spent on all federal elections (presidency, Senate, Congress)

Source: Kentucky Registry of Election Finance, annual reports

179

hand, the reports do not include the value of volunteer efforts made on behalf of candidates and issues. In addition, many out of pocket expenses borne by the candidates and their supporters are not reported.

Several interesting findings emerge from an analysis of Table 8.2. The Democrats tend to expend more resources contesting their primary elections than in the general election, while the opposite is true for the Republicans. Spending tends to increase in a hotly contested primary, in part, because it may be more influential there. Primary candidates must provide voters with a reason to vote for them, but in a general election, party identification plays a major role in shaping the vote. Republicans, to have any chance of winning in a traditionally Democratic area, must obtain a high level of name identification and provide the voters with a reason to support a member of the other party. These two goals require a great deal of resources. Members of the majority party, on the other hand, have an incentive to play down issues and personalities, while relying on party identification to carry the day. The data clearly support this interpretation.

A second reason Democratic primary campaigns have greater levels of spending is that more individuals become viable candidates in the primaries than in the general elections. It is not uncommon for three or more Democrats to seek their party's nomination for governor or other major offices. The inability of statewide constitutional officials to succeed themselves assures that in most cases there will not be an incumbent seeking reelection. Not only are there more actors, but Democratic primaries tend to heat up much sooner. In the general election, the candidates focus in on election day and seek to peak on that day. In a three- or four-way primary, however, a successful candidate must demonstrate viability early in order to attract support among the party's leadership and cadre. This requires the candidates to start spending in earnest much earlier to have an organization in place well before primary day.

Table 8.3 details the level of expenditure in Kentucky gubernatorial elections since 1967. The level of spending has not automatically increased over time. The expenditure levels in 1975, for example, were quite modest. Governor Carroll, after succeeding to the office in 1974, was running for reelection. He was clearly a popular candidate after easily winning the Democratic nomination. The Republican challenger, Robert Gable, was not able to raise a great deal of money to finance a serious campaign.

In 1967 and 1971 the eventual winners of the general election for governor expended *less* money than their opponents. The mere expenditure of money does not assure electoral success. The issues

180

TABLE 8.3

Campaign Expenditures—Gubernatorial Elections

Year	Primary Democratic	Primary Republican	General Democratic	General Republican
1967	628,338	242,905	689,993	444,289
1971	1,503,648*	266,133	953,193	1,354,561
1975	1,548,773	212,813	293,920	225,758
1979	5,817,043	476,820	1,863,250	1,225,148

*includes expenditures for both the governor's and lieutenant governor's races

Source: Kentucky Registry of Election Finance Annual Reports

and personalities of the candidates, as well as the tenor of the times in which the election is held, have a great deal to do with determining the eventual winners and losers.

In addition, expenditure totals alone do not tell the whole story. Campaign resources must be spent wisely and effectively. Resources must be allocated among a wide variety of items:

paid staff (press relations, researchers, headquarters coordinators, field staff, etc.)

overhead costs (rent for headquarters and associated costs, such as telephones, stationery, etc.)

candidate travel and lodging

postage

printing of brochures, pencils, matchbook covers, emery boards, etc.

survey research consultants

telephone "boiler room" operations

media consultants' "creativity fees"

costs of production for radio and television ads

radio and television air time

get out the vote organizational activities

A candidate may be able to raise enough money to carry an election but may lose because the money was spent improperly. Not only must the money be divided properly, the money must be spent effectively. All potential staff members are not equal. Some headquarters locations are conducive to attracting volunteers, and others are not. All television commercials are not equally persuasive. Television and radio time must be targeted to the appropriate audiences.

The costs of campaign-related activities are high, and they are getting higher. The inflationary pressures on Kentucky campaigns are complicated by strict limitations on how much an individual can give to a candidate. Table 8.4 presents a comparison of the costs associated with some typical expenditures in 1974, when the limits were enacted, and in 1983.

TABLE 8.4

A Comparison of Campaign-Related Costs—Kentucky 1974 to 1983

	1974	*1983*
Consumer Price Index (all items)[1]	147.7	292.1
Telephone[2]		
installations (per line)	$10.00	10.00
line connection	20.00	28.25
labor	15.00 (hr)	43.25 (¼ hr)
WATS line (state)	665.00 (month)	1080.00 (70 hrs)
Newspaper (cost per line)[3]		
Bowling Green News	$.111	.52
Corbin Times-Tribune	.11	.23
Covington-Kentucky Post	.33	1.28
Danville Advocate-Messenger	.10	.47
Frankfort State Journal	.16	.30
Fulton Leader	.065	.24
Glasgow Times	.12	.23
Harlan Enterprise	.11	.23
Henderson Gleaner	.16	.35
Hopkinsville Kentucky New Era	.12	.77
Lexington Herald-Leader (M-E)	.52	2.27
Louisville Courier Journal-Times (M-E)	1.50	5.13
Madisonville Messenger	.11	.36
Mayfield Messenger	.13	.29
Maysville Ledger-Independent	.13	.25
Middlesboro News	.13	.23
Murray Ledger and Times	.11	.26
Owensboro Messenger & Inquirer	.22	.44
Paducah Sun-Democrat	.21	.73
Richmond Register	.11	.22

Somerset Commonwealth-Journal	.13	.26
Winchester Sun	.10	.30

Radio (one minute spot, bottom of the card)[4]

Bardstown - WBRT	$2.00	3.25
Bowling Green - WBGN	2.75	5.30
Bowling Green - WDNS (FM)	4.15	5.90
Columbia - WAIN	2.35	5.75
Corbin - WCTT (AM and FM)	2.50	5.55
Fort Campbell - WABD	2.30	5.20
Frankfort - WFKY (AM and FM)	6.50	5.30
Harlan - WHLN	2.85	7.10
Hazard - WKIC	2.40	4.20
Hopkinsville - WHOP	4.40	8.40
Lexington - WLAP	8.00	26.00
Louisville - WAVG	31.00	60.00
Madisonville - WFMW	3.00	8.00
Morehead - WMOR	2.25	2.25
Murray - WNBS	3.75	6.50
Paducah - WDXR	5.00	11.75
Paducah - WPAD	7.00	13.55
Pikeville - WPKE	3.25	7.00
Richmond - WEKY	5.00	7.30

Television (thirty-second spots)[5]

Bowling Green		
WBKO - 6 P.M. News	$45.00	150.00
Lexington		
WKYT - Early News	60.00	81.00
WLEX - 5:30 News	24.00	100.00
WTVQ - 6:00 News	30.00	70.00
Louisville		
WHAS - Noon-News	45.00	200.00
WLKY - 6:30 P.M.	85.00	180.00
Paducah		
WPSD	15.00	15.00

Sources:

[1]*Statistical Abstract of the United States,* Vol. 44, p. 467; *Survey of Current Business,* Vol. 63, No. 2.

[2]phone conversation with Mr. Donald Stuart, South Central Bell, August 3, 1983.

[3]*Standard Rate and Data Service*—Newspapers May 12, 1974, pp. 259ff, and December 12, 1983, pp. 405ff.

[4]Standard Rate and Data Service—Radio May 1, 1974, pp. 353ff, and December 1, 1983, pp. 278ff.

[5]Standard Rate and Data Service—Television January 15, 1974, pp. 134ff, and December 15, 1983, pp. 111ff.

CONCLUSIONS

The system of campaign financing that operates in Kentucky is not perfect. There are several problems that are apparent. The consumer price index has doubled over the ten years; however, several of the essential expenditures of a campaign have more than doubled in cost. Telephone service is one example. The higher costs of phone service tend to be front loaded, that is, they occur at the beginning of the service—installation and the purchase or lease of the phone. The portion of the campaign that requires a heavy use of the phone (phone banks to identify likely voters and get out the vote drives) tends to be of a short duration. Campaigns, unlike many individuals, cannot reduce the cost of phone service by averaging these initial costs over several years, and the breakup of American Telephone and Telegraph has substantially increased costs for candidates for major offices. In order to control these costs, candidates will probably start to utilize professional "boiler room" operations in primaries and have their party headquarters house phone banks so that they can be used in general election campaigns. Large interest groups, such as organized labor or chambers of commerce, may purchase a large number of phones and make them available to candidates they support. These groups would then be able to average the costs of these phones over several campaigns.

The costs of taking out an advertisement in a local newspaper in Kentucky has generally more than doubled over the first decade since the ceiling on campaign contributions by individuals has been frozen. Table 8.4 reports that the cost of a line in the Louisville *Courier-Journal* and *Times* has increased 242 percent. A comparable advertisement in the Lexington *Herald-Leader* has increased 336 percent. An advertisement in the Kentucky *Post*, a paper serving northern Kentucky, has increased 287 percent over the decade. The Paducah *Sun* raised its advertising rates 247 percent. Many of the newspapers in smaller communities across the commonwealth have had increases comparable to the 100 percent increase in the cost of living.

The increase in the costs of advertising on radio and television stations in Kentucky have been irregular. In some markets the increases have far exceeded the consumer price index; in others the increases have been more moderate. Comparisons are made difficult because the size of the audience of the various stations vary over time, and many of the television stations have restructured their charges.

The Operation of the Kentucky Registry of Election Finance

The ability of the Kentucky Registry of Election Finance to insure compliance with the law is severely limited by its budget. The registry has an annual budget of $250,000 and is able to employ two full-time auditors. The agency is not able to perform a timely audit of the reports of each of the major contenders for high office.

Debts

Several candidates have finished their primary or general election campaigns deep in debt. These debts can raise questions about the compliance with the law. There are no legal problems if the debt is secured by the assets of the candidate, but the campaign contribution limitations may be exceeded if the loans are secured by others.

A secondary concern is generated by who pays these debts off. If the political party is obligated to pay off the debts of its losing candidates but has no control over the decision to go into debt, it may very well mortgage its ability to be competitive in future races. If the candidate with a debt is an officeholder, public policy decisions may be made with an eye to their consequences in fund raising.

On the other hand, if campaigns are forbidden to run a debt, then they may fall victim to cash flow problems. Late contributions may arrive after the deadlines to buy optimal television and radio time. Challengers may be forced to loan money during the early stages of their campaigns. If the campaign hits a responsive chord in the electorate and campaign contributions start to flow, why should the candidate not be able to recoup the money that was advanced? If the candidate were not allowed to recover the money, candidates of modest means might think twice about running.

Political Action Committees and Individual Contribution Limitations

Inflation has effectively reduced the real dollar value of maximum allowable campaign contributions. As a result, the importance of the political action committee, which is not limited in the amount of campaign contributions, has increased. Contributions by PACs have the benefit of disclosing which interest group supports which candidates. Reporters have a difficult time discovering which large individual contributions come from a particular industry. However, large PAC contributions may compromise an officeholder's independence.

185

Campaigns are big business in Kentucky. Campaign finance will be an issue in state politics for some time to come, no matter what action the general assembly takes. Public funding of elections would only shift the focus of the debate; it cannot end it.

FOOTNOTES

1. Herbert E. Alexander, *Financing the 1980 Election*, Lexington, MA: Lexington Books, 1983, p. 111.
2. "Politics and Money," *The New Yorker*, December 13, 1982, p. 76.
3. Ed Ryan, "Fund-raiser From Florence Says He's Available for Collins' Cabinet," *Courier-Journal*, August 21, 1983, p. A-1.
4. *Courier-Journal* editorial, "It's More than Simple 'Influence'," April 21, 1983, p. A-22.
5. *Courier-Journal*, editorial, "Paducah Road Flap is a Double Fiasco," August 13, 1983, p. A-6.
6. *Report of the Kentucky Registry of Election Finance*, 1973, Louisville, Kentucky, pp. 11, 128.
7. Kentucky Legislative Research Commission, Research Report No. 28, "Regulation of Campaign Contributions," Frankfort, Kentucky: November 1965, p. 2.
8. Herbert E. Alexander, *Financing Politics*, 2nd ed., Washington, D.C.: Congressional Quarterly Press, 1980, p. 26. Kentucky Legislative Research Commission, *op. cit.*, p. 2.
9. Kentucky Legislative Research Commission, *op. cit.*, p. 3.
10. 424 U.S. 1 (1976).
11. Kentucky Legislative Research Commission, *op. cit.*, p. 3.
12. *Ibid.*, p. 57 (KRS 123.030).
13. V. O. Key, Jr., *Politics, Parties & Pressure Groups*, 5th ed., New York: Thomas Y. Crowell Company, 1964, p. 489.
14. *Op. cit.*, p. 5.
15. *Ibid.*, p. 5.
16. Phone conversation between the author and Mr. Charles Tucker, a long-time political activist within the Jefferson County republican organization, August 3rd, 1983.
17. *Report of the Registry of Election Finance*, 1981, Frankfort, Kentucky.

18. *Dollar Politics*—3rd Edition, Wanig Lammers, ed. Washington, D.C.: Congressional Quarterly Press, 1982, p. 75.
19. *Report of the Registry of Election Finance*, 1979, Frankfort, Kentucky.
20. Bob Johnson, "Collins Campaign Raised Nearly $5 Million For Race," *Courier-Journal,* December 13, 1983, p. B-4.
21. *Ibid.*
22. Herbert E. Alexander, *Financing Politics*, 3rd Edition, Washington, D.C.: Congressional Quarterly Press, 1984, pp. 174-176.
23. Joel Goldstein, "Expansion of the Kentucky Political Party Tax Checkoff System" *Comparative State Politics Newsletter,* vol. 3, No. 5 (October, 1982) pp. 8-9.
24. Herbert E. Alexander, *Financing the 1980 Election,* Lexington, MA: Lexington Books, 1983, p. 423.
25. *Ibid.*
26. KRS 121.230.

Chapter 9

PUBLIC OPINION IN KENTUCKY

Michael A. Baer, Phillip W. Roeder,
and Lee Sigelman, University of Kentucky

In Kentucky, as in any other state, public opinion is a product of many different forces—geographical, historical, cultural, and political. Kentucky occupies the unique geographical position of being "the northernmost of the southern states and the southernmost of the northern states." Along the Ohio River, Kentucky is in many ways an extension of the Midwest, but along the Tennessee border it is part of the Old South. Within its borders Kentucky encompasses diversity on a scale exceeded only by such superstates as California and Texas. From the Appalachian coal fields of eastern Kentucky, through the rolling bluegrass of central Kentucky, to the farmland and strip mines of western Kentucky, the commonwealth is a land of striking contrasts—great beauty and terrible devastation, immense wealth and grinding poverty. Politically, Kentucky has in common with the states of the Confederacy the still largely unchallenged predominance of the Democratic party in politics at the state and local levels, although here again Kentucky is a land of contrasts: some counties in the southeastern part of the state are bastions of Republican strength, as they have been ever since the Civil War.

THE CULTURAL CONTEXT OF PUBLIC OPINION
IN THE COMMONWEALTH

Kentucky's unique placement and geographical and cultural characteristics shape its distinctive *political culture*—the general

188

pattern of orientations toward politics prevailing in the common-wealth. According to political scientist Daniel Elazar (1972), the foremost student of political cultures in the American states, Kentucky is highly "traditionalistic." The traditionalistic culture was carried into Kentucky during the eighteenth and nineteenth centuries by the southern stream of settlers migrating westward from Virginia and Carolina. One of the main features of tradition-alistic political cultures is a highly personalistic, rather than ideological, brand of politics. The primary purpose of government in such cultures is seen as the maintenance of the status quo rather than the fostering of major political and social change, and in that sense government is viewed negatively. Politics tends to be dominated by elites rather than by the masses, and political competition takes place among elite-dominated factions of the dominant party. The same has also been said about the Appalachian region of Kentucky, which has been characterized as a "destructive traditionalist subculture" that is "regressive" and resistant to change. Such descriptions have not gone unchallenged, however, for evidence has been found that Appalachians are activist progressives committed to individual achievement and social development rather than being traditionalistic, fatalistic, or reactionary. Speaking of another part of the state, Elazar also notes that there are pockets of an "individualistic" political culture along the Ohio River, especially in the southern suburbs of Cincinnati. The individualistic culture was carried westward by the middle stream of settlers from Pennsylvania, Maryland, and neighboring states. Politics in indi-vidualistic cultures focuses on tangible economic benefits. Political parties act as business organizations, doling out favors and respon-sibility. Politics is seen as dirty, to be left to those who soil themselves by engaging in it, often professional politicians.

The traditionalistic flavor of Kentucky's prevailing culture is quite evident in responses to a statewide opinion survey conducted in the spring of 1981 by the University of Kentucky Survey Research Center (UKSRC). (In this and its other statewide surveys, the UKSRC contacts via telephone members of more than 600 randomly selected households in the state.) Only 28 percent of those polled answered yes when asked, "Would you describe yourself as a person who likes change in your life?" and fully 73 percent agreed that "people who know you" would "be likely to describe you as a traditional person." Only 28 percent said they liked "a great deal of variety" in their lives, while 60 percent said they "like routine." A related but separate dimension of traditionalism shows up very clearly in the great pride Kentuckians take in their state. In the spring 1981 UKSRC statewide survey, 45 percent of those polled considered Kentucky an "excellent" place to live, with another 40 percent calling it "good"; only 13 percent said Kentucky was "fair" as a place to live, and a bare 2 percent termed it a "poor" place to live. For purposes of comparison, these responses are shown in Table 9.1 alongside the responses given to the very same question in statewide surveys conducted in 1981 by polling organizations in Alabama, Florida, Mississippi, New Hampshire, and New Jersey. According to Table 9.1, in none of these six states was there truly massive disenchantment, although levels of dissatisfaction were highest in Alabama, Mississippi, and especially New Jersey. Residents of New Hampshire stood out from all the rest in the pleasure they derived from living in their home state, but Kentucky, along with Florida, was rated very close to New Hampshire as a place to live.

TABLE 9.1

"Overall, how would you rate ——— as a place to live?"

Rating	Alabama	Florida	Kentucky	Mississippi	New Hampshire	New Jersey
Excellent	37%	40%	45%	38%	54%	17%
Good	44	42	40	40	38	51
Fair	16	14	13	18	7	26
Poor	3	4	2	5	1	7

Source: Spring 1981 UKSRC survey.

One other cultural feature of the commonwealth that must be borne in mind is the extent of religiosity in the state. Like every other southern state except Florida, Kentucky is overwhelmingly Protestant, with a strong element of evangelical fundamentalism. This element is quite evident in responses to the spring 1981 UKSRC statewide poll, in which 63 percent of the adult Kentuckians who were surveyed claimed to have had a "born-again" religious experience. In the same survey 67 percent of the respondents said they attended church services at least once or twice a month, and a like number said they had personally encouraged someone to accept Jesus in his/her life.

INTEREST IN GOVERNMENT AND POLITICS

Kentucky politics is often thought of as an unusually entertaining spectator sport; according to Jewell and Cunningham, Kentuckians like to think that their politicians are more flamboyant, their courthouse gangs more powerful, and their scandals more scandalous than anywhere else in the country. But, no matter how entertaining Kentucky politics may be, Kentuckians are no more interested in state politics than citizens of any other state about which comparable information is available. If anything, they may be less interested. As Table 9.2 reveals, in none of the six states for which information was available in 1981 did as many as half the people polled indicate that they were "very interested" in state politics, with the percentages ranging from a low of 26 percent in New Jersey to a high of 43 percent in Alabama. The 30 percent figure for Kentucky placed it above only New Jersey in this regard. On the other side of the coin, Kentucky outranked all the other states, including New Jersey, in the percentage of its citizens who professed to have no interest whatsoever in state politics.

TABLE 9.2

"How interested are you in ——— government?"

Interest Level	Alabama	Florida	Kentucky	Mississippi	New Hampshire	New Jersey
Very interested	43%	31%	30%	38%	32%	26%
Somewhat interested	36	44	41	38	47	46
A little interested	17	20	20	19	17	20
Not at all interested	4	5	9	5	4	7

Source: Statewide polls conducted in 1981.

All in all, levels of citizen interest in state politics seem to have varied relatively little from state to state. Still, there were some differences, as can be seen when the first two response categories ("very interested" and "somewhat interested") are combined into an overall index of interest in state politics. By that measure, citizen interest in state politics was lower—only slightly lower, to be sure, but lower nonetheless—in Kentucky than in any other state in which surveys were conducted.

One consequence of low levels of interest in state politics is widespread public ignorance of and/or misinformation about political issues. Little hard evidence is available concerning Kentuckians' knowledge of government and politics, but there are reasons to be pessimistic. In the first place, it has often been demonstrated that better educated people generally pay closer attention to and are more knowledgeable about public affairs. The fact that Kentucky ranks fiftieth among the states in the percentage of its adult citizens who are high school graduates can thus be taken as an indication of low levels of public awareness in the common-wealth.

One other relevant bit of evidence comes from a recent survey of students entering introductory geography courses at Eastern Kentucky University, the University of Kentucky, the University of Louisville, Morehead State University, Murray State University, Northern Kentucky University, and Western Kentucky University. These students were shown a map of Kentucky that had the numbers 1, 2, and 3 marked where the cities of Louisville, Frankfort, and Lexington should be. Statewide, 57 percent of the students could not identify Frankfort, the state capital; 43 percent missed on Lexington; and 30 percent were wrong on Louisville. At the University of Kentucky alone, 29 percent could not correctly identify Lexington. Nor was the students' poor preformance restricted to their knowledge of *Kentucky* geography. On a United States map, only 52 percent could identify Los Angeles, and on a world map only 11 percent identified the Persian Gulf. Of course, knowledge of geography is not the same thing as knowledge of politics and government, as it is conceivable that some people who cannot find Frankfort on a map are still reasonably well informed about state government, but the poor showing of Kentucky's "best and brightest"—the students in its state university system—on a simple map-reading exercise certainly provides little room for optimism in this regard.

PARTISANSHIP AND POLITICAL IDEOLOGY

One of the foremost nationwide political trends of recent years has been the erosion of traditional patterns of party control, such as the once solidly Democratic south. Over the years, more and more Americans have rejected any party label, while those who have persisted in calling themselves Republicans or Democrats have shown less and less hesitation about crossing party lines in particular elections. Still, the distribution of partisan sentiments is a, perhaps *the*, basic political fact of life in each state, including Kentucky. Although political scientists usually classify Kentucky as a two-party, or "competitive" state because of occasional Republican successes in races for governor and United States Senator and frequent Republican successes in races for president, in terms of sheer numbers the Democrats are much stronger in Kentucky than are the Republicans.

Table 9.3 shows the distribution of party identification in six states as of 1981. According to these figures, Kentucky stood out from every other state in two respects. First, the percentage of independents was lower in Kentucky than in any other state, and by a considerable margin. The independent share of the respondents varied from 22 percent in Kentucky all the way to 42 percent in New Hampshire. However, this does not mean that Kentuckians were of an antiparty frame of mind. Indeed, the second respect in which Kentucky stood out from the rest was in the unrivalled frequency with which citizens of the commonwealth identified with the Democratic party. More than half (52%) of all adult Kentuckians, according to these figures, considered themselves Democrats, a sharp contrast with the counterpart figure for any other state, including states traditionally dominated by the Democrats (most notably, Alabama and Mississippi).

TABLE 9.3

The Distribution of Party Identification

Party	Alabama	Florida	Kentucky	Mississippi	New Hampshire	New Jersey
Democratic	44%	40%	52%	45%	24%	32%
Independent	29	31	22	33	42	40
Republican	28	29	26	21	34	27

Source: Statewide polls conducted in 1981.

As a result of its unusually large concentration of Democratic identifiers and its unusually low percentage of independents, Kentucky ranked just behind Mississippi (where the Republican party remains very unpopular) as the state with the highest ratio of Democrats to Republicans. It is no mean feat for Kentucky

Republicans to win a statewide election when they start, as Table 9.3 indicates, with a two-to-one disadvantage in party identifiers. Their ability to do so depends on their success in getting out the vote among their party faithful and at the same time in rallying independents and Democrats to their cause, objectives that can be extraordinarily difficult to accomplish in all but relatively unusual circumstances.

According to national opinion polls, between 35 percent and 40 percent of the American public consider themselves moderates, or middle of the roaders, politically, approximately the same number call themselves conservatives, and the remainder—between 20 percent and 25 perent—think of themselves as liberals. Table 9.4 reveals that the national pattern of ideological self-placements is largely borne out in the six states for which we have comparable information, but with some interesting variations. The percentage of self-proclaimed middle of the roaders in 1981 varied from 35 percent in Alabama to 53 percent in New Hampshire, with Kentucky falling about midway between the extremes (45%). In every one of these states, including Kentucky, conservatives outnumbered liberals by a substantial margin. In four states the ratio of conservatives to liberals exceeded two to one, the exceptions being New Jersey and Kentucky, where liberal sentiments were more prevalent than in the other four states. In Alabama, there were actually more conservatives than moderates, by a 46 percent to 35 percent margin. In the two other southern states (Florida and Mississippi) and in New Jersey, there were almost even splits between conservatives and middle of the roaders. Only in Kentucky and New Hampshire did middle of the roaders significantly outnumber conservatives.

TABLE 9.4

The Distribution of Political Ideology

Self-Identification	Alabama	Florida	Kentucky	Mississippi	New Hampshire	New Jersey
Liberal	19%	18%	20%	16%	15%	22%
Middle of the Road	35	42	45	42	53	40
Conservative	46	40	35	42	32	38

Source: Statewide polls conducted in 1981.

Ideologically, then, Kentucky is less typical than several other states are of the overall American pattern of approximately equal moderate and conservative strength and lesser liberal strength. Kentucky's ideological distribution deviates from the norm largely in the unusually pronounced preference of Kentuckians for the middle of the road, a tendency that provides a fairly sharp point of contrast between Kentucky on the one hand and Alabama, Florida, and Mississippi on the other. So, even though Kentucky shares with these states a continuing preference for the Democratic party, Kentucky politics is marked by greater moderation and a less conservative tilt than politics in the remaining southern states. The reputations for ideological moderation established by so many of Kentucky's recent governors and United States Senators becomes more understandable in light of figures like those shown in Table 9.4.

PERCEPTIONS OF PROBLEMS
FACING THE COMMONWEALTH

It is not to say that Kentuckians feel that there are no important issues with which government must try to cope, only that Kentuckians tend not to be very doctrinaire in their preferences as to how government should try to cope with them. What are the problems about which Kentuckians are most concerned? In the spring of 1982, citizens of Alabama, Florida, and Kentucky were asked to name the most important problem facing their state. In Kentucky, 48 percent of those polled mentioned unemployment, 23 percent named inflation, and 8 percent cited taxes, bringing to 79 percent the total who mentioned economic problems of some sort. The ony noneconomic problem that gained any widespread mention in Kentucky was state government, the operation of which was perceived as the state's greatest problem by 9 percent. In Alabama there was an even greater tendency to single out unemployment, which 53 percent mentioned. Another 17 percent of the Alabamans pointed to inflation as the state's foremost problem, but taxes received only scattered mention as a pressing problem. Overall, then, Alabamans were somewhat less fixated on economic issues than were Kentuckians. Alabamans also mentioned other problems, such as education (9%) and crime (4%) much more frequently than Kentuckians did.

The Florida responses contrast sharply with those from both Kentucky and Alabama. Only 16 percent of the Florida sample

195

pointed to unemployment or inflation as great problems, reflecting the fact that the Florida economy was much more robust than that of either Kentucky of Alabama; indeed, 6 percent of those surveyed in Florida singled out the fact that economic growth was proceeding too rapidly as the state's greatest problem. In Florida by far the foremost problems were seen as crime (23%) and refugees (18%), in comparison to which all other problems, including economic ones, were seen as secondary.

Perceptions of problems fluctuate rapidly over time. It should hardly come as a great surprise to learn that in the midst of a national recession, which struck Kentucky particularly hard, most Kentuckians were worried about the economy. Presumably gradual economic recovery will ease these concerns somewhat. In fact, there are some recent signs that education may be replacing the economy as a priority problem in the minds of many Kentuckians. For the moment, though, it seems accurate to classify the foremost concerns of Kentuckians as being based on economic problems.

EVALUATIONS OF STATE GOVERNMENT

As just noted, some Kentuckians view their state government as the greatest problem presently facing the state. Indeed, very few Kentuckians assign high marks to Kentucky state government for its overall performance: according to a 1981 UKSRC poll, only 4 percent rated the quality of state government in Kentucky excellent, as opposed to good, fair, or poor. On the other hand, very few Kentuckians are acutely dissatisfied with the quality of state government, as evidenced by the fact that only 7 percent rated state government poor. By far the greatest number of Kentuckians indicated that in their view the quality of Kentucky state government was either good (46%) or fair (43%). So, it would appear that Kentuckians are in general reasonably well satisfied with the quality of state government they receive.

These figures become much easier to interpret in the context of responses to the same question by citizens of other states. In 1981 citizens of Alabama, Mississippi, New Hampshire, and New Jersey were asked the same question. Table 9.5 indicates that there were no large differences among states in the percentage of citizens who gave their state government a rating of excellent. However, the frequency of poor ratings did vary considerably, with Alabama standing alone in this regard; almost one Alabaman in five said that state government was poor in Alabama. More generally, residents of New Hampshire were most positive about their state government, and residents of Alabama and New Jersey were least positive about government in their states. Kentucky state government ranked alongside that of Mississippi—both somewhat behind New Hampshire but well ahead of New Jersey and Alabama. Thus, it is fair to say that Kentuckians are by no means as proud of their state government as they are of their state, but their evaluations of Kentucky state government are still fairly high relative to the evaluations expressed by citizens in some other states.

TABLE 9.5

Ratings of the Quality of State Government

Rating	Alabama	Kentucky	Mississippi	New Hampshire	New Jersey
Excellent	3%	4%	6%	7%	3%
Good	28	46	43	50	36
Fair	51	43	44	36	50
Poor	18	7	8	7	11

Source: Statewide polls conducted in 1981.

EVALUATIONS OF GOVERNMENT SERVICES

Do these fairly positive evaluations of state government reflect satisfaction with the services Kentuckians are receiving? In many instances citizens do not know which level of government is providing certain services. However, we can still get a general measure of their satisfaction with state government services by examining responses to a series of questions asked by the UKSRC in its statewide poll.

On several occasions the UKSRC has asked its respondents about their satisfaction with the "general quality of services for the taxes" they pay. Table 9.6 indicates the proportion of respondents who said they were satisfied with state services in general and in seven specific service areas in 1979, 1982, and 1983. We can see that a greater proportion of Kentuckians were satisfied with the general quality of government services in the latter two polls than in 1979. It is surely no coincidence that there was a change in gubernatorial administrations between 1979 and 1982.

TABLE 9.6

Kentuckians' Ratings of Government Services
(% Responding "Very Satisfied" or "Satisfied")

	Spring 1979	Spring 1982	Spring 1983
Quality of government services	42	58	51
Public libraries	83	84	86
Parks and other recreational facilities	80	83	81
Higher educational facilities	76	74	75
Consumer protection	62	71	68
Elementary and high schools	60	58	66
Public welfare system	36	33	36

Source: Statewide polls conducted in 1979, 1982, and 1983.

However, when one examines responses in the specific service areas, one sees that satisfaction increased dramatically only in the areas of the condition of roads and consumer protection. Both of these areas were emphasized by the Brown administration, including a strong consumer protection effort spearheaded by then-Attorney General Steven Beshear. Levels of public satisfaction with other services, including parks and recreation facilities, public libraries, elementary and high schools, higher educational facilities, and the public welfare system remained stable from 1979 to 1983. Only in the area of public welfare do we find less than a majority of respondents indicating satisfaction with state government services. On the basis of Table 9.6, then, it seems clear that although there is variation from service to service in the satisfaction Kentuckians expressed, these services were generally considered satisfactory.

OPINION ON TAXING AND SPENDING

Another means of evaluating satisfaction with services and assessing priorities among services is to ask people whether they want government to spend more, less, or about the same amount for various programs. In recent years public elementary and secondary schools and streets and highways have been the highest spending priorities of Kentuckians, with spending for colleges and universities, the environment, police, and prisons being viewed less favorably. In comparing these spending priorities with the service evaluations summarized in Table 9.6, it is difficult to ascertain whether people want government to spend more on services they are relatively satisfied with or on programs they consider deficient. However, the tendency seems to be more toward the latter than the former: Kentuckians rate the conditions of their roads as poor relative to other services and appear willing to spend more to improve them; on the other hand, they rate higher education highly and hesitate to spend more on it.

Table 9.7 reveals that the spending priorities of its citizens tend to differ from those of residents of other states. Along with Alabamans and Mississippians, Kentuckians are especially likely to want to spend more on public schools and streets and highways. Kentuckians are also unusually resistant to greater spending for police, higher education, and programs for the poor.

Of course, these services have to be paid for with public funds. If Kentuckians tend to be satisfied with the services they receive, are they equally positive about the tax moneys that are used to pay for these services? When confronted with the choice of cutting services or cutting taxes, how do they respond?

As in many other areas, the answer depends on the way one asks the question. When asked in 1980 whether taxes should be cut even if services had to be cut or whether "we need these public services even if it means paying the same taxes," only 21 percent of Kentuckians advocated cutting taxes, and 67 percent said "we need the services." However, when told in 1981 that the state would lose 10 percent of the money it planned to spend on numerous programs and then asked whether the state should raise taxes or "cut back further on services," 58 percent said services should be cut further. A similar question was asked in 1982, and a similar proportion (53%) said they preferred to reduce services. Thus, it appears that when presented with a trade-off between raising taxes and reducing government services, most Kentuckians prefer reducing services. However, when the choice is between maintaining services with the same level of taxes or reducing taxes, a majority favors the status quo. These

199

TABLE 9.7

Spending Priorities in Six States

Spending On	Alabama	Florida	Kentucky	Mississippi	New Hampshire	New Jersey
Environment						
More	25%	49%	30%	44%	38%	57%
Same	58	44	53	39	45	33
Less	18	8	18	17	17	10
Programs for the Poor						
More	54	42	42	48	42	49
Same	31	41	37	36	41	36
Less	15	17	22	16	18	16
Public Schools						
More	73	61	62	74	46	52
Same	24	35	32	22	40	40
Less	4	4	6	4	14	9
Streets and Highways						
More	58	38	52	63	30	43
Same	35	54	42	32	60	47
Less	7	9	6	5	10	10
Police Forces						
More	61	81	48	64	34	55
Same	33	17	46	29	58	39
Less	6	2	7	7	8	6
Higher Education						
More	43	49	42	63	40	47
Same	49	46	48	32	50	41
Less	8	5	11	5	10	12

Source: Statewide polls conducted in 1981.

responses reflect in large measure Kentuckians' overall feelings about the taxes they pay. About half of the citizens of Kentucky (48%) consider the state and local taxes they pay too high, while another half (49%) call their taxes about right. As Table 9.8 reveals, this pattern contrasts markedly with those found in Florida, where only a small minority view their state and local taxes as too high, and New Jersey, where almost two-thirds of the public believes taxes are too high.

TABLE 9.8

Opinions on State and Local Tax Levels

Tax Level	Alabama	Florida	Kentucky	Mississippi	New Hampshire	New Jersey
Much Too High	15%	3%	21%	18%	17%	33%
Somewhat Too High	25	10	27	23	26	31
About Right	53	83	49	55	53	35
Too Low	6	4	2	4	5	1

Source: Statewide polls conducted in 1981.

OPINIONS ON EDUCATION-RELATED ISSUES

A major responsibility of state and local governments is education. This is a matter of special concern in Kentucky, which presently ranks last among the fifty states in the proportion of persons twenty-five or older who are high school graduates and which ranks forty-third in spending per pupil.

Surveys conducted by the UKSRC show increasing concern with education. In response to identical questions asked in 1979 and 1983, the proportion of Kentuckians who identified education as the most important or the second most important problem facing the state climbed from 17 percent in 1979 to 34 percent in 1983. Nonetheless, Kentuckians tend to be relatively well satisfied with their schools. However, in spite of this increased concern, a majority (53%) of Kentuckians in late 1983 expressed satisfaction with their local school system, and three Kentuckians out of every four were satisfied with the state's higher education system.

Other education-related issues are related to the traditionalism and religiosity of the state. For example, in 1981 a substantial majority (71%) of Kentuckians supported prayer in the public schools, slightly above the counterpart figure for the nation as a whole. Moreover, an overwhelming majority (87%) favor displaying a copy of the Ten Commandments in public school classrooms, and there is also fairly widespread support for the teaching of scientific creationism, which is favored by 50 percent and opposed by 36 percent.

Once again, however, these opinions are more complex than they may initially seem. In spite of their strong preference for posting the Ten Commandments on the walls of public school classrooms, 60 percent of Kentuckians agree that the Supreme Court decision disallowing this practice should be obeyed. There is, then, a conflict between the pull of religious convictions, on the one hand, and the deeply held conviction that the law should be obeyed.

Along these same lines, about 70 percent of Kentuckians believe that sex education should be part of the public school curriculum. This indicates widespread support for a nontraditional aspect of education, but it should also be recognized that Kentuckians are less supportive of sex education than are Americans in many other parts of the country; in the nation as a whole, a 1981 NBC News survey uncovered 75 percent approval of sex education in the schools.

OPINION ON CONTROVERSIAL POLITICAL
AND SOCIAL ISSUES

We noted earlier the unique geographical placement of Kentucky, which provides the setting for differences that carry far beyond the contrast of natural beauty and demolished landscapes into political philosophy, party ideology, and clashes between the modern and the traditional. How, then, does Kentucky stack up on today's most controversial political and social issues? Are these contrasts still apparent, or have Kentuckians taken positions that distinguish them as highly traditionalistic?

Issues that may clarify Kentucky's political position today include abortion and the Equal Rights Amendment. In a traditionalistic society one might expect widespread support for the status quo rather than for sweeping social change. Positions on both abortion and the ERA are related to conceptions of traditional family, work, and social roles. Support for the ERA can be interpreted as indicating a willingness to change the existing social structure. Support for legal abortions might indicate a recognition that women need not be placed only in the traditional positions of childbearer and homemaker.

Kentuckians are in the American mainstream on the ERA. UKSRC respondents were asked in 1981, "Do you strongly favor, favor, oppose, or strongly oppose the Equal Rights Amendment—also known as the ERA—the constitutional amendment concerning women?" Fifty-three percent of those surveyed favored the ERA. The same question was asked of a national sample by the CBS News/*New York Times* poll in 1980 and received positive responses from 53 percent of the respondents—exactly the same as in Kentucky.

Abortion is a more complex issue. There is a whole range of positions that one may take on abortion, including total freedom for unlimited abortion, permitting abortion only under conditions of health, incest or rape, permitting abortion only if it is not publicly funded, or making abortion illegal under any circumstances. The spring 1981 UKSRC Poll asked whether the decision to have an abortion should be left to a woman and her physician. Sixty-three percent of Kentuckians said that it should. In the same survey, respondents were asked whether they would favor a constitutional amendment to allow Congress and the states to restrict or prohibit abortions. Fifty-one percent said they would favor such an amendment. To add to the confusion, on the same poll 57 percent indicated that they believe abortion is wrong, and of those who considered it wrong about three-fifths said it should be illegal. Of all Kentuckians, 37 percent said abortion should not be legal.

How do these attitudes toward abortion compare with those of other Americans? According to Table 9.9, Kentuckians are unusually supportive of a constitutional amendment outlawing abortion—almost twice as supportive as Americans in general and much more supportive than citizens of any other state for which comparable data are available.

TABLE 9.9

Opinions on a Constitutional Amendment to Allow Prohibition of Abortions

Position	Kentucky	U.S.	Illinois	New Jersey	New York	Ohio	Pennsylvania
In favor	51%	32%	29%	27%	27%	31%	34%
Opposed	43	58	55	58	60	53	50
No opinion	6	10	16	15	13	16	16

Source: Fall 1981 UKSRC poll and September-October CBS/*New York Times* surveys.

A final controversial issue is gun control. In Kentucky only the federal requirement that a handgun purchaser be a resident of the state is in force, though a few counties have local ordinances that are slightly more stringent. However, a spring 1983 UKSRC poll found that 50 percent of those surveyed favored stricter laws regulating the sale of handguns. Even so, support for gun control remains lower in Kentucky than it is nationwide; according to a 1981 NBC News/ Associated Press poll, 70 percent of Americans favor a law that would require a person to obtain a police permit before buying a handgun.

CONCLUSION

We are unable in this chapter to consider the fascinating and important question of opinion differences *within* Kentucky. Is the Appalachian region really distinctive in terms of the political and social views of its inhabitants? Are residents of northern Kentucky really northerners, politically speaking, while those who live in the southern part of the state hold positions more typical of southerners?

The data summarized here simply do not address these questions. Nor do they permit us more than a fleeting glimpse of how Kentuckians' attitudes and opinions have evolved over the course of time. Is Kentucky becoming less distinctive politically than it may once have been, melding into a middle American homogeneity? Are new issues coming to the fore and old ones dropping by the wayside? These are important questions for which we have no ready answers.

Our data do, however, indicate that the widely held view of Kentucky as a traditionalistic political culture is both accurate and inaccurate. It is accurate in terms of certain general tendencies, but it is inaccurate as a stereotype. There is an overriding status quo orientation in Kentuckians' attitudes toward their own lives as well as toward political institutions and public policies. Kentucky is not a hotbed of mass political activity; as is true of traditionalistic political cultures in general, levels of political interest in Kentucky are relatively low, and Kentuckians are apparently not very knowledgeable about public affairs. Most Kentuckians continue to identify with the dominant Democratic party, though they often defect to the Republicans in state and national elections. Kentuckians are most concerned about the same political issues that most concern the citizens of other relatively underdeveloped southern states such as Alabama and Mississippi—most notably, schools and roads. They are far less concerned about quality of life issues such as higher education and environmental protection. They generally are satisfied with the quality of their state government and the specific government services they receive and would resist increasing the taxes they pay to support these services. On a number of controversial political and social issues, they do not speak with a single voice, but their overall opinions are somewhat more conservative than those found in many other parts of the country.

These tendencies toward traditionalism and conservatism should not be overstated, however, for they are only tendencies — and not always very strong ones at that. Public opinion in Kentucky does display certain traditionalistic elements, but Kentucky is by no means an unalloyed example of the traditionalistic culture. The geographical and cultural diversity of the state has made far too deep an impression on its political life for public opinion in the commonwealth to be so readily categorized.

Chapter 10

BLACKS IN KENTUCKY POLITICS
An Overview

Cassie Osborne, Jr., with assistance from James Graves,
Kentucky State University

The political history of blacks in Kentucky in many respects has reflected the political experiences of blacks in the nation at large and the South in particular. To be sure, the inhumane institution of slavery and lynching were dominant facets of Kentucky's early political history, leading to a rigid Jim Crow system for much of the twentieth century. Blacks in Kentucky have enjoyed the right of suffrage with little resistance from whites after 1870. However, the state has generally taken a "southern approach" to race relations. Notwithstanding the fact that Kentucky is a border state with a small black population, the struggle for full political equality has reflected the black struggle for political equality in the Deep South. It would be unwise, nevertheless, to begin our discussion with a superficial comparison of the political experience of black Kentuckians with the political status of blacks in the Deep South. Our focus will be on those factors which are unique to the political history of blacks in Kentucky, for such an approach will enhance our understanding of the historical as well as the contemporary status of blacks in the state.[1]

As often is the case, most literature on black politics has suffered from a narrow conceptualization of black political life in the United States. Consequently, it has often been atheoretical and journalistic in nature, resulting in a lack of understanding of the political experience of black Americans.[2] Thus, in our effort to avoid such shortcomings and to conform to techniques designed to add theoretical import, we will not only look at ways in which blacks have affected politics in Kentucky through traditional political methods

205

(registration, voting, and officeholding) but also focus on ways in which they have indirectly affected the politics in Kentucky.[3] As Prestage and Williams have noted, "The latter consideration has received only limited attention in the literature of black politics.[4]

The political history of blacks in Kentucky will be discussed within five historical periods: (1) slavery, 1770 to 1861; (2) Civil War, 1861 to 1865; (3) Reconstruction, 1865 to 1890; (4) post-Reconstruction and the formal reimposition of white supremacy, 1890 to 1954; (5) the struggle for full social and political equality—the contemporary epoch—1954 to the present. These periods represent distinct segments in the political life of black Kentuckians. Within each period the political forces acting on blacks and black reactions to them were markedly different.[5]

THE PERIOD OF SLAVERY
(1770 to 1861)

When Kentucky became the nation's fifteenth state in 1792, slavery as an economic institution was well entrenched in the political culture of the United States. Although there was considerable controversy over the slavery issue at Kentucky's first constitutional convention, the proslavery forces were successful in including a proviso in the state's constitution that prohibited the legislature from enacting statutes that would emancipate slaves without the consent of the slaveholder.[6] Thus, Kentucky, like many of her sister states, succumbed to the oppressive proslavery forces, and thereafter the status of slavery in Kentucky became one of the chief issues in Kentucky's political life until this institution was finally eradicated by the national government through the Thirteenth Amendment to the United States Constitution in 1865.[7]

The exact date marking the entry of slavery in Kentucky is unknown, but it is generally believed that slaves were among the first settlers of the state.[8] When Captain John Cowan recorded the number of settlers living in Harrod's Fort in 1777, 19 of the population of some 198 were blacks. Twelve of the slaves were age ten or older, while seven were less than ten years of age. From that day on, the slave population in Kentucky increased rapidly. In 1790 when the first census was taken, almost twelve thousand of nearly seventy-five thousand inhabitants living in Kentucky were slaves, and some one hundred were free blacks.[9] This population of slaves and free blacks continued to increase; by 1860 there were 225,483 slaves and 10,684 free blacks in Kentucky (Table 10.1).[10]

TABLE 10.1

The Growth of the Black Population in Kentucky from 1790 to 1860

	Slaves	Percent Increase	Free Blacks	Percent Increase
1790	11,830		144	
1800	40,343	241.02	741	550.00
1810	80,561	99.69	1,713	131.17
1820	126,732	57.31	2,759	61.06
1830	165,213	30.36	4,917	78.21
1840	182,258	10.31	7,317	48.81
1850	210,981	15.75	10,011	36.81
1860	225,483	6.87	10,684	6.72

Source: "Slavery in Kentucky" by Ivan E. McDougle in *The Journal of Negro History* (III July, 1918).

It is constructive to note that the slave population increased faster than the white population in Kentucky from 1790 to 1830.[11] After 1830, however, the slave population declined, due in part to the 1833 Nonimportation Act, which forbade the importation of slaves in Kentucky other than for personal use.[12]

Slavery in Kentucky, as in other slaveholding states, was a minority institution, for the majority of white Americans did not own slaves. In Kentucky, only 28 percent of white families owned slaves. The 1850 census shows that the 38,385 slaveholders had 210,981 slaves, or an average of 5.4 for each owner.[13] Table 10.2 reveals the classification of slaveholders in Kentucky according to the number of slaves held. The data indicate that 22,528, or 58 percent, of Kentucky's slaveholders held fewer than five slaves and that 96 percent of the slaveholders owned fewer than twenty slaves.[14]

As the slave population increased in the state, slave labor became increasingly important, and Kentucky, as well as other border states, began to breed slaves for the Southern market.[15] Slave trading became a major commercial enterprise between Kentucky and the Deep South. It is difficult to establish the specific date for the beginning of the relationship between Kentucky and Southern slave traders, but as early as 1818, slaves were being sold to Mississippi.[16] In any event, by 1843 slave trading became a well-established economic enterprise in Kentucky. The city of Lexington, located in the heart

TABLE 10.2

Classification of Slaveholders by
the Number of Slaves Owned, 1850

Holders of 1 slave	9,244
Holders of over 1 and less than 5 slaves	13,284
Holders of 5 and under 10 slaves	9,579
Holders of 10 and under 20 slaves	5,022
Holders of 20 and under 50 slaves	1,198
Holders of 50 and under 100 slaves	53
Holders of 100 and under 200 slaves	5
TOTAL	**38,385**

Source: "Slavery in Kentucky" by Ivan E. McDougle in *The Journal of Negro History* (III July, 1918).

of the bluegrass region, where the agricultural system demanded a larger enslaved populace, was by now a major slave-trading center. In addition to Lexington, slave trading occurred throughout the bluegrass, including the city of Louisville, the state's largest urban area.[17]

The slave trade in Kentucky was enhanced when, in 1849, the legislature repealed the anti-importation law and exonerated from punishment all those who had violated the act.[18] Slave traders were given further insurance in 1849 with the adoption of a resolution denouncing abolition by the Kentucky House of Representatives.[19]

Slave trading, and the inhumane institution of slavery, was motivated by economic rewards. The importance of the slave trade to Kentucky's economy is indicated by the fact that in 1859 Kentucky objected strongly to reopening the African slave trade.[20] A number of the state's newspapers printed editorials on the impact reopening the African slave trade would have on Kentucky's economy. A typical example is an editorial sent to a Vicksburg newspaper by a Kentuckian stating that reinstituting African trade would ruin Kentucky because the slave trade was a major source of revenue for the state.[21] To underscore this point, it is estimated that Kentucky sent from 2,500 to 4,000 slaves annually to the southern market.[22]

The highest percentage of slaveholding families in Kentucky was found among the bluegrass counties, where economic conditions were more favorable to the slave system. In the mountain areas of the state, few slaves were found because the institution was unprofitable.

For example, in 1860 at the time when slaves made up a sizable proportion of Kentucky's population, the smallest number of slave-holding families was found among eastern Kentucky counties (Table 10.3).

TABLE 10.3

**Slaveholding Counties with
the Lowest Number of Slaves in 1860**

Counties	Number of Slaves
Jackson	7
Johnson	27
Magoffin	71
Perry	73
Pike	97

Source: *Slavery Times in Kentucky* by J. Winston Coleman, Jr. Copyright 1940 The University of North Carolina Press. Used with permission of the publisher.

Slaves were concentrated on small plantations and farms, where "political life was determined by the object of economic gain."[23] Hence, every aspect of slave life was conditioned by economic considerations, and whatever activity the master perceived would contribute to the productivity of slave labor was employed. In an effort to increase the productivity of slaves, whipping, sexual exploitation, overwork, and other excessive and cruel methods were common. Family life as we know it today did not exist for slaves, and the black father-husband role had no legal status.[24] Slaves often worked from sunup to sundown, and in many cases they were required to do chores in the master's house during times usually considered to be their own.[25] The bulk of slaves in Kentucky were engaged in field and domestic work on small plantations; others worked in nonskilled and skilled trades. They worked in iron, salt, and lead mines and in specialized occupations such as mechanics, engineering, and other skilled trades.

In most slaveholding states, education had no legal status; however, Kentucky was one of the few slave states that never passed any statutes forbidding education for slaves or freedmen. As a result, some slaves learned to read, but very few learned to write, for it was felt that they might be tempted to forge passes in their owner's names. One study that analyzes runaway slave advertisements in Kentucky found only 71 of 350 cases in which the advertisement mentioned slaves who could read and only 27 instances in which slaves could write.[26]

Although members of the slave community had no political rights and could not participate in traditional political activities, it is clear that slaves did not constitute an inactive element in Kentucky from 1770 to 1865.[27] In Kentucky, as elsewhere, slaves rebelled against their oppressive status. This action manifested itself through a number of nonpolitical acts such as work slowdown, destruction of the master's property, self-mutilation, suicide, escape, revolt, and often violence against slave owners. Kentucky had its share of these forms of nonpolitical expression.[28] According to Herbert Aptheker, there were more than ten instances of organized defiance to the institution of slavery from 1810 through 1860.[29] In 1862 a group of slaves who had been sold to slave traders from the Deep South overpowered and killed their new masters. Furthermore, in that same year a massive slave revolt took place in Kentucky when a group of seventy-five slaves on a ship headed to New Orleans gained control of the ship and guided it to the Indiana shores. The oppressive nature of slave life and the closed society in which slaves operated added a distinctly political component to these actions.

Slaves in Kentucky had considerable indirect influence on the formal political process of the state. They were the subject of a substantial body of laws designed to regulate their behavior and upkeep. The first slave codes in Kentucky were modeled after the slave code from Virginia, and it was not until the legislative session of 1798 that an omnibus slave code was enacted. The 1798 legislature enacted forty-three articles involving almost every legal consideration in connection with the institution. These articles remained the basis of all legal provisions throughout the entire slavery period in Kentucky. These codes, however, were periodically amended by the state legislature consistent with its views of what was needed to control slaves.[30] Kentucky's slave codes restricted the movement of slaves. Slaves were not allowed to leave the master's plantation without written permission and were forbidden to carry weapons, engage in riots, or to assemble without the presence of a white man. Strict punishment was provided for those who broke the law, including the imposition of the death penalty for such acts as arson, poisoning the master's food, and taking the life of the master.[31] The central point, as it relates to the slave codes in Kentucky, is not what they contained but rather what they delineated as formal public policy and what this policy necessitated as "structures and processes for formulation, implementation, and enforcement."[32]

In addition to the slaves, free blacks made up a sizable proportion of Kentucky's population during the period of slavery in Kentucky. As has been noted, there were 144 free blacks in Kentucky in 1790, and by 1860 that number had risen to 10,684.[33] The status of free blacks was only somewhat better than slaves—they were social and economic misfits in a slaveholding community. Their presence was a potential threat to the slave system in Kentucky, and they lived in constant fear of being sold into slavery. These were legitimate fears, as there were several instances where free blacks were sold back into slavery because their free papers had been lost or destroyed.[34]

Laws governing the behavior of free blacks were very strict. Free blacks could not associate with their enslaved brethren, and their relations with whites were conditioned by economic considerations. In its effort to prevent interaction between free blacks and slaves, the legislature established severe penalties for free blacks who furnished forged free papers to slaves, aided runaway slaves, assisted slaves in their escape, and attended meetings with slaves without the presence of whites. Free blacks were subject to the death penalty for burning public buildings and tobacco houses or for the rape of white women.[35] Moreover, free blacks could be sold into servitude for two to ten years if they were convicted of keeping a disorderly house or of not having a visible means of subsistence. If a free black left the state to go into a nonslavery state, he was held to have forfeited his right to live in Kentucky. When the white majority felt threatened by free blacks, they were dealt with harshly. Often their homes were raided by slaveholders searching for runaways and for free blacks who entered the state from other political subdivisions in the United States, as blacks were not permitted to emigrate to Kentucky from other states.

Many of Kentucky's free blacks were small businessmen or skilled artisans; some were well educated, and many became considerably wealthy.[36] Businesses established by free blacks included barbershops and other businesses that catered exclusively to free blacks. These businesses were found, for the most part, in urban areas of the state where employment opportunities were greatest, where most free blacks were concentrated, and where their freedom was least noticeable.[37] This class became the core of the black leadership in Kentucky during the Reconstruction and the post-Reconstruction periods.

Kentucky's free blacks were not happy with their *de jure* status of quasi freedom. Thus, they engaged in several activities designed to ameliorate their oppressive condition and to some degree that of their enslaved brethren.[38] Many free blacks fled to nonslaveholding states when restrictive regulations were enacted by the state legislature in 1830 and just before the Civil War. In addition, free blacks aided by the Kentucky Colonization Society migrated within the borders of the United States, and others went to Africa and Canada. In an effort to remove free blacks from Kentucky, the state legislature passed a law appropriating $5,000 annually to the Kentucky Colonization Society.[39] This was a losing cause, however, because the society enjoyed limited success in its efforts to export free blacks out of the state.[40]

There is little evidence that free blacks in Kentucky struggled for the right to vote after the constitutional convention of 1799 restricted the right to vote to white males. Thus, although free blacks in Kentucky did not participate in the formal governmental apparatus, they did have an indirect impact on the political system during the slavery era. They were the subject of a sizable body of legal codes and were active in movements designed to influence the nature and character of the political system in Kentucky.

CIVIL WAR
(1861 to 1865)

The Civil War, one of the most important political events in the history of the United States, had a profound impact on the political experience of black Americans and the nation at large. Kentucky played a decisive role in this internal conflict. As a border and a slaveholding state espousing a political philosophy heavily grounded in the slave political economy, Kentucky repudiated secession from the Union and was one of the few slave states that remained faithful to the Union during the Civil War.[41] Kentucky's support for the Union was predicated on the premise that the Civil War was an effort to save the Union and the institution of slavery. At the same time, Kentucky's position of neutrality and her support for the Union produced sharp political fragmentation within the state, as some of her citizens supported the Confederacy.[42]

When Kentucky was invaded by the Confederate forces, she abandoned her position of neutrality and reaffirmed her support for the Union, reiterating her stand that "no slaves would be set free by any military commanders."[43] Because Kentucky never abandoned the Union, slavery continued throughout and for sometime after the

Civil War.[44] Moreover, during this period the legislature maintained and expanded its efforts to control free blacks and slaves by enacting statutes rejecting the national government's efforts to abolish slavery in the United States.

Unlike free blacks and slaves in some of the states of the Deep South, who were encouraged to enlist in the Union Army after 1862, all blacks in Kentucky were prohibited from participating in the Union Army, and slaves were returned to their masters.[45] To support this policy, the legislature produced a resolution in 1861 that reinforced the notion that "slavery was a state institution guaranteed by the federal constitution and that the National government to which we are intended to be loyal, shall undertake no action to emancipate slaves against the will of the slaveholding states."[46] Thus, with this action Kentucky again claimed its traditional position on state rights. Free blacks and slaves were not accepted into the Union ranks officially before 1864, but there developed in Kentucky a policy of using runaway slaves on military projects. As a result, a large number of slaves were used to construct fortifications, to repair railroads, and to bring military supplies for Union forces.[47] In the central part of Kentucky, a large number of slaves were put to work on roads, and by the middle of 1863, officials of the Union Army were calling for 6,000 slaves to extend the railway from Lebanon to Danville.[48]

In the western section of the state, Union forces raided plantations and recruited into the army slaves who desired to leave their masters.[49] When Union soldiers appeared in Lexington at several slave churches, all black men were arrested and lodged in jails until they could be sent to work on military projects.[50] In the spring of 1863, it was estimated that slaves deserted the fields in the midst of the growing season at a rate of 100 a day in many parts of the state. In Madison County, a black regiment was used to scour the fields and force slaves into the Union Army. By the end of 1863, over ten thousand slaves had left their masters.[51] For all practical purposes, the enlistment of slaves in the Union Army ended the slave system in Kentucky, although legally slavery still existed. Yet, in 1863 the Kentucky legislature refused to ratify the Thirteenth Amendment and passed legislation to nullify its execution.[52]

In 1864, when Kentucky officials changed state policy on black enlistment in the Union Army, blacks found themselves with the first legal opportunity to act against their oppression through direct enlistment in the Union Army.[53] Both slaves and free blacks responded quickly to this new opportunity and enlisted in large numbers. According to one historian, Kentucky supplied the second largest number of black soldiers to the Union Army.[54] Of the 178,975 black soldiers who fought within the Union ranks, 23,073 came from Kentucky. The state was outnumbered only by Louisiana, from which 24,053 blacks decided to join the Union Army.[55]

Black soldiers who served in the Union ranks were given few opportunities for combat. One account states that blacks were used behind combat lines to dig trenches, haul supplies, rebuild damaged railroads, and do the menial work, thereby freeing more white soldiers for battle.[56] When blacks were afforded the opportunity to participate in combat, they distinguished themselves valiantly on the battle field.[57] However, many black soldiers paid the ultimate price: casualty rates were heavier for black soldiers than for their white counterparts because of inadequate medical treatment, and the Confederate troops carried out their policy of murdering black soldiers rather than taking them prisoners.[58]

The number of blacks from Kentucky who enlisted in the Confederate Army has never been accurately determined, but the Confederacy was the first to recognize black labor as a military factor in the Civil War.[59] At first, however, only a few blacks were permitted to use guns, and like their brethren in the Union Army, they were involved in little combat.[60] Blacks who served in the Union and Confederate Armies were considered to constitute a Jim Crow class, for discrimination existed in pay between black and white soldiers, and blacks were generally segregated in colored regiments commanded by white officials.[61] In sum, it is clear that blacks influenced the political system in Kentucky directly during the Civil War through their participation as soldiers both in the Union and Confederate armies and through the development of organized protest movements against their legal status in the antebellum society.[62]

RECONSTRUCTION
(1865 to 1890)

By 1863, slavery had been abolished in most areas of the United States by various methods. In the Confederate states, the institution was abolished by the Emancipation Proclamation and policies of the Union Army.[63] In West Virginia, Maryland, and Tennessee the institution was abolished by the state legislatures. Nevertheless, in Kentucky and Delaware slavery continued after the Civil War, and Kentucky rejected every effort to abolish slavery. Indeed, public sentiment against the Thirteenth Amendment within the state was so strong that when the Amendment was submitted to Congress for ratification, Kentucky's senators voted against it. Moreover, when the amendment was presented for ratification in the Kentucky State Legislature, it was rejected by a vote of fifty-seven to twenty-eight in the house of representatives and twenty-one to twelve in the senate.[64] In spite of this opposition, the Thirteenth Amendment was ratified by twenty-seven states in 1865.

With the institution of slavery no longer part of the Kentucky political culture, blacks took steps to gain full political equality. Because Kentucky was not subject to the Reconstruction policies of the federal government as the secession states were, black political participation as voters and officeholders was retarded in Kentucky during the Reconstruction era. Nevertheless, this was the first period in which black Kentuckians were given the legal opportunity to participate in any form of traditional political involvement after the Civil War.[65] Blacks in Kentucky, as elsewhere in the American South, were very active during this period. They developed political organizations, participated in political partisan activities, and pressed for full political, economic, and social equality. Although blacks were given the right to vote by the Fifteenth Amendment, they did not contest for public offices during the Reconstruction era because they were prohibited from doing so by policies of the Republican and Democratic parties. As a result, black empowerment did not become a reality in Kentucky as it did in the Reconstructed states; nevertheless, the direct and indirect influence of blacks on the state's political system was considerable during Reconstruction. As early as 1865, blacks held protest meetings throughout the state and agitated for the right to vote, as well as for equality under the state constitution. In December of 1865, black leaders met and organized a political rally that was held in Louisville during January to celebrate the Emancipation Proclamation.[66] The celebration was attended by nearly 5,000 blacks from all areas of the state. At the meeting blacks adopted several resolutions petitioning the Kentucky State Legislature and the United States Congress for political equality.

The Kentucky legislature responded to the black demands for equality by passing a civil rights bill. While the civil rights bill generally conferred the same civil rights that whites had, the law put blacks in an inferior position in that they were denied the right to vote, the right to testify against whites in Kentucky courts, the right to serve on juries, and the right to an equal educational system. In addition, the 1866 Kentucky Civil Rights Act placed blacks in a dependent position as the economic arrangement gave former slaveholders firm control over the freedman. Thus, with the passage of the Kentucky 1866 Civil Rights Act, black Kentuckians were left in a semislave status; consequently, black political activities during this period were designed to change that position. Obtaining the right to vote was at the center of black political activity during this period.

Kentucky's political parties and the general population were against full equality for blacks, and this resistance often became a primary issue in political campaigns during the post-Civil War era.[67] In 1866, the Republican party of Kentucky, which remained the minority party during the Reconstruction period, took a state's rights position with respect to the black suffrage question by adopting a resolution favoring the right of each state to set qualifications for voting.[68] The Kentucky Republican opposition to black suffrage conflicted with the national Republican party's position on this issue. At the same time, resistance to black suffrage by white Democrats was almost cohesive, but not exclusively so. Strands of support for black suffrage were present in the ranks of the Democratic party; however, this position was supported by a small minority. For example, in 1867 the Democratic controlled Kentucky House of Representatives passed a notion supporting the position that the people of Kentucky were opposed to black suffrage.[69]

In 1867 blacks in the secession states were granted the right to vote by the Reconstruction Act of 1867; this action only intensified the struggle to secure the right to vote in Kentucky. Indeed, the right to vote became the dominant focus of many discussions at black political conventions, and attaining this right was believed to be the chief factor in gaining full equality in every area of Kentucky's public life.

After 1867 the Republican leadership began to hold discussions with blacks concerning the vote and the role of blacks in the Republican party. A number of meetings were held between blacks and Republican party elites; consequently, a black state Republican Central Committee was organized. The committee called for a state convention to be held on November 26, 1867, in Lexington for the purpose of discussing steps to secure the right to vote. This action was motivated by the desire to unseat the Democrats, who controlled the political system in Kentucky. While some members of the Republican party supported black suffrage, it was clear that support by the rank and file in the party was limited. When the Republican State Convention met in 1868, the Republican party refused to permit black delegates to be seated. The Democratic position on black voting remained negative, and the Democrats often criticized the Republican party for trying to gain political power on the strength of the black vote. Kentucky blacks were finally given the right to vote in 1870, when the Fifteenth Amendment was ratified.

The Republican effort to take advantage of the black vote intensified.

Not all Kentuckians welcomed the black vote. In an effort to minimize the potential impact of the black vote, several political jurisdictions developed methods to delay black voting. A plan was considered by bipartisans in Kentucky to delay the congressional election, which was scheduled to be held in November 1870, until August 1871. This proposal was approved by the house, but was rejected in the senate by a vote of nineteen to thirteen. However, white resistance to the exercise of the ballot by blacks did not die. Several cities took measures to disfranchise potential black voters. In Lexington, where blacks constituted a large proportion of the city's population, a charter was obtained from the legislature that allowed the city to move the date of the 1870 election up from August to February, to increase the term of office from two years to three, and to elect city officials before the Fifteenth Amendment became functional on March 30, 1870. Continued resistance to black voting manifested itself in other political subdivisions, where blacks constituted a sizable portion of the political electorate.

In Paris and Nicholasville, efforts were made to prevent blacks from voting by gerrymandering.[70] The most radical attempt to counteract the potential voting impact of blacks occurred in Danville, where the city charter was amended to allow county residents to vote in municipal elections only if they owned property in the city limits.[71] On the eve of the 1870 city election in Danville, ninety-three county residents purchased a lot with twenty-three feet frontage, divided the property into lots four inches wide, and sold them to Boyle County Democrats. This tactic diluted the impact of the black vote and ensured the Democratic party its political control in Danville.

Immediately after blacks in Kentucky gained the right to vote, they began exercising that right with aggressive intent. At the same time, the black vote was held as the panacea for changing the Democratic control in Kentucky by some Republicans. However, the prediction of Republican empowerment did not become a reality. The black vote in some local jurisdictions did, nevertheless, enable the Republican party to become competitive in some state and local races. For example, in the Seventh Congressional District, the Republican vote increased from 2,373 in 1866 to 10,916 in 1870, the first time black Kentuckians cast the ballot. In that same year the Republican nominee for governor polled 52,000 more votes than the Republican nominee in 1868.[72]

Although the Republican party encouraged the black vote, it was not welcomed by the Democrats. Democrats resisted black voting in some areas, particularly in many counties in the bluegrass areas of the state and in areas where the new black electorate was in a position to change the balance of political power in local jurisdictions. Thus, clashes over the right to vote for blacks became an intense political issue. Often this contention was reflected in the Democratic and Republican parties' disposition toward black voting. As Williams Gillette noted:

> With the negro either as an issue or as a voter in Kentucky politics, there was bound to be trouble. Indeed, differences between the races were transmitted into differences between the parties, and a speaker told the Kentucky Democratic Convention of 1871 that he wanted "no nigger voters, and that is the principle on which" he wanted Democrats to stand.[73]

White resistance to black voting during the early 1870s often was reflected in violence against black voters. Terror in Kentucky, for the most part, was found in counties with moderate or high levels of blacks and often manifested itself on the eve of elections. One aspect of this violence was lynching. In most areas in the United States where slavery was once a prominent institution, lynching became commonplace. Between 1882 and the mid-twentieth century, 4,730 lynchings took place in the United States. During this period, 205 occurred in Kentucky, and of this number 142 were black.[74]

Blacks protested against mob violence in Kentucky, but the state took little action to combat these lawless acts. The general assembly in 1872 did pass legislation prescribing punishment for acts of violence, but the legislation was ineffective because local and state officials refused to prosecute offenders who committed crimes against blacks. Black leaders appealed to the United States Congress, and on March 27, 1871, a group of black leaders presented a petition on behalf of black citizens of Frankfort and vicinity listing over 100 cases of racial violence against blacks between 1867 and 1869.[75] The petition did not bring an end to mob violence against black Kentuckians, but the fact that the petition was presented to Congress suggests that blacks were willing to seek recourse outside the state when the state did not take appropriate action to end violence.[76]

During the period when mob violence against black Kentuckians reached its peak, blacks were denied protection against violence in Kentucky's courts. As noted, Kentucky was the first state to pass a civil rights act after slavery, yet the state denied blacks fundamental civil liberties—the right to testify against whites in state courts and the right to serve on juries. After increasing federal intervention in the judicial affairs of Kentucky, the legislature in 1872 amended the 1866 Civil Rights Act, thus allowing blacks the

218

right to testify in Kentucky's courts against persons without references to race; in 1882 the right to serve on juries was granted.[77]

It is evident that blacks had a considerable impact on politics in Kentucky both directly and indirectly during the Reconstruction period. For example, a great deal of the indirect impact that blacks had on the political process in Kentucky was through protest activities. Although direct impact on the political process in Kentucky during the Reconstruction era was, at best, negligible because black empowerment in Kentucky did not become a reality as it did in the Reconstructed South, blacks did affect the political process in Kentucky as voters.

POST-RECONSTRUCTION AND THE FORMAL REIMPOSITION OF WHITE SUPREMACY (1890 to 1954)

By 1870, blacks were citizens and were entrusted to vote without discrimination and empowered with all other constitutional rights and privileges possessed by whites. However, in 1876 the social tides had begun to shift, and between 1877 and 1883 the Supreme Court eliminated, for the most part, all federal protection bestowed on blacks by ruling that the federal government had no legal authority to obviate private discrimination by individuals and groups.

It was not until the 1900s that Kentucky began to pass legislation adopting a Jim Crow policy in line with other southern states. Segregation in public education had been the state public policy since its Civil Rights Act of 1866. Thus, Kentucky office-holders were bent on establishing segregation in private education and in other areas of Kentucky's public life.

The tone of black existence in Kentucky during this period was set in 1891, when a bill was introduced in the general assembly requiring separate coaches for blacks and whites on interstate railroads. In an effort to prevent the legislature from enacting the separate coach bill, black leaders appeared before a joint committee of the senate and house asking them not to pass the separate coach bill. A delegation of black women also presented petitions to the general assembly. Nevertheless, the separate coach legislation was adopted by the general assembly on March 15, 1892.[78] In response to the separate coach law, black leaders from throughout the state met in Frankfort and made plans to test the constitutionality of the law, and less than a year after its passage, blacks tested the constitutionality of the Jim Crow law in the United States district court.[79] On June 4, 1894, the court held that the separate coach law was unconstitutional because the Kentucky law preempted the commerce powers of the federal government.[80] Blacks were jubilant over the court decision; however, the victory was short lived, as the Supreme Court legalized Jim Crow public facilities in *Plessy v. Ferguson* (1896).

The decision in *Plessy v. Ferguson* put the protection of civil rights for blacks under the dominion and control of state governments. The Kentucky legislature took advantage of the *Plessy* decision and enacted laws to strengthen the Jim Crow system in the commonwealth. In 1904, the legislature passed a major Jim Crow law that required segregation in private education. The Day Law, as it was called, forbade the teaching of blacks and whites in public or private schools at the same time. However, the statute did authorize an institution to teach both races if they maintained separate facilities twenty-five miles from the institution that taught exclusively one race.[81]

At the local level, Jim Crow legislation was passed in several cities. In 1914, the Louisville Board of Aldermen passed a residential segregation ordinance. The ordinance provided that if the majority of the residents in a given community was of one race only that race would occupy homes in that community.[82] Blacks in Louisville, as they had done with the separate coach law, challenged the constitutionality of the Residential Segregation Law. The test case was put in motion when William Warley, black editor of *The Louisville News*, purchased a lot in a predominantly white community from Robert Buchanan, a local white citizen. In the sale agreement, Warley made it clear that he was buying the lot with the intention of erecting a house for himself and his family and that unless he was given the right to occupy the house he could not issue Buchanan his commission.[83] Under the Louisville ordinance, Warley could not live in the community; therefore, when Warley did not pay for his lot, Buchanan sued him, claiming that the ordinance was unconstitutional because it interfered with his right to sell his property. Buchanan appealed his case to a local court and the Kentucky court of appeals. Both courts held that the law was constitutional; consequently, Buchanan appealed to the United States Supreme Court. In a historical decision, the Court in 1917 distinguished between Jim Crow laws in cities and those involving private property rights. In the former, the Court stated that no property rights were threatened while in the latter they were. Consequently, the Supreme Court held that the Louisville housing ordinance was

220

unconstitutional because it limited Buchanan's rights to dispose of his property. This ruling did not, however, have any measurable effect on residential segregation in Kentucky inasmuch as segregation remained in force in most communities until 1968.

The effort to gain black empowerment in Kentucky during this period continued to be a protracted struggle. Indeed, the Democratic and Republican parties maintained their position of not allowing blacks to run for political office under the party label. For example, even though black votes constituted 45 percent of the total Republican electoral vote in Louisville, they were not successful in getting the Republican party to nominate a black for public office in Louisville and Jefferson County, even in predominantly black districts.

In 1921 black alienation against the Republican party manifested itself in the organization of the Lincoln Independent party. The Republican party, which had the most to lose from a successful black independent party in Louisville, denounced the Lincoln party and charged that it was supported by the Democrats and that the "Democratic party in Louisville stood for black disfranchisement just as it did in Mississippi."[84] In spite of this indictment, the Lincoln party nominated an all-black slate of candidates for all public offices in Louisville and several offices in Jefferson County for the general election. The Lincoln party also selected black aspirants for seats in the senate and house in the Kentucky General Assembly.

The party adopted a civil rights platform that confirmed the party's commitment to equality of opportunity, proportional representation on public and appointed bodies, and nonpartisan support and allegiance to either political party in Kentucky. Thus, the Lincoln Independent party undertook an aggressive campaign to acquire political empowerment in Kentucky. The party's struggle was, however, unavailing as the party enjoyed limited success in enticing blacks to leave the Republican party. In fact, on election day the Republican party won all public offices in Louisville and Jefferson County. The Lincoln party polled only 274 votes.[85] Yet, the actual impact of the Lincoln party on party politics in Kentucky was probably underestimated inasmuch as black voters were beaten away from the polls by city policemen, and officials of the party were not represented at the counting of the ballots.

The Lincoln Independent party served as the primary impetus for black empowerment in Kentucky, and members from the Lincoln party continued their struggle for empowerment in Louisville and in other areas of the state. In 1929, A.C. Edward, a black doctor, ran for a seat in the Kentucky house of representatives from the predominantly black Fifty-eighth Legislative District. Of course, he did not receive the support of the Republican party, and in the primary he was defeated by a white Republican.

In 1935, however, blacks in Louisville gained a major concession for the Republican and Democratic parties when they nominated black candidates for the house of representatives from a predominantly black district. Charles Anderson, an attorney, was nominated by the Republicans, and Eubanks Tucker, also an attorney, was the Democratic party nominee. In the intrablack community contest, Tucker was outpolled by Anderson, the Republican nominee, by a vote of 2,373 to 956.[86] The Anderson election marked the first time that a black was elected to the Kentucky legislature in the history of the commonwealth and also the first time that a black was elected to a southern state legislature in the United States since Reconstruction.[87]

The election of Anderson as the first black representative generally regenerated the black struggle for full political equality in Kentucky. Moreover, for the first time, the struggle for political equality was taken to the state legislature. Hence, the issue of political equality became part of the public agenda from 1935 to the 1960s.

From 1935 to 1948, Charles Anderson together with the NAACP was the primary spokesman for full equality among black Kentuckians. During his tenure in the house of representatives, Anderson sponsored several bills designed to secure full equality and to reorder the socioeconomic status for blacks in Kentucky. One of his most publicized bills was the 1944 bill to repeal the Day Law, which segregated public and private schools in Kentucky. The bill passed in the house but was defeated in the senate. In his ten years in the house, Anderson sponsored many bills, several of which did not deal with racial identification, but it is evident from the nature of bills he sponsored that he saw his role as custodian of the black interest in the Kentucky General Assembly. In fact, a number of the bills he backed were designed to gain the black community a more equitable share of services and benefits provided by the government. In 1946 Anderson resigned from the Kentucky House of Representatives and was appointed assistant commonwealth's attorney for Jefferson County. (In 1959 he was selected by President Eisenhower to serve as an alternate delegate to the United Nations General Assembly.)[88]

In 1947 Anderson was succeeded in the house of representatives by Dennis Henderson, who became the second black in the history of the state to serve in the state legislature. Henderson, a Republican like his predecessor, saw his role as advancing the cause of full equality for blacks in the house of representatives. In an interview just after his election, Henderson stated that he would introduce legislation to repeal the Day Law, which he saw as a major impediment to political rights for blacks.[89]

As the pace of black political activity heightened during the late 1940s, the black community experienced a modification of the Jim Crow system in Kentucky, particularly in the educational domain and public accommodations. The NAACP in 1947 assisted P.S. Sweeney in his bid to integrate Louisville's public golf course, which was closed to blacks. After Sweeney was denied permission to play on the city-owned golf course, he filed suit in federal court against the city of Louisville.[90]

The NAACP also continued its active push for the removal of impediments to black educational opportunities, especially in higher education. In response to mounting pressure from blacks, elected officials, along with officials from the NAACP, developed a plan in Kentucky whereby blacks were offered graduate and professional studies at Kentucky State College, the only institution of higher education open to black Kentuckians. The graduate courses were offered by the University of Kentucky through professors traveling from Lexington to Kentucky State College in Frankfort. The first such classes began in 1948 when professors from the University of Kentucky Law School drove from Lexington to Frankfort to teach John Hatch, a black who was refused admission to the University of Kentucky Law School because of his race. This arrangement was not well received by blacks, however, and the following year it was challenged by Lyman T. Johnson, a social science teacher in Louisville, with a master's degree from the University of Michigan, who was declined admission to graduate classes at the University of Kentucky. Johnson refused to take graduate courses offered by the University of Kentucky at Kentucky State College in Frankfort. Instead, he and the NAACP filed suit in federal court against the state, charging that it did not provide separate but equal education as defined by the Supreme Court in *Plessy v. Ferguson*. In May 1949, the federal court ordered the University of Kentucky to admit blacks to its graduate and professional schools.

Four years later, the Sixth Circuit Court held that blacks must be admitted to Paducah Junior College. In 1949 the college denied black students admission to the school, claiming that such admittance was prohibited by the Day Law. In early 1954, a proposal repealing the Day Law was introduced in the Kentucky General Assembly, but the proposal did not gain approval. However, in that year the Day Law was nullified by the United States Supreme Court in its historic decision *Brown v. Board of Education* on May 17, 1954.

CONTEMPORARY EPOCH
(1954 to the Present)

The Brown decision marked the beginning of the contemporary epoch in Kentucky's black politics. Blacks in Kentucky, as they were in the American South, were involved in various forms of electoral and nonelectoral activities designed to gain inclusion in all phases of Kentucky's public life. The contemporary era is also the first period in which a large number of black Kentuckians took part in traditional forms of political participation. One indication of this participation is the increase in black Kentuckians who contested and won political offices from 1960 to the present. In addition to electoral participation, the drive for equality continued to be a distinguishing feature of black political activity during the contemporary epoch, particularly up to 1968.

This period also saw an increase in civil rights organizations; the NAACP, which had traditionally been in the forefront of the black struggle for political equality in Kentucky, maintained that position. During the early half of the 1960s, however, the struggle for equality was borne by other local civil rights groups, such as the Congress of Racial Equality (CORE), Student Nonviolent Coordinating Committee (SNCC), Southern Christian Leadership Conference (SCLC), and the Urban League. Each group was either affiliated with or patterned after national civil rights organizations.

On the national scene, blacks won major civil rights victories as Congress passed several civil rights acts between 1957 and 1968. In Kentucky, blacks were equally successful. In 1963, Governor Combs issued a governor's code of fair practice, marking the first statewide effort to deal with employment discrimination. In the general assembly, a public accommodations bill was introduced by one white and two black representatives. The bill died in the house since the majority of the Kentucky assembly was against this proposal.

The failure of the legislature to pass the public accommodations bill intensified black protest activities. On March 5, 1964, black Kentuckians from throughout the state held a march on Frankfort, demanding that the legislature enact a statewide public accommodations bill. The mass demonstration of over 10,000 people was addressed by national civil rights leaders, including Dr. Martin Luther King.[91] Nevertheless, the Frankfort demonstration did not induce the 1964 general assembly to accommodate black demands for a statewide accommodations bill.

By 1966, the social trend had shifted, and when the general assembly met civil rights groups had secured support for a public accommodations bill. The bill was supported by Governor Edward T. Breathitt, Jr., and key legislative leaders in the general assembly. Jesse Warders, the only black legislator, introduced the bill and spoke on its behalf. After Warders's speech, the house of representatives voted 76 to 12 in favor of the bill, and the senate passed the bill by a vote of 36 to 1.[92] The historic bill was signed by Governor Edward T. Breathitt, Jr., making Kentucky the first southern state to pass a comprehensive civil rights act in modern history. The Kentucky Civil Rights Act prohibited discrimination by employers who employed eight or more employees. Furthermore, the act required all places of public accommodations to cease discrimination against blacks.

Two years later, Kentucky became the first state in the South to pass a fair housing act. The statewide housing bill was introduced in the senate by Senator Georgia Powers, and in the house by representatives Mae Street Kidd and Hughes McGill. The bill passed the senate by a vote of 27 to 3 and the house by a vote of 54 to 17.

Concurrent with civil rights gains during this period, the black community in Kentucky made notable electoral gains from 1960 to 1981. Although the black community had been represented in the state legislature since 1936, there were few city and statewide black officeholders, and these blacks generally represented political jurisdictions with a majority black electorate. For example, the only black state legislator in the 1940s was from a predominantly black district in Louisville.

With the advent of the sixties a new phenomenon developed: black officeholders were elected from political subdivisions with predominantly white constituencies. This development saw a progressive push for black empowerment in many areas where blacks had not attempted to win public office before. For example, Woodford Porter was the first black elected to the Louisville Board of Education in 1958. In addition, in 1963 Harry N. Sykes was elected the first black city commissioner in Lexington, where 80 percent of the electorate was white.[93] Moreover, in 1968 in an unprecedented development, Luska J. Twyman of Glasgow became Kentucky's first black mayor and one of the few blacks to be elected chief executive of a major biracial city in the American South. What is more impressive about the Twyman election is that blacks made up less than 10 percent of the city's population and that Twyman defeated a white opponent.

At the state level, the black community witnessed an increase in the number of black state legislators. In 1968 Georgia M. Powers was elected to the senate, making her the first black and first woman to serve in that body. In that same year, Senator Powers was joined by another black female when Mae Street Kidd was elected to the house. Hughes E. McGill was also elected to the house the same year as Representative Kidd, increasing the number of black state legislators to three.

In the 1970s a significant increase in black political participation in Kentucky was evidenced by the number of blacks contesting and winning political offices (Table 10.4). As Table 10.4 shows, black Kentuckians held only twenty-six public offices in 1969. However, by 1972 the number of black officeholders in Kentucky had risen to fifty-six, and by 1980 that number swelled to eighty, the highest ever in the state's history.

The steady growth in the number of black officeholders from 1969 to 1980 was reversed in 1982, when only seventy-one blacks were elected to public offices in Kentucky.[94] As represented in Table 10.4, the present black officeholders include one senator, three state representatives, three mayors, forty city councilmen, two circuit court judges, one district judge, one sheriff, one magistrate, two constables, one jailer, and sixteen school board members.[94]

During the contemporary period blacks have also been appointed to major positions in state government by the last three governors. In 1978 Charles Lambert was appointed Deputy Secretary of Finance by former Governor Julian Carroll, and later he served as Acting Finance Secretary. In 1980 blacks gained a major cabinet level appointment when George Wilson became Kentucky's first black secretary of corrections. Wilson was appointed by former Governor John Y. Brown, Jr., and was reappointed in 1983 by Martha Layne Collins, Kentucky's first female governor. Wilson is the only top-ranking official from the Brown administration to be retained by Governor Collins.

TABLE 10.4

Black Elected Officials in Kentucky, 1969–1982

Office	1969	1972	1973	1974	1975	1976	1977	1978	1980	1981	1982
State	3	3	3	3	3	3	3	4	4	4	4
County	3	9	9	10	10	10	10	11	8	8	8
City	16	37	37	40	39	45	46	46	52	52	43
School	4	8	9	9	12	13	16	17	16	16	16
TOTAL	26	57	58	62	64	71	75	78	80	80	71

Source: 1982 Kentucky Directory of Black Elected Officials, Sixth Report, Kentucky Commission on Human Rights, Frankfort, Kentucky, p. 1.

At the national level, Kentucky's United States Senators and Representatives have supported the appointment of blacks to the federal bureaucracy. For example, they supported the appointment of W.A. Butts, former president of Kentucky State University, as director of Title III in the United States Department of Education in 1982. In addition, blacks have also been appointed to boards and commissions in recent times by Kentucky's governors. Blacks continue to be involved in partisan political activities and have been represented among campaign workers for both political parties. They have served on the state central committees, on county executive committees, central committees for gubernatorial races and delegates to national party conventions. While black participation transcends political parties in Kentucky, blacks have a more positive relationship with the state and local Democratic party than with the Republican party. Participation by blacks in Republican partisan politics has declined since the late 1930s but not to the extent that it did in the Deep South. To be sure, in Louisville black Republican partisans remained strong throughout the 1930s and until 1967. However, Louise Reynolds was the only black elected that year. Reynolds, a Republican and the first woman to serve as alderman in the city's history, was elected in 1961. Black support for the Republican party in Louisville was in part a result of the Democratic party's not mounting an aggressive campaign to solicit the black vote and because the Republican party had traditionally appointed blacks to positions in city and county governments.

Blacks developed political organizations during the contemporary era, as they did during Reconstruction. These organizations developed primarily in response to the increased number of blacks contesting for political office and to the desire of some black leaders to extract a more equitable distribution of the political spoils for the black community. In 1981, a group of black influentials in Louisville formed a political action committee (PAC-10). The primary purpose of the committee was to influence politics in Louisville and Jefferson County. Since 1981, PAC-10 has contributed money to black and white candidates from Louisville and Jefferson County. In addition, PAC-10 has spearheaded voter education projects and registration drives and has interviewed candidates seeking the committee's endorsement. PAC-10 has become a major political force in Louisville and Jefferson County, and along with the NAACP, several black and white organizations, and black and white elected officials, it has played a major role in defeating an attempt by Louisville and Jefferson County business and economic elites to consolidate Louisville and Jefferson County governments. The antimerger coalition was headed by Senator Georgia Powers, the dean of Kentucky's black politicians. Under Senator Powers's leadership, the antimerger coalition, with limited resources, twice defeated the well-financed promerger coalition of political and financial leaders in Louisville and Jefferson County.

In Kentucky, as well as in the nation as a whole, blacks do not hold public office in proportion to their numbers, nor is black officeholding in Kentucky significant in any category other than at the city council level. Even there, black officeholders do not constitute electoral equality inasmuch as the forty black city councilmen represent only 1.5 percent of Kentucky's city officials.[95] Also, in many political jurisdictions where blacks constitute a sizable proportion of the population, they have not been successful in converting their votes into political power, and black candidates for public office have not been able to gain approval from their predominantly white electorate (Table 10.5).

TABLE 10.5

Percentage Black of Total Population in Cities Without Black Officeholders and with 10 Percent or More Black Population

Percentage Blacks	Number of Cities
10–14.9	21
15–25.9	12
26–39.9	7
TOTAL	40

Source: 1982 Kentucky Directory of Black Elected Officials—Sixth Report, Kentucky Commission on Human Rights, Frankfort, Kentucky, p. 6.

As Table 10.5 indicates, in 1982 there were forty political subsystems where the percentage of the black population was greater than 10 percent yet had no black officeholders.[96] Of the forty political subdivisions with no black elective officials, twenty-one have black populations less than 15 percent. Another twelve have populations from 15 to 25 percent, while seven have populations from 26 to 39 percent. County and state totals are much the same. For example, all four black officeholders in the general assembly are from predominantly black districts in Louisville's west end. The extent to which this number will remain constant is problematic in light of the 1982 reapportionment, since two of the present black representatives will run for reelection in the 1984 Democratic primary in two districts that have white incumbents.

In sum, blacks have had significant direct impact on the politics of Kentucky from the 1960s to the present. Much of this impact has been through black elected officials and as a result of the increased black voter participation. Blacks have also indirectly influenced the political process, as black campaign workers have become commonplace in most political contests. In addition, blacks have secured positions on most executive and legislative units and on boards and commissions. At the national level, Kentucky's United States Senators and Representatives have supported the appointment of a black as director of Title III in the United States Department of Education as well as other federal positions.

SUMMARY AND CONCLUSIONS

Blacks in Kentucky have exercised the vote since 1870, when Congress passed the Fifteenth Amendment; however, black participation was circumscribed, since blacks were not allowed to contest for public office under the Democratic and Republican party labels. As a result, black political participation, to a large degree, has reflected black participation in the nation and the South in general. Black electoral participation has increased radically since the 1960s as measured by black officeholding and increased registration and voting. As a result, blacks have exercised substantial political influence since the 1960s. Blacks have also influenced the political process in the state indirectly through various protests of public policy designed to deny them equality under the state constitution. Consequently, black political activity has generally vacillated between traditional electoral politics and nontraditional protest politics.

Even though black officeholding in Kentucky has not reached electoral equality, it has made an impact on the state's political systems. Black officeholders in some political subdivisions have shown a willingness to introduce policies that address salient problems besetting the black community. These proposals have been designed to gain increased employment opportunities and an equitable distribution of public projects sponsored by state and local governments. The proposals, for the most part, have been successful in Louisville and Lexington and in political subdivisions where black officeholders were elected from predominantly black constituencies. In addition, some black elected officials have fought proposals that they perceived would diminish black political influence in Kentucky politics.

Finally, some general projections are needed concerning the future of black politics in the state. As has been noted, most blacks holding public office in the state are elected from at-large districts serving predominantly white communities. This political phenomenon is contrary to black officeholding in the nation—the majority are generally elected from districts with majority black constituencies. If black officeholding is to remain at its present numerical level, black aspirants for public office must continue to appeal to both black and white constituencies. At the same time, black officeholders will be expected to enter aggressively the bargaining process both individually and collectively to secure aid and services that will improve the socioeconomic status for their constituents. Failure to do so will retard black political development in Kentucky.

FOOTNOTES

1. Mack H. Jones, "A Frame of Reference for Black Politics" in Lenneal J. Henderson, Jr. (ed.), *Black Political Life in America* (San Francisco Chandler, 1972) pp. 7-20; Jewell L. Prestage and Carolyn Sue Williams, "Blacks in Louisiana Politics," in James Bolner (ed.), *Louisiana Politics* (Baton Rouge: Louisiana State University Press, 1983) p. 385.

2. Cassie Osborne, Jr., "Black Empowerment in Rural Mississippi: The Cases of Mound Bayou, Fayette, Bolton, Shelby and Tchula" (unpublished Ph.D. dissertation, Department of Political Science, Atlanta University 1982) pp. 1-12; Jones, "A Frame of Reference for Black Politics," 7-20; Hanes Walton, Jr., *Black Politics: A Theoretical and Structural Analysis* (Philadelphia: J.A. Lippincott, 1972) pp. 1-25.

3. Prestage and Williams, "Blacks in Louisiana Politics," p. 286.

4. *Ibid.*

5. *Ibid;* Mack H. Jones, "Black Politics: From Civil Rights to Benign Neglect" in Harry A. Johnson (ed.), *Negotiating the*

Mainstream: A Survey of The Afro-American Experience (Chicago: American Library Association, 1978) pp. 164-195.

6. *Kentucky Constitution* (1792), art. 6; J. Winston Coleman, Jr., *Slavery Times in Kentucky* (North Carolina: The University of North Carolina Press, 1940).

7. *Ibid;* Frank E. Mathias, "Slavery, The Solvent of Kentucky Politics" (*Register of Kentucky Historical Society,* vol. 79) p. 2.

8. Coleman, *Slavery Times in Kentucky,* p. 3.

9. *Ibid.,* p. 2; *Kentucky's Black Heritage: The Role of the People in the History of Kentucky from Pioneer Days to the Present* (Frankfort: Kentucky Commission on Human Rights, 1971) p. 1.

10. Ivan E. McDougle, "Slavery in Kentucky" in *The Journal of Negro History* (III July, 1918) p. 8.

11. *Ibid.*

12. *Ibid.,* p. 221; Wallace B. Turner, "Abolitionism In Kentucky," *Register of the Kentucky Historical Society,* vol. 69.

13. McDougle, "Slavery in Kentucky," p. 221.

14. *Ibid.*

15. Coleman, *Slavery Times in Kentucky,* pp. 144-45.

16. Coleman, *Slavery Times in Kentucky,* pp. 144-45; T.D. Clark, "The Slave Trade Between Kentucky and the Cotton Kingdom," *The Mississippi Valley Historical Review,* 21, pp. 291-297.

17. *Ibid.*

18. Wallace Turner, "Kentucky Slavery in the Last Ante-Bellum Decade"; Clark, "The Slave Trade Between Kentucky and The Cotton Kingdom," p. 337.

19. *Ibid.*

20. T.D. Clark, "The Slave Trade Between Kentucky and the Cotton Kingdom," p. 341.

21. Coleman, *Slavery Times in Kentucky,* pp. 173-194; Turner, "Kentucky Slavery in the Last Ante-Bellum Decade."

22. Coleman, *Slavery Times in Kentucky,* pp. 193-194.

23. Prestage and Williams, "Blacks in Louisiana Politics," p. 386.

24. John Hope Franklin, *From Slavery to Freedom* (New York: Knopf, 1974) p. 144; Prestage and Williams, "Blacks in Louisiana Politics," p. 386.

25. *Ibid.*

26. McDougle, "Slavery in Kentucky," p. 289.

27. Prestage and Williams, "Blacks in Louisiana Politics," pp. 286-290.

28. *Ibid.*
29. Herbert Aptheker, *Slave Revolts* (New York: International Publishers, 1952) pp. 277-278; Coleman, *Slavery Times in Kentucky*, pp. 85-112.
30. Prestage and Williams, "Blacks in Louisiana Politics," p. 288.
31. Coleman, *Slavery Times in Kentucky*, p. 262; McDougle, "Slavery in Kentucky," pp. 248-249.
32. Prestage and Williams, "Blacks in Louisiana Politics," p. 288.
33. McDougle, "Slavery in Kentucky," p. 218.
34. Coleman, *Slavery Times in Kentucky*, p. 205 and pp. 135-139.
35. McDougle, "Slavery in Kentucky," pp. 248-249.
36. Alice A. Dunnigan, *The Fascinating Story of Black Kentuckians: Their Heritage and Tradition* (Washington, D.C.: The Associated Publishers, Inc., 1980) pp. 14-15.
37. *Ibid.*
38. Prestage and Williams, "Blacks in Louisiana Politics," p. 289.
39. Dunnigan, *The Fascinating Story of Black Kentuckians: Their Heritage and Tradition*, pp. 39-44; Henry Ellis Cheaney, "Attitudes Of The Indiana Pulpit and Press Toward the Negro 1860-1880," (unpublished Ph.D. dissertation, Department of History, The University of Chicago, 1961) pp. 82-83; Mathias, "Slavery, The Solvent of Kentucky Politics," (*Register of The Kentucky Historical Society*, vol. 70) p. 2.
40. Lowell H. Harrison, *The Civil War in Kentucky* (Lexington, Kentucky: The University Press of Kentucky, 1975) p. 12; Ross A. Webb, *Kentucky in the Reconstruction Era* (Lexington, Kentucky: The University Press of Kentucky, 1979) pp. 1-10.
41. E. Merton Coulter, *The Civil War and Readjustment in Kentucky* (Gloucester, Mass.: Peter Smith, 1966) pp. 18-35.
42. *Ibid.*
43. Coulter, *The Civil War and Readjustment in Kentucky*, p. 156; Harrison, *The Civil War in Kentucky;* W.E.B. DuBois, *Black Reconstruction in America 1860-1880* (New York: Atheneum Publishers, 1935) pp. 566-579.
44. DuBois, *Black Reconstruction in America 1860-1880*, pp. 566-579; Coulter, *The Civil War and Readjustment in Kentucky*, pp. 247-248.
45. Coulter, *The Civil War and Readjustment in Kentucky*, p. 156; DuBois, *Black Reconstruction in America 1860-1880*, pp. 566-579; Coulter, *The Civil War and Readjustment in Kentucky*, p. 157.

46. *Ibid.*
47. Coulter, *The Civil War and Readjustment in Kentucky,* p. 157.
48. *Ibid.,* pp. 158-159; DuBois, *Black Reconstruction in America 1860-1880,* p. 567.
49. *Ibid.*
50. DuBois, *Black Reconstruction in America 1860-1880,* p. 567.
51. *Ibid.*
52. Dunnigan, *The Fascinating Story of Black Kentuckians: Their Heritage and Tradition,* pp. 74-84.
53. Prestage and Williams, "Blacks in Louisiana Politics," p. 290.
54. Dunnigan, *The Fascinating Story of Black Kentuckians: Their Heritage and Tradition,* pp. 72-74.
55. *Ibid.*
56. *Kentucky's Black Heritage: The Role of the Black People in the History of Kentucky from Pioneer Days to the Present,* pp. 8-33.
57. *Ibid.*
58. *Ibid.*
59. *Ibid.*
60. *Ibid.*
61. *Ibid.*
62. Victor B. Howard, "Negro Politics and the Suffrage Question in Kentucky, 1866-1872," *(Register of Kentucky State Historical Society)* vol. 72, pp. 111, 1974.
63. *Ibid.*
64. Victor B. Howard, *Black Liberation in Kentucky—Emancipation and Freedom, 1862-1884* (Lexington, Kentucky: The University Press of Kentucky, 1983) pp. 12-45; Ernest Collings, "The Political Behavior of the Negroes in Cincinnati, Ohio, and Louisville, Kentucky," (unpublished Ph.D. dissertation, Department of Political Science, University of Kentucky, 1950) pp. 134-173.
65. Prestage and Williams, "Blacks in Louisiana Politics," pp. 293-297.
66. Howard, *Black Liberation in Kentucky—Emancipation and Freedom, 1862-1884,* pp. 146-156.
67. *Ibid.,* 148.
68. *Ibid., Louisville Democratic,* January 2, 1967.
69. *Ibid.*
70. Richard O. Curry, *Radicalism, Racism, and Party Realignment* (Baltimore, Maryland: The Johns Hopkins Press, 1969) p. 280;

Kentucky's Black Heritage: The Role of the Black People in the History of Kentucky from Pioneer Days to the Present, pp. 46-49.

71. *Ibid.*

72. *Ibid.*

73. William Gillette, "Anatomy of a Failure: Federal Enforcement of the Right to Vote in the Border States During Reconstruction" in Curry's (ed.) *Radicalism, Racism, and Party Realignment,* p. 294; *Kentucky's Black Heritage,* pp. 46-49.

74. Curry, *Radicalism, Racism, and Party Realignment,* p. 272.

75. Dunnigan, *The Fascinating Story of Black Kentuckians: Their Heritage and Tradition,* p. 96.

76. Howard, *Black Liberation in Kentucky—Emancipation and Freedom, 1862-1884; Kentucky's Black Heritage,* p. 53.

77. *Kentucky's Black Heritage,* p. 53.

78. *Ibid.,* p. 37.

79. *Ibid.,* pp. 54-59.

80. *Ibid.,* pp. 54-59.

81. *Ibid.,* p. 56.

82. Loren Miller, *The Petitioners—The Story of the Supreme Court of the United States and the Negro* (New York: The World Publishing Company, 1967) p. 200.

83. *Kentucky's Black Heritage,* p. 65.

84. Curry, *Radicalism, Racism, and Party Realignment;* Collings, "The Political Behavior of The Negroes in Cincinnati, Ohio and Louisville, Kentucky," pp. 100-180.

85. *Crisis,* 23, no. 3. (January, 1922), p. 114.

86. Collings, "The Political Behavior of The Negroes in Cincinnati, Ohio and Louisville, Kentucky," pp. 20-100.

87. *Kentucky's Black Heritage,* pp. 89-119.

88. *Ibid.,* p. 87.

89. Collings, "The Political Behavior of The Negroes in Cincinnati, Ohio and Louisville, Kentucky," pp. 100-178.

90. *Kentucky's Black Heritage,* p. 119; In 1954, the federal court ruled that the city must allow blacks to play on the city's golf course.

91. *Ibid.,* p. 121.

92. *Ibid.,* p. 121.

93. "1982 Kentucky Directory of Black Elected Officials", Frankfort, Kentucky, Kentucky Commission on Human Rights, p. 1; *Kentucky's Black Heritage,* p. 119.

94. *Ibid.,* p. 5.
95. *Ibid.,* p. 4.
96. *Ibid.,* p. 4.

Chapter 11

THE QUEST FOR EQUALITY
Women in Kentucky Politics
Mary Hawkesworth, University of Louisville

Women have a long tradition of political activism in Kentucky. This chapter will examine three areas of women's political involvement: (1) the prolonged battle for equal rights under the state and federal Constitutions, (2) women's participation in the political process, as voters, party workers, lobbyists, and government officials, both elective and appointive, and (3) women's efforts to engage in politics as a means of self-protection, that is, to use the political process to protect and promote specific interests of women.

THE CONSTITUTIONAL QUEST FOR EQUALITY

In the nineteenth and early twentieth centuries, women were defined as citizens of the commonwealth of Kentucky and of the United States, but citizenship was conceived as a flexible concept that accorded different rights to individuals on the basis of age, sex, race, and ethnicity. Despite the formal equality of the title of citizenship, women were denied the right to vote and to hold public office.[1] Upon marriage, women experienced "civil death," a legal arrangement that merged a woman's interests and identity with that of her husband. According to both state and federal laws, the husband had legal custody of his wife's body. A married woman could not own property, make contracts, engage in gainful employment without her husband's permission, or retain earnings derived from her employment. She could not testify, sue, or be sued in court.

236

She had no legal custody of the children she bore. If she tried to escape from her husband's dominion, he could use the force of the law to reclaim her. In addition to these legal restrictions, women encountered formidable constraints upon their actions in the form of religious and social customs. It was the custom that only males be admitted to educational institutions, public or private, and to the professions. Tradition mandated that only men be allowed to speak in religious ceremonies, at public meetings, and before legislative assemblies.

Kentucky women first mobilized for sustained political action in response to these legal and traditional restrictions.[2] Although demands for women's rights were aired in the state as early as 1853, it was not until the 1880s that an effective women's political network was established to attack the "disadvantages of inferior education, dependence, poverty and political disability" that circumscribed women's lives.[3] From the earliest organizational efforts, the leaders of the state campaign defined their goals broadly, in terms of the achievement of "absolute equality with men in the right to free enjoyment of every opportunity ... that civilization, the joint work of both sexes, offers to the development of individual capacity."[4] To achieve this goal, a wide range of tactics was employed. In 1881, the Kentucky Woman Suffrage Association was founded as the first state suffrage society in the South.[5] In the following years, repeated efforts were launched to organize local chapters of the Equal Rights Association in order to raise the issues of property rights, divorce, custody, inheritance, educational opportunity, and suffrage across the state. In 1889, the Kentucky Equal Rights Association established the Kentucky Lecture Bureau, which provided knowledgeable speakers on the entire range of issues relating to women's legal, political, and economic status for lecture engagements throughout the state. Mary C. Roark, Ellen B. Dietrick, Mary Barr Clay, Laura Clay, and Eugenia Farmer travelled throughout Kentucky arguing for the revision of state laws in order to advance the industrial, educational, legal, and political rights of women.

In addition to organizing grass roots support for women's rights and educating the public about the pressing need for reform of state laws pertaining to women, Laura Clay and Josephine Henry initiated a woman's rights lobby during the 1890 session of the Kentucky General Assembly. Armed with petitions bearing over 10,000 signatures, these representatives of Kentucky's Equal Rights Association demanded the full enfranchisement of women, the repeal of laws barring women from elective office, the creation of equal property laws for men and women, the provision of educational, professional, and occupational opportunities for women, the passage of equal custody laws, and an increase in the age of "protection" (the age at which females could consent to marriage) from twelve to eighteen.[6]

Although this lobbying effort did not produce the full range of reforms sought, the persistence of Clay and Henry did culminate in one piece of legislation that was essential to the economic independence of married women in the state. The 1890 general assembly passed a law that required employers to pay wages earned by married women to the women themselves rather than to their husbands. In addition to this legislative victory, the first decade of systematic political activism in the cause of women's rights closed with two other notable accomplishments. Women were admitted to the State Agricultural and Mechanical College and Normal School at Lexington, which was later renamed the University of Kentucky.[7] The Kentucky court of appeals struck down legislation that prohibited women from dispensing medicines and affirmed the principle that all professions and occupations should be open to women.[8]

When the constitutional convention was convened to revise Kentucky's constitution in 1890, the Kentucky Equal Rights Association delegated a committee, consisting of Laura Clay, Josephine Henry, Eugenia Farmer, Isabella Sheppard, and Sallie Clay Bennett, to pressure the convention to produce a document that afforded women the equal protection of the laws. Despite hours of testimony before the convention's Committee on Women's Rights, intensive lobbying, educational sessions concerning the plight of women in the home and the work place, and a major address before the entire convention delivered by Laura Clay, Kentucky's revised constitution afforded women neither property rights nor suffrage. Members of the Kentucky Equal Rights Association continued to lobby the state legislature for justice for women. Hundreds of articles on women's rights were published in newspapers throughout Kentucky, letters were written to individual legislators, and the aid of Governor John Young Brown was solicited. Josephine Henry delivered an eloquent address on "American Citizenship" before a packed audience in Representative's Hall in Frankfort.[9] But, it was not until 1894 that the intensive lobbying of the women's rights advocates produced its second major legislative victory. The legislature passed and the governor signed the Married Women's Property Act, which enabled married women to control their own personal property and real estate, to make wills, and to engage in business ventures independent of their husbands. This law also eliminated gross inequities in the inheritance law by equalizing curtesy and dower, "It gave the wife the same one-half life interest in her deceased husband's property (dower) as he had in her property under reverse circumstances (curtesy).[10] Twenty-two years after the first woman addressed the Kentucky legislature to demand property rights for women, Kentucky took its first step toward equalizing the property and inheritance rights of marriage partners.

The 1894 general assembly also responded to the Equal Rights Association's demands for suffrage by extending school suffrage to women in second-class cities. Kentucky had initiated this partial suffrage, which enabled widows with children of school age to vote for school trustees in rural districts, in 1838. This franchise was extended in 1888 to allow "taxpaying widows and spinsters" to vote on school taxes. This partial school suffrage was not, however, available either to married women in the rural districts or to any women in Kentucky's first-, second-, third-, or fourth-class cities. When these city charters were being revised following the adoption of Kentucky's 1890 constitution, the equal rights associations of the state's three second-class cities (Covington, Newport, and Lexington) orchestrated massive letter-writing campaigns for the extension of school suffrage to all women. In response to this pressure, the general assembly approved charters for the second-class cities, which made women eligible to vote in school board elections and to be elected to serve on school boards. The lobbying efforts of the State Equal Rights Association, however, was not successful in its attempt to secure the school suffrage for first-, third-, and fourth-class cities.[11] Moreover, the school suffrage attained by women in second-class cities was secured for less than a decade. In an action justified on the grounds of the protection of white supremacy in the state, the 1902 general assembly revoked the school suffrage of women in second-class cities because more black women than white had exercised their democratic rights in the spring election in Lexington.[12]

Despite their frustration at the recalcitrance of the legislature, members of the Equal Rights Association continued to press their cause. Throughout the early years of the twentieth century, speakers continued to travel the state to sustain interest in women's rights. Under the leadership of Madeline McDowell Breckinridge, local chapters of the Equal Rights Association were organized across Kentucky. By 1914, only one county in the state was without an active women's rights league. Local rights activists set up booths at county fairs to publicize their views. Hikes for suffrage were organized along the Cincinnati-Southern Railroad. Essay contests were held at state colleges and universities, offering prizes of $100 for the best treatment of the topic of equal rights for women. Mass meetings, rallies, and demonstrations for suffrage became regular occurrences throughout the state. In 1913, 200 Louisville suffragists held the first public suffrage march in the South.[13] Regularly, legislation pertaining to women's suffrage was introduced to the general assembly, only to die in committee or to meet defeat on the floor.

During this forty-year period of intense political activism in the cause of women's rights, few dates stand out to register successes for the women's rights movement. In 1896, the first women were appointed to serve on the board of directors of the newly created House of Reform for Girls. In 1898, legislation was passed that required women physicians to care for female patients in state institutions for the insane. In the same year, the first police matrons were hired to oversee female prisoners at state institutions. In 1910, the general assembly passed a Co-Guardianship Act, which gave mothers and fathers equal custody of their children. In 1911, the first maximum hour legislation was passed to regulate the conditions of the employment of women in factories. School suffrage was again extended to women in the state in 1912, but the literacy test incorporated into the provision insured that only a small proportion of the state's female population would qualify to exercise the franchise. The United States Senate passed the Nineteenth Amendment to the Constitution, which accorded women full citizenship, the right to vote and to hold elective office in June 1919. The Kentucky General Assembly ratified the Nineteenth Amendment on January 6, 1920, the first day of its legislative session. With a vote of 72 to 25 in the house and of 30 to 8 in the senate, Kentucky became the twenty-third state to ratify the Women's Suffrage Amendment.[14]

It did not take women in Kentucky long to realize that full citizenship did not imply the full equality that had been the goal of the women's rights movement from its inception. Despite ratification of the Nineteenth Amendment, Kentucky statutes were riddled with provisions that treated men and women differently. The Kentucky constitution's Bill of Rights proclaimed that "all men are equal," but ignored the existence of women citizens within the state.[15] In 1923, the League of Women Voters (the name adopted by the Equal Rights Association following the ratification of the Nineteenth Amendment) launched an effort to strike the word *male* from the election clause of the state constitution. The skilled lobbying of league members resulted in an amendment passed by the legislature without a single negative vote. However, when the constitutional amendment was submitted to the voters for ratification, it was defeated by a margin of 11,000 votes.[16]

In the absence of a strong public consensus on the meaning of full equality for women, advocates of women's rights have had to wage piecemeal campaigns against the worst inequities perpetuated

240

by state laws. For example, in 1936, Charles Anderson, the first black elected to the Kentucky legislature, introduced and secured the passage of legislation to allow public school teachers in Kentucky to retain their teaching positions after marriage.[17] Due to the high concentrations of women in public instruction, the benefits of this legislation accrued primarily to women. Despite small gains of this sort, piecemeal efforts failed to alter laws pertaining to marriage, divorce, employment, credit practices, and criminal proceedings, which reflected and promoted male interests. For the greater part of this century, Kentucky marriage laws reflected the assumption that husbands would treat their wives benignly under all circumstances.[18] State divorce statutes allowed men several grounds for divorce such as "lewd and lascivious behavior on the part of the wife without proof of adultery," and "habitual drunkenness on the part of the wife for one year," while requiring much more stringent requirements to sustain the wife's petition for divorce (e.g., proof of the husband's adultery and proof that the husband's drunkenness undermine's his capacity to support the wife).[19] Rape statutes reflected greater interest in protecting men from false accusation than in protecting women from physical assault. Credit, pension, and insurance legislation afforded advantages to men in the state while simultaneously disadvantaging women. All such differences in the treatment of men and women by state law existed even though Section 446.020 (2) of Kentucky's Revised Statutes provides "that ... words importing the masculine gender only *may* extend and be applied to females as well as males."[20]

In 1965, Governor Ned Breathitt established the Governor's Commission on the Status of Women to "review and research the progress of women in Kentucky" and "to make recommendations for constructive action" in the areas of public and private employment practices, women's political and civil rights, labor laws, education and training opportunities, and state social insurance, tax, and inheritance laws. The commission's report, issued two years later, revealed that the median level of education for women in Kentucky was 9 years, while that of men was 8.6 years, that 18.7 percent of the women in the state completed high school compared with 14.2 percent of the men, and that 3.9 percent of Kentucky's women graduated from a four-year college compared with 5.9 percent of Kentucky's men. Women constituted 30 percent of Kentucky's nonagricultural work force in 1965, heavily concentrated in the service sectors, especially in hospital and educational services. The median income of women in the state was 54 percent that of their male counterparts. Moreover, the average Kentucky woman with a college education earned 20 percent less than the average Kentucky

241

male with a high school diploma, and the average Kentucky woman with a high school diploma earned 12 percent less than the average Kentucky man with an eighth-grade education.[21]

Although the commission's report made reference to specific instances of discriminatory legislation still in effect in the state, it was the general consensus of the commission that "Kentucky presents no legal barriers to the advancement of women."[22] The two factors identified by the commission as the major obstacles to women's progress were "(1) the traditional role of women as conceived by men, the community and our society in general; and (2) the view of women held by women themselves."[23] By attributing the major causes of women's condition to amorphous social attitudes beyond government control, the Commission on the Status of Women both minimized the seriousness of the problems created for women by Kentucky's discriminatory laws and undermined possible legislative strategies for the amelioration of women's position in the state.

In 1971, an *ad hoc* committee for women's rights mobilized to demand "Legislative Action for Women" (LAW).[24] The initial objective of the LAW forces was to have the Kentucky Civil Rights Act of 1966 extended to prohibit discrimination against women. In order to demonstrate the need for such legislation, Constance C. Woosley completed extensive research on the discriminatory provisions in state decisional law. Woosley's systematic research constituted the core of LAW's proposed legislative reforms, which were introduced in the 1972 general assembly. Under the joint leadership of Mary K. Tachau, Marcia Segal, Suzy Post, Anne Fremd, and Connie Woosley, LAW supporters sold bumper stickers sporting the "Legislative Action for Women" theme, both to publicize their cause and to raise funds to sustain an intensive lobbying campaign. Each day during the 1972 legislative session, LAW supporters travelled to Frankfort to attend committee meetings, to testify, and to buttonhole legislators. Governor Wendell Ford, Lieutenant Governor Julian Carroll, Speaker of the House Norbert Blume, and Senate Majority Leader Dee Huddleston publicly announced their support of LAW's proposals and worked with the LAW lobbyists to secure passage of the legislation. After forming a coalition with senior citizen activist Arthur Kling to lobby for a statute that would prohibit both age discrimination and gender discrimination, the LAW forces emerged victorious in the final hours of the legislative session. As amended in 1972, the Kentucky Civil Rights Act prohibits discrimination on the basis of race, color, religion, national origin, age, and sex. Primary responsibility for enforcement of the act rests with the Kentucky Commission on Human Rights.

The research, lobbying, and publicity-generating activities of the LAW supporters heightened public awareness of and increased legislators' sensitivity to gender-based discrimination in Kentucky. This advance work was to prove crucial in the subsequent effort to ratify the federal Equal Rights Amendment (ERA). When the proposed Twenty-seventh Amendment to the United States Constitution was passed by the Congress in June 1972, the Kentucky General Assembly was already convened in special session to consider school financing proposals. With the support of the governor and the majority leaders of both houses, the special session undertook the consideration of the ERA. In June 1972, Kentucky became the sixteenth state to ratify the federal amendment designed to insure that "equality before the law shall not be denied or abridged by the United States or any state on account of sex."

From 1972 to 1974, the general assembly passed a series of laws that attempted to eradicate gender-based discrimination within the state. The general assembly created the Kentucky Commission on Women as a separate administrative body within state government with a mandate to assist in the establishment of local programs designed to meet the needs of women in Kentucky communities.[25] The assembly passed a no-fault divorce law, which establishes the grounds for divorce to exist when a "marriage is irretrievably broken" and there are "no reasonable prospects for reconciliation."[26] The omnibus bill, House Bill 368, amended various sections of Kentucky's Revised Statutes to "eliminate discrimination on the basis of sex and thereby insure equal rights for men and women."[27] Legislation was passed to insure the extension of equal credit to women through the adoption of nondiscriminatory practices and through the elimination of personal questions from credit applications. Public accommodations legislation was revised to guarantee that men and women have access to the same public facilities. Taken in conjunction, this legislation constituted a significant attempt to purge laws and regulations that discriminate on the basis of gender from Kentucky legal and administrative codes.

Unfortunately, the achievements of the early 1970s did not represent a permanent commitment to the full equality of women in the state. Anti-ERA forces, including a Kentucky contingent of "Pink Ladies," began a campaign to persuade state legislators to rescind Kentucky's ratification of the proposed Twenty-seventh Amendment. Claiming that the Equal Rights Amendment constituted an "attack on motherhood" that would "destroy the American family," anti-ERA lobbyists successfully pressured the 1978 general assembly to pass a rescission resolution. Lieutenant Governor Thelma Stovall, acting as governor in the absence of

Governor Julian Carroll, vetoed the rescission resolution. Despite Stovall's principled attempt to protect women's rights, the federal Equal Rights Amendment met defeat on June 30, 1982, when it fell three states short of the required three-fourths majority for state ratification of a constitutional amendment.

After 150 years of political struggle to achieve full equality, women in Kentucky are still without constitutional guarantees at the state and federal levels that they will be treated as equals before the law. The Supreme Court of the United States has consistently ruled that the equal protection clause of the Fourteenth Amendment *is* compatible with differential treatment on the basis of sex. The Supreme Court's failure to declare sex a suspect classification allows states to pass laws that treat men and women differently as long as the states can demonstrate that they have a "reasonable basis" for the differential treatment,[28] that it serves an "important governmental objective," and that the discriminatory means employed are "substantially related" to the achievement of the governmental objective.[29]

In recognition of the precarious status of women's rights as a result of the defeat of the Equal Rights Amendment, Governor John Y. Brown, Jr., established the Governor's Commission for Full Equality on July 30, 1982. Charged with the responsibility to examine Kentucky's statutes, regulations and constitution in order to discover whether differential treatment on the basis of gender exists in the state and to recommend methods for remedying any discriminatory practices identified, the Governor's Commission on Full Equality undertook a year-long study of the legal, economic, political, and social conditions of women in Kentucky. Their report issued in December 1983, asserts unequivocally that

> in order to guarantee that the basic rights established in our federal and state Constitutions are also extended to women, we believe that it is necessary to amend both the federal and state Constitutions to reflect recognition of women as full citizens. Women's rights must be guaranteed in perpetuity as well as protected from regressive legislative and court action. Furthermore, a constitutional provision prohibiting the denial of rights under the law on the basis of sex would benefit both women and men. It would insure that people would be treated in accordance with their individual abilities and needs.[30]

The Kentucky Women's Legislative Network comprised of more than 400 women representing diverse women's organizations throughout the state is mobilizing at this time to continue the constitutional quest for full equality.

FROM POLLING PLACE TO PUBLIC OFFICE:
Women's Political Participation in Kentucky

Social science research consistently indicates that voting is the predominant form of political participation among United States citizens. In Kentucky, 71 percent of the women over eighteen are registered to vote. The 1983 voter registration rolls revealed that 64,000 more women were registered than men.[31] Moreover, since 1980 women have been outvoting men, casting 55.9 percent of the ballots in the state.[32] Of the women voters in the state, 71.3 percent identify with the Democratic party, 27.4 percent identify with the Republican party, and 1.3 percent describe themselves as independents.[33]

A recent statewide survey of the political attitudes and activities of Kentucky women revealed that women are concerned about issues and about the way their elected officials were voting on the issues. Forty-seven percent of the women polled shared the belief that the Republican administration in Washington was insensitive to the needs and interests of women; 48 percent expressed doubt that Reagan's economic policies would improve the conditions of working-class and unemployed people; 49 percent feared that the current administration's policies toward Latin America would lead the United States into war. One year after the defeat of the Equal Rights Amendment, 62.5 percent of Kentucky's women expressed support for a constitutional amendment to guarantee equality for women.[34] In a year that witnessed repeated efforts by legislators to impose restrictions upon women's reproductive freedom, 52 percent of the women surveyed stated opposition to the human life amendment and to any attempt to make all abortions illegal in the United States.[35] The survey results suggest that women in Kentucky are growing increasingly concerned about the ability of their elected officials to represent the interests of the majority of women in the state.

Women in Kentucky have demonstrated a consistent willingness to engage in more demanding forms of political activity, such as donating money to candidates and assisting in political campaigns. As Table 11.1 indicates, working and retired women, not the mythic housewife-volunteers, donate the greatest amounts of time and money to political campaigns. It is also interesting to note that in Kentucky a greater percentage of black women donate time and money to political campaigns than white women.

TABLE 11.1

**Percent Women Contributing to Political Campaigns in
Time and Money Broken Down by Occupation**

| | % Who Have Donated to Political Campaigns | |
Occupation	Money	Time
Executive, Professional, Teacher	26.1	19.6
Clerical/Sales	20.6	18.6
Blue-collar	19.1	12.8
Housewife	11.5	4.6
Retired	23.5	11.8

Perhaps the most interesting finding of this survey of Kentucky women concerns attitudes toward women candidates for elective office. The women surveyed expressed grave concerns about the underrepresentation of women in public office, about discrimination against women in the work place and about the feminization of poverty, the increasing proportion of women among the poor. A large majority of the respondents agreed that "we need more women in politics to pass laws to end discrimination on the basis of sex." Indeed, when asked what they would do to help increase the number of women in politics, 41 percent of the women noted that they would be willing to contribute money to a female candidate's campaign, and 39 percent of the women of all ages and 47 percent of the women under thirty said that they would volunteer time to assist the election efforts of a female politician. Interviews with women in state elective office substantiate this commitment. Several of Kentucky's female legislators indicated that 75 to 80 percent of their campaign work had been done by women volunteers.

Leaders of the state Democratic and Republican parties have described women as the backbone of local party organizations. From the moment that women gained suffrage and turned their energies to party work, they have proven themselves to be great grass roots organizers who have incomparable skills at turning out the vote. Indeed, as long ago as 1923, Leigh Harris, editor of two Kentucky newspapers noted in an editorial that "we will have to take off our hats to the women for they have proved themselves better political workers than men."[36] Since the 1950s women have comprised from 33 to 60 percent of the precinct captains of both the Democratic and

Republican parties.[37] Functioning as party stalwarts, women serve primarily as middle management officials, who maintain the party organization from one election to another.[38] These female party workers tend to manifest stronger party loyalty and to be active longer in the party organization than their male counterparts.[39]

Although few women in the United States have achieved positions of party leadership, the Democratic party in Kentucky can boast of two women who have functioned for extended periods of time as the local party boss. "Miss Lennie" McLaughlin served as a chief party functionary of the Jefferson County Democratic machine from 1938 to 1964.[40] Marie Roberts Turner orchestrated the affairs of Breathitt County for nearly half a century through the Turner Machine, initially working in conjunction with her husband, Judge Ervine Turner, but assuming sole charge upon his death in 1968.[41] Both women fulfilled the traditional role of political boss by building their strength upon precinct organization and using primary returns as the mechanism for controlling the nominating process. Marie Turner has also played a central role in the state Democratic party hierarchy, serving as vice-chair of the Democratic State Central Executive Committee.

Despite their valuable contributions as party workers, remarkably few women have won their party's nomination for elective office in Kentucky. Political parties have not functioned as escalators for women who aspire to candidacy for public office in the state.[42] Interviews with women in elective office at both state and federal levels indicates that for many "winning the election is far easier than capturing the nomination."[43] The refusal of male party leaders in Kentucky to field female candidates for safe or winnable seats in electoral contests seems to reflect the belief discovered by Duverger thirty years ago that "to give a post to a woman is to deprive a man of it and in these circumstances, the posts given to women are cut down to the minimum required for propaganda purposes."[44] Both major political parties in Kentucky have tended to meet this minimal nominating requirement by nominating female candidates for seats that are unwinnable or for contests in which the opposing candidate is also a woman.

One consequence of this dearth of female candidates in the state is the drastic underrepresentation of women in elective office. Although women constitute 51.3 percent of Kentucky's population, women hold only 6.5 percent of the seats in the general assembly,[45] which is roughly half the national average of 13.4 percent. At the local level, women comprise only 4 percent of the elected officials, one-third of the national average of 12 percent. In 1983, Kentucky elected its first female governor, Martha Layne Collins, the only woman to serve as the chief-executive of any state in the nation in 1984. Collins' victory highlights the fact that it is not women's unpopularity at the polls that impairs their political prospects. On the contrary, women have proven themselves to be strong vote winners ever since Emma Guy Cromwell, the first woman to win a statewide election to the office of secretary of state, outpolled the Democratic candidate for governor in 1923.[46] The major obstacle to the increased representation of women in elective office in Kentucky remains party leaders' reluctance to accord female candidates viable opportunities to beat the opposition.

Once elected to public office, women officials report that "their conduct is always under scrutiny."[47] They must work much harder than their male counterparts to gain credibility, for to prove themselves they must "free the minds of some who were bound by the old traditions to the chivalric attitudes of the past."[48] The standards by which women in office are judged are often substantially different from those applied to their male counterparts. If a male official demonstrates emotion on the job, he may be described as "compassionate" or "sensitive to the plight of his constituents"; if a female official manifests the same response in the same set of circumstances, she may be labelled "weak" or "unable to cope with the pressures of office."[49] Moreover, if a male politician proves himself to be corrupt or incompetent, he alone suffers the consequences of his failures; however, if a female politician proves corrupt or incompetent, her failure may be cited as evidence that women do not belong in politics.

Women in office may also be subject to forms of harassment from which their male colleagues are exempt. Working outside of the long established "old boy" networks, female officeholders may be penalized for decisions that disrupt the status quo. For example, while Emma Cromwell was serving as Kentucky's first female state treasurer (1928 to 1932), she initiated a policy to require that all banks handling state funds be bonded to the full amount. Despite the fact that this decision safeguarded Kentucky from the worst ravages of the Depression, Cromwell was subjected to a humiliating grand jury investigation for initiating this sound fiscal policy.[50] Women's exclusion from the informal advantages of "old boy" networks can also impair their chances, as members of the general assembly, for important assignments on powerful committees and impede their effectiveness in serving their constituents.[51]

Despite the obstacles that confront women in public office, Kentucky's female officeholders have made significant contributions to the state and to their constituents. Women have served ably on school boards and boards of aldermen, as judges, mayors, school superintendents, clerks of the court of appeals and the supreme court, state treasurers, auditors of public accounts, secretaries of state, lieutenant governors, and state representatives and senators.[52] Women also have a long history of service in appointive positions in state government. Although their service had been largely restricted to postions related to the State Library and Archives, the Kentucky Historical Association, and the Department of Public Information during the first half of this century, by 1975 women were serving on 44 percent of the 181 state boards and commissions.[53] The administration of Governor John Y. Brown, Jr., manifested its commitment to affirmative action by appointing Jackie Swigart as the first woman to serve as secretary of a cabinet (Department of Natural Resources and Environmental Protection) and June Taylor as the first woman to serve as chief of staff of the governor's office. Between December 1979 and July 1983, the Brown administration had increased the number of women in top management positions in state government from 66 to 124 and had appointed more than 450 women to positions on the state's boards and commissions.[54] With the advent of Governor Martha Layne Collins to the chief executive's office, Kentuckians have the opportunity to witness a woman "prove her worth by performance" in the highest political office in the state.[55]

POLITICS AS A MEANS OF SELF-PROTECTION: The Defense of Women's Interests in Kentucky

One of the strongest arguments for the extension of the franchise in democratic political systems has been self-protection. According full voting rights to individuals equips them with a weapon for the protection and promotion of their own interests. Early American suffragists explained "woman's need of the ballot: that she may hold in her own right hand the weapon of self-protection and self-defense."[56] Testifying before the House Judiciary Committee in 1884, Kentuckian Mary Barr Clay eloquently expressed women's desire to represent their own interests: "Gentlemen, if your protectors were women and they took all your property and your children and paid you half as much for your work... would you think much of the chivalry which allows you to sit in street cars and picks up your pocket handkerchief? ... women need the ballot for self-protection."[57] In 1984, when one out of every four women in Kentucky is a victim of rape and one in every five women in the state is a victim of domestic violence; when one in every three female Kentuckians experiences sexual harassment in the work place on a regular basis;[58] when white women earn only 54 percent and black women earn only 47 percent of the median income of men in Kentucky; when the median income of Kentucky's male executives is $20,285 while that of female executives is $11,120;[59] when women constitute the fastest growing poverty group in the state, with 34 percent of the female headed families living below the poverty level;[60] women need to use the ballot for self-protection more than ever.

In recent years an increasing number of women's organizations, interest groups, and political action committees have emerged in Kentucky to press for programs to protect women's interests. A brief enumeration of these groups would include the following: The Business and Professional Women's Political Action Committee, the Coalition of Labor Union Women, the Coalition for Reform of Rape Laws, Kentucky Black Women for Political Action, Kentucky Chapters of the National Organization for Women, the Kentucky Civil Liberties Union Women's Rights Committee, the Kentucky Coalition Against Rape and Family Violence, the Kentucky Domestic Violence Association, Kentucky's Pro-ERA Alliance, Kentucky Women's Legislative Network, Kentucky Women's Political Caucus, the League of Women Voters, the Older Women's League, the Religious Coalition for Abortion Rights, the Women's Alliance and the Women's Equity Action League. Working in conjunction with the Kentucky Commission on Women and key legislators in the general assembly, these groups have achieved a number of significant accomplishments. In 1976, the general assembly passed a rape shield law designed to develop programs for rape victims and to provide training for police to increase their sensitivity toward rape victims. In 1978, the general assembly established a legal requirement that all hospitals in the state conduct rape exams and inform victims of rape-relief services available in the locality. In 1980, the appropriation for the budget of the attorney general's office was increased by $166,000 to provide funds for payment for rape exams in hospitals. (The fees for this exam, which range from $90 to $250, had been imposed on the rape victim.)

In 1978, the Kentucky Commission on Women received a $50,000 grant from the Law Enforcement Assistance Administration (LEAA) to conduct a statewide victimization study to determine the level and types of crimes committed against women and the elderly in Kentucky. The study's finding that 80,000 Kentucky women, one in ten, had experienced some degree of violence by their partners in one year and that 169,000 Kentucky women, 21 percent of the state's female population, had experienced domestic violence at some point in their lives provided the impetus for the enactment of legislation that altered the procedures for dealing with cases of family abuse.[61] In 1980, domestic violence was established as a crime, a class A misdemeanor, and police were authorized to make warrantless arrests in cases where officers had probable cause to believe that wanton physical abuse had occurred or would continue to occur. Legislation was passed to enable victims of domestic violence to file for protective orders in court for themselves and for their children, to petition for court-ordered custody and child support without filing for divorce, and to insure that abandonment of the home by a victim of spouse abuse could not be counted against the victim in custody cases. Seven state-funded spouse abuse centers were established in Kentucky, and in 1982 a Spouse Abuse Shelter Funding Bill was passed, which raises revenue for shelters by increasing the fee for marriage licenses by $10.

More than 39,000 Kentucky women fall within the category of displaced homemakers, persons who have lost their primary source of livelihood through the death of a spouse, divorce, separation, or abandonment. In July 1980, the Kentucky Employment and Education Transition Program for Homemakers began offering remedial education, graduate equivalency degrees, vocational training, associate degree programs, on-the-job training programs, and work experience opportunities to state displaced homemakers who were economically disadvantaged and unemployed or underemployed. In addition to the creation of the Displaced Homemaker Program, two other pieces of legislation of importance for women's economic condition were passed in 1980. A law that prohibits wage discrimination on the basis of sex in establishments that employ two or more workers and a law that requires that women affected by pregnancy, childbirth, and related medical conditions receive the same benefits as other workers similar in their ability or inability to work were added to the Kentucky statutes.

The lobbying efforts of coalitions of women have not all been successful. Legislation to shield the names of rape victims was killed in committee. Legislation to establish rehabilitation programs for sex offenders was defeated. Legislation to allow married women to use their birth names or hyphenated names on motor vehicle operator's licenses failed to win the approval of the general assembly. Legislation passed in the 1970s prohibits the use of state funds for abortions, except in cases where the woman's life is endangered, and also prohibits health insurance coverage for elective abortions, except where coverage derives from an optional rider purchased at an additional premium. Moreover, the 1982 general assembly passed an antiabortion measure (HB 339) that drastically curtails women's reproductive rights in this state. Because this law undermines the constitutional rights of women repeatedly upheld by the United States Supreme Court, its constitutionality is currently being challenged in the courts.

Many laws that protect women's rights and interests are inadequately enforced in Kentucky. For example, sexual harassment, any unwelcome sexual advance, request for sexual favors, or other verbal or physical conduct of a sexual nature by an employer or other employees that is made by intent or effect a term or condition of employment or promotion, is a form of illegal discrimination on the basis of sex prohibited by both the Kentucky Civil Rights Act and Title VII of the federal Civil Rights Act. Yet, in a study entitled "Sexual Harassment of Women in Kentucky," Kimberly Greene and Susan Tatnall found that 95 percent of their 2,150 respondents believed that sexual harassment was a problem on the job; 55 percent of these considered it a "serious problem." Fifty-six percent of the women interviewed had experienced sexual harassment; of these, 79 percent reported that they experienced sexual harassment on a regular basis. Although sexual harassment adversely affects women's economic situation, work opportunities, mental and physical health, and self-esteem and although it is illegal, 70 percent of the women surveyed believed that reporting sexual harassment would bring about no result other than labelling them as troublemakers.[62] The public's propensity to tolerate illegal forms of discrimination is not restricted to sexual harassment; on the contrary, it extends to gender-based discrimination in hiring, promotion, wage levels, and employee benefits.

In a 1983 report, the governor's Commission for Full Equality recommends a wide range of legislative and policy reforms designed to protect women's interests by securing full equality under the law for both men and women. Their recommendations include the addition of an equal rights amendment to the state and federal Constitutions, the reform of pension law and insurance law to prohibit discrimination on the basis of sex, the amendment of the inheritance tax law to exempt a surviving spouse from inheritance taxes, the adoption of administrative procedures more efficient than judicial proceedings for the determination of child support, the use of mandatory wage assignments and liens in the event of default on child support payments, the creation of programs to insure equal treatment of male and female juveniles within the juvenile justice system, the systematic implementation of existing regulations concerning equal opportunity in employment by state contractors, the institutionalization of procedures to guarantee due process for state employees filing discrimination complaints, the passage of legislation to encourage employer-sponsored child care facilities through tax credits, consideration of adoption of the concept of comparable worth in order to achieve pay equity for male and female state employees, encouragement of flexible work hours and job sharing programs to accomodate the needs of working parents in state government, passage of an equal opportunity in public education act to prohibit discrimination in education on the basis of race, color, religion, national origin and sex, the revision of Kentucky's criminal code to make it a crime to use forcible compulsion to engage a spouse in sexual intercourse, the amendment of the law to insure that all rape examination fees would be paid for by the office of the attorney general, the passage of legislation to increase individual's protection against domestic violence and to provide services for victims of domestic violence, and the review of all state regulations for the identification and elimination of language that is discriminatory on the basis of sex. The wide-ranging reforms recommended by the Commission for Full Equality are likely to serve as a catalyst for continuing efforts to protect women's rights and interests in the state.

CONCLUSION

In the past hundred years, Kentucky women have worked diligently to translate the title of equal citizenship into meaningful equality. Their intense participation in the political process as members of interest groups, lobbyists, voters and party workers must dispell the outmoded stereotype of women as disinterested in politics. However, women's underrepresentation in elective office attests to the persistence of the tendency to deploy women's political interest in the activities of making coffee rather than policy and licking envelopes rather than the opposition. Perhaps the growing evidence of the gender gap in Kentucky, coupled with the status of women as the voting majority in the state, will serve as the final stimulus to the achievement of full equality conceived in terms of demographic representation and full protection of women's economic, political, and social interests.

FOOTNOTES

1. In *Minor v. Happersett*, (88 U.S. [21 Wall] 162, 22 L. Ed. 627 (1874)), the United States Supreme Court ruled that women were "citizens" but that citizenship did not necessarily involve voting rights. In both the *Bradwell* case (83 U.S. 130 (1873)) and *In Re Lockwood* (154 U.S. 116 (1894)), the Court held that women were not "persons" under the Fourteenth Amendment.

2. The best sources on the history of the women's rights movement in Kentucky are Paul E. Fuller, *Laura Clay and the Women's Rights Movement* (Lexington, Kentucky, The University of Kentucky Press, 1975); Helen D. Irvin, *Women In Kentucky* (Lexington, Kentucky, The University of Kentucky Press, 1979) esp. pp. 89-126; Susan B. Anthony and Ida Husted Harper, *History of Woman Suffrage (Vol. 4) 1883-1900* (New York, Arno Press, 1969) esp. pp. 665-677; and Melba Dean Porter, "Madeline McDowell Breckinridge: Her Role in the Kentucky Woman Suffrage Movement, 1908-1920," *The Register of the Kentucky Historical Society* 72 (October 1974): 342-363.

3. Fuller, *op. cit.*, pp. 11-30.

4. *Ibid.*, p. 31.

5. *Ibid.*, pp. 25-26.

6. Anthony and Harper, *op. cit.*, p. 452.

7. *Ibid.*, p. 676.

8. *Ibid.* Although the Court affirmed the principle of occupational opportunity for all regardless of sex, it did not require Kentucky to purge all labor laws that discriminated against women. It is interesting to note in this connection, that women were prohibited by law from tending bar in Kentucky until the late 1970s.

9. Fuller, *op. cit.*, pp. 46-47.

10. *Ibid.*

11. Anthony and Harper, pp. 670-671.

12. *Ibid.*, pp. 674-675.

13. Irvin, *op. cit.*, p. 103.

14. *Ibid.*, p. 91.

15. Although this phrase is taken from Section 3 of Kentucky's constitutional Bill of Rights, it is representative of the entire document, which is cast in sexist language. Only Section 145, which deals with "Suffrage and Elections," has been revised to substitute the term, person for man, and even in this section, all

persons are referred to in the exclusive terminology of masculine gender. Those who believe that the term *man* has always been used to refer to women might wish to review recent scholarship on this question, which indicates that it was only in 1850 that an all-male British Parliament enacted legislation that decreed that *he/man* should stand for women. For a full account of this development see Ann Bodine, "Androcentrism in Prescriptive Grammar," *Language and Society* 4 (2): 129-156, Spring 1975.

16. Fuller, *op. cit.*, p. 165.
17. Alice A. Dunnigan, *The Fascinating Story of Black Kentuckians* (Washington, D.C., Associated Publishers, Inc., 1982) p. 357.
18. Ellen B. Ewing and Patricia W. Owen, "The Legal Status of Homemakers in Kentucky," Homemakers Committee National Commission on the Observance of International Women's Year. (Washington, D.C., Government Printing Office, 1977) p. 1.
19. Governor's Commission on the Status of Women, *Kentucky Women* (Frankfort, Kentucky, May 12, 1966) p. 30.
20. *Ibid.*, p. 29.
21. *U.S. Census of the Population,* 1960, Vol. I, Characteristics of the Population, Part 19—Kentucky (Washington, D.C., Government Printing Office, 1963) p. 322, 151. By 1980, 53 percent of Kentucky's men and women over twenty-five and 72 percent of the men and women aged eighteen to twenty-four completed high school; 14.1 percent of Kentucky's women compared with 17.6 percent of Kentucky's men graduated from a four-year college; and 4 percent of Kentucky's women compared with 6 percent of Kentucky's men had some post-graduate training. By 1982, women constituted 40 percent of the nonagricultural labor force. (*U.S. Census of the Population,* 1980, Vol. I, Characteristics of the Population, Part 19—Kentucky, Table 66.) Although the median income of women in the state had dropped to 44 percent of the median male income by 1976, by 1983 it had returned to the 54 percent level. However, the average Kentucky woman with a college education still earns $2,629 less than the average Kentucky male with a high school diploma, and the average Kentucky woman with a high school diploma still earns $1,127 less than the average Kentucky male with an eighth-grade education. The average Kentucky woman with a high school education earns $6,800 less than the average male high school graduate, and the average female college graduate in the state earns 56 percent of her male counterpart. (Kentucky Commission on Women, *Annual Report,* 1980.)

22. Governor's Commission on the Status of Women, *Kentucky Women*, p. 9.

23. *Ibid.*

24. The information for the following paragraph was provided by Dr. Mary K. Tachau, Department of History, University of Louisville, in an interview with the author on January 3, 1984. In addition to the women mentioned in the text, the following women deserve recognition for their contributions to the LAW campaign: Maxie Nay, Emily Homeister, Nancy Ray, Pat Elam, Debby Grayson, Katie McCarthy, Pam Elam, Rebecca Westerfield, Barbara Froula, Jerre Shaw, Parry Burnes, Charlotte Zerof, Marcia Lipetz, Kate Cunningham, Linda Glick, Celeste Callahan, Mary Zubrod, and P.H. Starks.

25. Kentucky Commission on Women, *Annual Report*, 1974-1975.

26. Ewing and Owen, *op. cit.*, p. 9.

27. The Governor's Commission for Full Equality Report to Governor John Y. Brown, Jr., *The Crumbling Pedestal* (Frankfort, Kentucky, December, 1983) p. xii.

28. *Reed v. Reed*, 404 U.S. 71 (1971).

29. *Mississippi University for Women v. Hogan*, 102 S.Ct. 3331 (1982).

30. Governor's Commission for Full Equality Report, *op. cit.*, p. 2.

31. The exact numbers were 951,703 women registered to vote and 887,670 men registered to vote in Kentucky. Nationwide, 64 percent of the women over eighteen are registered to vote.

32. Evans Witt, "Women Imperil G.O.P. in South, Study Says," Lexington *Herald-Leader*, Tuesday, August 9, 1983, p. A8.

33. The figures in this section are drawn from a statewide survey of women in Kentucky conducted by Research Analysis Corporation of Boston, Massachusetts, in August 1983. The study was financed by Kentucky's Business and Professional Women's Clubs (KBPW) and was designed to gather information that would enable the KBPW's Political Action Committee to provide technical assistance to candidates in the 1984 election. I am indebted to Heidi Margulis, President of the KBPW, for sharing the results of this survey with me.

34. *Ibid.* Only 27 percent of those surveyed registered disapproval of the ERA.

35. Only 38 percent of the respondents indicated any support for the human life amendment.

36. Emma Guy Cromwell, *Woman in Politics* (Louisville, Standard Printing Co., 1939) p. 74.

37. Carolyn Luckett Denning, "The Louisville (Kentucky) Democratic Party: Political Times of 'Miss Lennie' McLaughlin," M.A. thesis, University of Louisville, 1981.

38. Harold D. Clarke and Allan Kornberg, "Moving Up the Political Escalator: Women Party Officials in the United States and Canada," *The Journal of Politics*, 41 (1979): 442-447.

39. Edmond Constantine and Kenneth H. Craik, "Women As Politicians: The Social Background, Personality and Political Careers of Female Party Leaders," *Journal of Social Issues*, 28 (1972): 217-235.

40. Denning provides a systematic overview of McLaughlin's career in her thesis.

41. Vicki Dennis, "Profiles of Women In Kentucky Politics: Marie Roberts Turner," Kentucky Commission on Women, unpublished essay. I am grateful to Ms. Dennis for sharing this information with me.

42. This metaphor is borrowed from Clarke and Kornberg, *op. cit.*

43. M.M. Lee, "Why So Few Women Hold Public Office: Democracy and Sexual Roles," *Political Science Quarterly*, 91 (1976): 297-314; and Susan Welch, "Women As Political Animals: A Test of Some Explanations for Male-Female Political Participation Differences," *American Journal of Political Science*, 21 (1977): 711-730.

44. M. Duverger, *The Political Role of Women*, UNESCO, 1955. For a review of Duverger's findings see Joni Lovenduski, "Toward the Emasculation of Political Science: The Impact of Feminism," in *Men's Studies Modified*, Dale Spender (ed.) (Oxford, Pergamon Press, 1981) pp. 83-97.

45. National Women's Political Caucus, *National Directory of Women Elected Officials*, Washington, D.C., 1983.

46. Cromwell, *op. cit.*, p. 74. Cromwell had already defeated three other candidates in the Democratic primary that year.

47. *Ibid.*, p. 98. In preparing this article, I interviewed a number of Kentucky's women officials about their experiences in public office. Their responses were remarkably similar to those articulated by Cromwell in her memoirs and documented by social scientists' studies of female officeholders throughout the United States. Rather than risk jeopardizing the political interests of those women who were willing to discuss their experience with me, in the following notes I shall cite published material that corroborates their statements.

48. Cromwell, p. 62.

49. M.E. Currell, *Political Woman* (London, Croom Helm, 1974); J. Jacquette (ed.), *Women in Politics* (New York, John Wiley and Sons, 1974); Elizabeth Valance, *Women in the House* (Humanities Press, 1982).

50. Cromwell, *op. cit.*, pp. 180-193.

51. Judith Cummings, "Women in State Legislatures Speak Out," *New York Times*, December 5, 1983, p. 21.

52. For the names of the women who have served in these posts, see Annie Harrison, *Women in Kentucky State Government 1940-1980: A Chart of Commissioners and Other Appointees, Elected State Officials and Members of the General Assembly* (Kentucky, Department of Library and Archives, Spring, 1981).

53. *Kentucky Commission on Women Annual Report*, 1974-1975 (Frankfort, Kentucky, 1975) pp. 5-7.

54. Governor's Commission on Full Equality Report, p. 48; *Kentucky Woman: A Year End Report*, Kentucky Commission on Women, vol. 4 (1):5, 1983.

55. Cromwell used this phrase to describe the fundamental opportunity that women in politics seek, *op. cit.*, p. 45.

56. Elizabeth C. Stanton, "The Kansas Campaign of 1867" in *The History of Woman's Suffrage*, reprinted in *The Feminist Papers*, Alice S. Rossi (ed.) (New York, Bantam Books, 1973, p. 463.)

57. Fuller, *op. cit.*, p. 26.

58. "Rape Fact Sheet," Rape Relief Center, YWCA, Louisville, Kentucky, 1981; "LEAA Victimization Study," 1979-80 Annual Report, Kentucky Commission on Women (Frankfort, Kentucky, 1980) pp. 2-3; Kimberly Greene and Susan Tatnall, "Sexual Harassment of Women in Kentucky," *1979-80 Annual Report*, Kentucky Commission on Women, p. 11.

59. Governor's Commission on Full Equality, p. 36.

60. *Ibid.*, p. xiii.

61. Louis Harris and Associates, *A Survey of Spousal Violence Against Women in Kentucky* (Kentucky Commission on Women, July, 1979).

62. The findings of Greene and Tatnall's study are discussed in the Kentucky Commission on Women *Annual Report 1978-1979*, pp. 11-12 and in the Kentucky Commission on Women, *Annual Report 1980-1981*, p. 3.

Chapter 12

LOCAL GOVERNMENT IN KENTUCKY

Allen Singleton, Eastern Kentucky University
and
Joel Goldstein, University of Louisville

COUNTY GOVERNMENT

The county serves essentially as a subdivision of the state. Despite local needs, great variances in size (from 100 square miles in the smallest county to 725 square miles in the state's largest county), and great differences in population (ranging from 2,000 in Robertson County to over 690,000 in Jefferson County, with its over ninety city governments), each county—with the exception of Fayette County— is governed under the organizational structure established in the constitution. Although the general assembly has been given the authority to adjust these functions, duties, and compensation for counties and their officials, it must do so uniformly.

The county in Kentucky has historically played and currently plays a significant role in the politics and culture of the common-wealth. Two recent events have done more to alter the pre-eminence of the county during the past ten years than in the preceding 200 years: (1) the completion of the east-west interstate road network, which linked Ashland to Fulton and Paducah, that for the first time made reasonable east-west communication possible and (2) the adoption of the present judicial article of the constitution.

The background to this first event is complex. An observer of Kentucky must recognize the pre-eminence geography has played in the state's political and cultural history. From the earliest days of the commonwealth, east-west travel has been difficult. Even during the formative period when settlers traveled overland, such as along Boone's Trace, their journey ended at such places as Boonesboro, Harrodsburg, or at the Falls of the Ohio (Louisville). Early railroads were designed to cut through Kentucky on a north-south axis, for example, the Illinois Central in far-west Kentucky and the Louisville and Nashville, and the Cincinnati Southern in the central portions of the state. Anyone who has visited the region recognizes that roads have always been a problem in eastern Kentucky. Thus, the terrain of Kentucky early dictated isolation of sections of the state from communication with each other.

Often, interstate focal points attracted the interest of many Kentuckians. Three such examples follow: northern Kentucky was drawn into Cincinnati's sphere of influence, the purchase area was more closely linked to Memphis and St. Louis than to any other part of Kentucky, and Bowling Green and its surrounding areas were attracted to Nashville. With only minimal east-west linkages established, it was natural for this centrifugal process to be a dominant element in a great many cultural factors. With the final construction of an east-west interstate/parkway system, the overland journey between the eastern and western extremities of the state finally became a reasonable trip, not only from Paducah to Frankfort or Ashland to Frankfort but from Paducah to Ashland.

New communications linkages have always required time to nurture and develop, especially in the face of established tradition, but what is most important is that it is now not only feasible but reasonable for intrastate east-west communications to develop. The significance of this physical linkage is heightened by the increasing importance of the media in statewide politics.

The adoption of the present judicial article was one of the most sweeping changes ever to occur in local government in Kentucky. This change was precipitated by the passage of the 1975 constitutional amendment creating the present judicial system for the state. An integral segment of that amendment was the elimination of the judicial function of the office of county judge, thereby making that office the county judge/executive.

In the period preceding the general election, during which voters had time to consider the amendment, very few people perceived the import that the judicial amendment would have on county government. Most of the campaigning surrounding the article debated the "reform" or "modernization" of the state's court system. That the article also effectively separated the judicial and executive functions at the local level was largely ignored. It is quite likely that a great many of the county judges were not particularly upset at the prospective loss of their judicial authority because that authority could quite easily become a two-edged sword. Although some political power was given to the individual holding the office of county judge simply because of the judicial power involved, a county judge could quite easily have political pressure leveled against him about a judicial decision in a case appearing before his court.[1]

It seems likely that at least some segment of the county judges' constituencies were disappointed with the new arrangement. This seems evident from the rear-guard conflicts between fiscal courts and the newly created district and circuit courts and from stories of grassroots proposals to rescind the judicial amendment. Most major newspapers in the state routinely carried articles relevant to the post-amendment activities for several months. But, by mid-1980, such stories had all but disappeared from press reports.

The general assembly did not leave the newly revised position of county judge/executive in a total vacuum. During the 1976 and 1978 sessions, the legislators strengthened the position of the county judge/executive by providing that office with additional administrative and financial powers. For example, through KRS 67.710, the county judge/executive is recognized as the "chief executive officer of the county" and is assigned substantial appointive powers (KRS 67.710 [7] and [8]). The county judge/executive is also given the specific power of preparing the county budget and of estimating county receipts (KRS 68.240).[2]

Even with these two factors altering the Kentucky political scene, the importance of the county in the politics of Kentucky is not to be minimized. This is especially true in relation to the political linkages that are necessary to construct winning coalitions for election to statewide political office—in particular, the offices of governor, lieutenant governor, and United States Senator. Additionally, the county is significant in representing the citizen in the legislative process. The functioning of the general assembly essentially is based upon county units, even though the election district may not coincide with the county boundaries. Reality dictates that the county represents the basic political unit, and the linkages are between the representative and the elected officials of the county, especially since the county unit is the administrative unit used by executive agencies and by federal and state programs.

The county has been particularly hampered by the tradition of Dillon's Rule, i.e., that the state legislature is supreme over activities of local units of government. This principle is reinforced in the Kentucky constitution and has been made even more complicated by the tradition of county politics in Kentucky, e.g., the formation of smaller counties, many of which were generated because of a political factions seeking representation.[3]

The popular concept of what a county government is to do is another factor limiting governmental action by county governments. Traditionally in the United States, the county has not been organized as nor has it been perceived by the electorate as, an active governing body. This is probably a legacy of the rural nature of the institution. In more recent times, the imposition of extraterritorial planning powers (up to a five-mile distance from the city limit) has helped to stifle the growth of county governmental functions in Kentucky.

The fiscal court, with elected representatives chosen either on a district or an at-large basis and with the county judge/executive as its presiding officer, is the chief administrative and policy-determining body of the county. Although the general assembly has tried to confer some form of home rule to the fiscal court, the nature of the state constitution dictates that the chief agency of county government is constrained in its formal powers. The Kentucky supreme court in the case of *Fiscal Court of Jefferson County v. City of Louisville, et. al.*, 559 S.W. (2nd) 478 (KY 1977), said that "the General Assembly must grant governmental power to Fiscal Courts with the precision of a rifle shot and not with the casualness of a shotgun blast."[4]

The fiscal court does derive a considerable amount of authority because it serves as the governmental board regulating allocations of funds. In this role, the extent of cooperation that exists between the county judge/executive and the majority of members of the fiscal court plays the key role in determining the programs with which the county actually becomes involved.

In addition to the county judge/executive and the fiscal court, there are eight other constitutionally designated officials of county government in Kentucky: county clerk, county attorney, sheriff, jailer, coroner, surveyor, property valuation administrator, and constable—one constable for each magistrate's (fiscal court member) district in the county.[5]

Other county officials are appointed by the county judge/executive, including some that are appointed with the approval of the fiscal court. This includes statutory officials such as a county treasurer, road engineer or supervisor, dog warden, or any of the independent boards or commissions that various counties have established, e.g., "Airport Board, Parks and Recreation Board, etc."[6]

AREA DEVELOPMENT DISTRICTS

Despite the complicating factors, the legislative and executive branches in Kentucky have intensified intergovernmental contacts between state agencies and local units of government. In fact, they have increased the number of points at which the county units serve as the administrative unit for state programs. This growth has been paralleled by an increase in the amount of funds available to local governments through state administered programs. This has increased counties' arena of intergovernmental cooperation, although they are still dominated by state agencies, and has become the principal means through which county governments provide services to its citizens. In the past few years a new entity, the area development district, has increasingly served as a clearinghouse for state and local governments.

In other states these agencies are called "councils of governments" (COGs), and they are often thought of as being associated with metropolitan areas. The state was divided into fifteen of these area development districts by the general assembly in 1972 (KRS 147A .050 to .120). As was true nationally, the ADDs were in response to congressional legislation aimed at providing planning and coordination for fragmented governments and the federal grant-in-aid programs.

The mechanism for implementing the ADDs is the A-95 Review Process. In distributing funds for local governments, both those originating from the national government as well as those from state-generated funds, the ADDs utilize a review process initiated by the United States Office of Management and Budget. Labeled Circular A-95, issued July 24, 1969, the circular has four basic parts: (1) state and area agency review of federal aid applications, (2) federal agency consultation with state and local governments prior to undertaking direct federal development programs, (3) gubernatorial review of federally required state function plans before submission to the federal funding agency, and (4) coordination of federally supported planning programs at the substate (regional) level.[7] This process, then, is designed to achieve coordination of efforts, to avoid overlapping/duplication of efforts, and to provide a more effective use over a wider geographic area of reviews.

The operations, structure, staffing, and programs of each of the ADDs is as varied as the agencies. ADDs do not have legislative taxing authority. They derive their funds from activities that receive state and federal funding, from the contributions by the city and county governments they serve, and from fees from administrative/consulting services provided by their staff. Each ADD has an administrative or executive staff and a governing board comprised of elected and lay representatives from the governmental units the ADD serves. Each ADD functions according to the manner in which its role is defined by the executive staff and its board of directors. This applies to staffing and policy initiatives. In a sense, the ADD is forced to react to demands from state and federal agencies, as well as demands for services from its constituent governments. Obviously, the ADDs are constantly besieged by pressures from both directions regarding policies and activities.

During 1982 several of the smaller, rural ADDs were consolidated into larger planning units, resulting in a total of eight planning units in the state. Preliminary response to this arrangement seems to be positive.

MUNICIPAL GOVERNMENTS

The Kentucky constitution provides for a classification system for cities that is based on population.

Class	Population
1st	Over 100,000
2nd	20,000 to 99,999
3rd	8,000 to 19,999
4th	3,000 to 7,999
5th	1,000 to 2,999
6th	Under 1,000

There are over 400 incorporated cities in Kentucky. Less than ten of these are classed as first- or second-class cities. Therefore, most cities in Kentucky are not highly urbanized areas. (This point is almost a question of semantics, however, since quite a number of cities of the third through sixth class are located in a metropolitan [SMSA] area. This is especially true of Jefferson County and the northern Kentucky areas.)[8]

Throughout the twentieth century, the labyrinth of legislation relative to cities seemed to be deepened at the end of each session of the general assembly. Many forces in the state had long struggled to bring some sense out of this chaos. In 1976 the general assembly created the Municipal Statute Review Commission. This com-

264

mission's efforts represented a two-stage task. The first task was to identify and make retrievable (i.e., make known and knowable) all existing legislation relating to municipal governments in the commonwealth. The second task, with input from all interested parties, was to prepare a model municipal code for Kentucky. The code thus created was not adopted by the 1978 session of the general assembly; however, the 1978 general assembly did establish the Local Government Statute Revision Commission. The 1980 session of the legislature then enacted a series of statutes that essentially redefined municipal government in Kentucky. This was followed by clarifying legislation in 1982.

Basically, the 1980 and 1982 statutes provided for either one of three forms of city government to be adopted by the cities of the state: the mayor-council plan, the commission plan, or the city manager plan.[9] The mayor-council plan provides separation of executive and legislative powers. The commission plan provides for an integration of executive and legislative powers. Finally, the city manager plan provides for professional administration for the city.

In restructuring the municipal law of Kentucky, the general assembly attempted to give the greatest flexibility possible to allow the diverse cities of the commonwealth to meet and cope with problems in ways that are locally prescribed and not otherwise in conflict with state or national law. This attempt flies in the face of the much more restrictive character of Dillon's rule (previously cited) and the traditionally interpreted concepts of Kentucky's present constitution. If the courts of the state allow the legislation to stand, it will indeed mark the transformation of local municipal government in Kentucky from chaos to attainability.

LOUISVILLE AND LEXINGTON

Introduction

The phrase that dominated local politics in Kentucky's two largest cities over the past decade was "government reorganization." The voters in Lexington and Fayette County adopted a charter that merged their governments in November of 1972. The next decade was devoted to establishing the new urban county government and ironing out its details. The voters in Louisville and Jefferson County rejected proposed charters for a reorganized local government in November 1982 (by a margin of 1,400 votes) and November 1983 (by the more substantial margin of 5,000 votes). The politics of Louisville and Jefferson County during the late 1970s and early 1980s was initially devoted to a debate over the need for a merged government and then to the specifics of the 1982 and 1983 charters.

The politics of Louisville and Jefferson County in the rest of the 1980s will be focused on the alternatives to a merged government, and Lexington will continue to iron out the nuances surrounding Kentucky's first urban county government.

Background

Local governments in Kentucky are creatures of the state. Section 156 of the 1891 Kentucky state constitution created six classes of cities based upon their population. The state constitution also established the basic governmental structure for these cities. The at-large electoral system for Louisville's aldermen and the one-term limit for the mayor, for example, are mandated by the 1891 constitution. Any changes desired by the people of Louisville would require a constitutional amendment, which must be approved by the general assembly and by the voters of the entire commonwealth. Urban county governments, like Lexington/Fayette County, on the other hand, are not subject to these constitutional constraints and consequently can take any form desired by the residents of the county.

There are 125 local governments operating in Jefferson County. A single county government, 97 city governments—1 city of the first class (Louisville), 10 cities of the fourth class (Douglas Hills, Hurstbourne, Jeffersontown, Lyndon, Middletown, Newburg, Shively, St. Matthews, and St. Regis Park), 15 cities of the fifth class, and 71 cities of the sixth class. In addition, there are nineteen volunteer fire department districts and eight sanitation districts. There are also nineteen joint city-county boards and commissions, ranging from the Air Pollution Control District to the Zoological Commission.

Fayette County

The governmental framework in Lexington/Fayette County even prior to merger was considerably simpler than in Louisville/Jefferson County. Fayette County never developed a large number of small cities. Generations of piecemeal annexations by Lexington resulted in crazy-quilt borders: there were many streets in which one or two houses would be in the city, the next two or three in the county, and then some in the city again. The problems arising from the irregular borders created political pressures that supported merger.[10]

Merger passed in Lexington for several reasons. The primary reason was that the status quo was not a feasible alternative. The local government structure had to change regardless of the outcome of any specific merger vote. The change was the product of two forces. The first came as a result of the 1970 census. Lexington's population exceeded the 100,000 mark. Consequently, it would change from a city of the second class to a city of the first class. The structure and laws written to apply to Louisville would automatically apply to Lexington as soon as the legislature recognized its population growth. This would mean that the city would no longer retain its manager form of government. It would have to replace its five-member commission elected in a nonpartisan election with a merger-twelve member council elected at large in partisan elections.[11] Second, the city felt the reality of a massive court-ordered annexation of the developed fringe area surrounding the city. Large segments of unincorporated Fayette County were scheduled to be annexed by Lexington in 1975 and 1980. These areas faced larger tax increases without necessarily larger additions to the level of municipal services.[12] The charter's creation of partial urban service districts enabled these residents to soften the tax blow that annexation would have created.

A third element that made the passage of government reorganization in Fayette County easier was the support of the black community. In many urban areas, including Louisville and Jefferson County, merger is seen as a vehicle to dilute the budding political power of the black community. This was not the case in Lexington. The Lexington black community was not large enough to have hopes of becoming a majority of the city's population. This expansion of black power would be further weakened by the major annexations of white areas scheduled in 1975 and 1980. Lexington's current nonpartisan, at-large five-member commission electoral system, or the alternative twelve-member board of aldermen elected at-large in partisan elections, did not provide much hope for making political inroads. The charter's council consisting of twelve members from districts and three at-large provided the black community an opportunity to elect one or two members of the new city council.

A fourth factor favoring the adopting of the charter arose out of the political infighting among the county judge, Lexington's mayor, and commission. The Underwood-Stephens battles, as well as the factional disputes among the city's commissioners, set the stage for the public acceptance of the argument that merger was needed to end the battles and to get the city moving in one direction. The new charter created a strong mayor and a chief administrative officer to run the city. The division of power between the mayor and the CAO was an issue that created political tension over the next decade.

The charter stripped most of the powers of the constitutionally created county officials (the sheriff, county commissioners, etc.). These positions, however, could not be abolished. The 1980s saw the development of a political battle between the sheriff, looking to expand his political power by taking a law-enforcement role, and the metropolitan police department.

Jefferson County

None of the forces that helped pass the Fayette County merger was present in Louisville a decade later. The political map was confused by the existence of the ninty-plus small municipalities. The bill that granted Jefferson County the right to attempt to pass a new charter specifically guaranteed the continued existence of those small cities. Although the leadership supporting merger argued that these cities did not create the major problems facing local government, many of the opponents of the first charter charged that since only the city of Louisville was to be dissolved, annexations of the wealthier areas of Louisville would be attempted by these cities. The result would be an even more chaotic structure.

Many of the small municipalities lie in the eastern quadrant of the county. The opponents of the charter had their strength centered in the southern and southwestern portions of the county. The continued existence of the small cities provided support for the argument that the merger was an upper-class, east end plot to saddle an additional burden on the working class areas of the county.

The threat of annexation by the city of Louisville caused some suburbanites to support the merger. However, the annexations were not yet approved, and the legal battles over the attempts promised some hope of victory by the citizens on the city's fringe. In addition, many of these residents realized that they could end the threat of annexation by incorporating into small cities or by being annexed by one of the existing small cities. Consequently, the political status quo could be maintained with a minimum of disruption.

Louisville's large black community mobilized against the proposed charter. The black community had four of the twelve aldermen in the city of Louisville, in addition to a larger number of the city's department heads. They saw merger as a threat to their power base. In addition, they maintained the hope of eventually electing a black mayor of Louisville.

The city and county Fraternal Orders of Police also mobilized against the plan. The county police, a 400-member force, were threatened with being overwhelmed by the 700-member city police lodge. The city police saw a potential threat to their favorable pension plan, and the county saw the loss of their take-home cars as one of the potential economy moves the new government would be quickly forced to adopt.

The political infighting between the county judge and mayor, which was a major force in the early 1970s did not continue in the 1980s. Judge Mitch McConnell got along well with Mayors Stansbury and Sloane. The mayor and county judge appeared together to push the plan. The conflict between the two governments was not obvious to the average voter.

The city and county developed joint agencies to handle many communitywide services. Table 12.1 reports the population figures for Fayette and Jefferson Counties and their major cities. Louisville's population peaked in 1960, while the population in the balances of the county grew, and by 1980 they exceeded that of the central city. The failure of the Mallon plan, a referenda to create a countywide government in 1956, resulted in the expansion of the county's tax base through the imposition of an occupational tax on workers in areas outside Louisville and the creation of joint city-county agencies. The average citizen did not see the problems of accountability created by these agencies. The question of tax inequity created by the city resident's paying twice for services the county residents paid for only once was reason for the county taxpayer to support the status quo. City residents were told that merger would end the tax inequity. County taxpayers could only assume that they would somehow have to pick up a larger portion of the tab.

TABLE 12.1

Population of Louisville/Jefferson County and Lexington/Fayette County
1900–1980

Year	Louisville	Jefferson Co. Balance	Lexington	Fayette Co. Balance
1900	204,731	27,818	26,369	15,702
1910	223,928	38,992	35,089	12,626
1920	234,890	51,478	41,534	13,130
1930	307,745	47,605	45,736	22,807
1940	319,077	66,315	49,304	29,595
1950	369,129	115,486	55,534	45,212
1960	390,639	220,308	62,810	69,096
1970	361,706	333,349	108,137	66,186
1980	298,451	386,342	204,165	————

Source: U.S. Department of Commerce Census Reports

The trauma of court-ordered busing for desegregation, which was associated in the public's mind with the merger of the city and county school system in 1975, also helped to defeat the proposed charters. The school system's merger did not result in quick economies in its operating budget. Rather, the residents of Jefferson County saw a doubling of the administrative superstructure. Why, the opponents thought, would the proposed merger of the two governments be any different?

The influence of these forces led to the defeat of both merger attempts. Local politics will concentrate in the rest of the 1980s on the attempts by the city of Louisville to shift some of the fiscal burden to the county. There will be continued court battles over annexation attempts by Louisville. There will be political games of chicken played by the board of aldermen and fiscal court to see how the joint agencies will be funded. The city may eventually stop offering some services currently offered by the county to the residents in the balance of the county (EMS for example) with the expectation that the county government will be forced to absorb the related costs.

FOOTNOTES

1. William Berge and William Ellis, County Oral History Project, Eastern Kentucky University, interview February 1984.
2. For further discussion of these powers see Prentice Harvey, *County Government in Kentucky*, revised edition, Legislative Research Commission Informational Bulletin No. 115, Frankfort, Kentucky, May 1979.
3. Robert Ireland, *The County in Kentucky History* (Lexington: University Press of Kentucky, 1976).
4. Quoted from 5 NORTHERN LAW REVIEW 107 (1978).
5. See Legislative Research Commission Informational Bulletin No. 115 for a discussion of each of these offices.
6. Detailed information on county government and its officials is contained in LRC Bulletin No. 115 and Ireland, *op. cit.*
7. A. Lloyd and J.A. Singleton, *Kentucky Government*, Legislative Research Commission, Frankfort, 1979.
8. *Ibid.*, pp. 102-108.
9. For a discussion of each of these forms of government see any standard text in state and local government, such as Thomas

Dye, *Politics in States and Communities*, 4th ed. (Englewood Cliffs: Prentice-Hall, 1982).

10. W.F. Lyons, *The Politics of City-County Merger* (Lexington: University Press of Kentucky, 1977) p. 20.

11. *Ibid.*, pp. 31-32.

12. *Ibid.*, pp. 29-30.